John Duncombe

The Works of the Emperor Julian

Vol. I

John Duncombe

The Works of the Emperor Julian
Vol. I

ISBN/EAN: 9783337185992

Printed in Europe, USA, Canada, Australia, Japan

Cover: Foto ©ninafisch / pixelio.de

More available books at www.hansebooks.com

SELECT WORKS

OF THE

EMPEROR JULIAN,

⁎ The inauspicious name of JULIAN is stamped on the memory of all ages, not more by the extent of his dominions than by the infamy of his deserting the Christian religion: that great and eternal blot, that single stain, which has totally sullied all his other graces and accomplishments; adorned, as he was, with every endowment of nature, genius, learning, and eloquence, surrounded by a noble train of attendant virtues, temperance, continence, liberality, moderation in his mode of life, and distinguished also by the renown of valour and success in war. But as it was by no means my intention, I will not say to erase or remove (for what Christian would attempt that?); but in the least to disguise or extenuate, the blemish that his name has thus contracted, by paying some respect to his other virtues; so that elogium of uncommon erudition and elegance which his lucubrations in various branches of literature have received from so many past ages, should not, I thought, on that account be with-held from them.

SPANHEIM, in Dedic.

THE WORKS
OF THE
EMPEROR JULIAN,
AND
SOME PIECES
OF THE
SOPHIST LIBANIUS,

TRANSLATED FROM THE GREEK.

WITH

Notes from PETAU, LA BLETERIE, GIBBON, &c.

TO WHICH IS ADDED,

The HISTORY of the EMPEROR JOVIAN,

From the French of the Abbé DE LA BLETERIE.

By JOHN DUNCOMBE, M.A.

IN TWO VOLUMES.

THIRD EDITION CORRECTED.

  Him Poefy, Philofophy, deplore,
The fcepter'd Patriot, who diftinctions wav'd,
Lord of himfelf, by Pagan rites enflav'd;
Whom all, but Chriftians, held their common friend,
Whofe very errors had a virtuous end.———IRWIN.

VOLUME THE FIRST.

LONDON,
Printed for T. CADELL, in the STRAND.

1798.

CONTENTS OF VOL. I.

	Page
Preface	v
Annals and Pedigree of Julian	xxxv
Gallus Cæsar to his Brother Julian	1

Select Works of Julian, viz.

1. Epistle to Themistius — 4
2. A Consolatory Oration on the Departure of Sallust
3. Epistle to the Emperor Constantus — 54
4. ——— to the Senate and People of Athens — 59
5. An Allegorical Fable (from Orat. VII.) — 105
6. The Duties of a Priest (from the Fragment) — 118
7. The Cæsars
8. The Misopogon, or the Antiochian — 223

XVI Epistles of Libanius to Julian. — 303

PREFACE.

THE Abbé de la Bleterie publiſhed, in 1735, *La Vie de l' Empereur Julian*, 12mo.* To this he added, in 1748, *L' Hiſtoire de l' Empereur Jovien, et Traductions de quelques Ouvrages de l' Empereur Julien*, in two volumes, ſmall 8vo. Both theſe works are executed with uncommon elegance and judgement, and have been very ſerviceable to me in the following tranſlations. With great ſagacity the Abbé has explained and enlightened ſeveral ambiguous and obſcure paſſages; and many others he has happily illuſtrated, though, in general, by endeavouring to give the idea of his author as he preſumes " Julian himſelf would have ex-" preſſed it, if he had written in French,"

---

* Bleterie's Life is indeed a very elegant one, and writ with much candour and impartiality. He is no deep man in the learning of thoſe times, but his good ſenſe generally enables him to ſeize the right.   WARBURTON.

PREFACE.

his verſion is too free and paraphraſtical. If I have ſteered between the extremes of thoſe " literal verſions," thoſe " homely copies," which he condemns, and the beautiful, but flattering, likeneſs which he has drawn, I ſhall have ſucceeded to my wiſh, being deſirous of repreſenting this Imperial author juſt as he is, as far as the idiom of the two languages will admit, in which the Engliſh, in point of analogy to the Greek, has the advantage of the French. Moſt of the annotations of M. de la Bleterie I have adopted, and the rather, as few of them have before appeared in Engliſh. A tranſlation of his " Life of Julian," by ſome ladies *, was publiſhed in 1746, under the inſpection of Mr. Bowyer; but the " Hiſtory of Jovian" has till now been to our country " a fountain " ſealed." Were the learned Abbé ſtill living, I ſhould, however, deſpair of ſatisfying him in this attempt, having traced him more cloſely than he has tranſlated Julian, or wiſhed to be tranſlated himſelf.

The occaſion, and the motives, that engaged me in this undertaking being the ſame

---

* Mrs. Williams, a blind lady, aſſiſted by two ſiſters of the name of Wilkinſon. *Anecdotes of Bowyer*, p. 185.

with

PREFACE.

with those of this French academician, I cannot so well express them as in the same words:

"Having lately met with the works of Julian, notwithstanding the just horror with which I was inspired by his apostacy, I found them equally eloquent and ingenious, and perhaps more worthy to be read than many of the ancient Pagan writers. Besides, his morality being more refined than theirs, because it has retained a tint of ours, I perceived in his writings a multitude of particulars useful for history, and others, contrary to the intention of the author, very advantageous, and highly honourable, to religion. It seemed grievous to me, that ill-founded scruples should prevent translating into our language that which deserved it. 'The Emperor Jovian,' said I to myself, 'very zealous as he was for the faith, did not think the adorning the tomb of Julian, and honouring, even in the ashes of that apostate prince, his rank as a man and an emperor, incompatible with the true spirit of Christianity. Would it therefore be criminal not to neglect the productions of his genius, and to draw them from the obscurity

PREFACE.

' of the learned languages?' The excellent
" Latin version of Father Petau *, has already
" placed Julian within the reach of those
" who are not sufficiently acquainted with
" Greek to read the original; and the cele-
" brated Satire of THE CÆSARS, published
" in French by M. Spanheim †, with a long
" and

---

* PETAU DIONYSIUS [or PETAVIUS], a Jesuit, was one of the most learned men of his age. He was born in the city of Orleans, and honoured it by his merit. He was a vast genius, formed for literature, and rendered himself a prodigy of knowledge. For, besides the learned languages, which he wrote and spoke with the greatest fluency, there never was a divine more profound, an historian better informed, an orator more eloquent, a critic more judicious, a poet more ingenious and more flowery. In short, of nothing in literature he was ignorant. His excellent works leave no room to doubt this truth. Father Petau entered among the Jesuits in the year 1605, which was the 22d of his age. He was professor there of eloquence, and afterwards of sacred literature, and during the forty-eight years that he lived there in a most exemplary and edifying manner, he was the ornament of his society, the friend of all men of learning, the admiration of foreigners, and, in a word, one of the most excellent geniuses in France in the xviith century. F. Petau died in the college of Clermont, at Paris, on the 11th of December, 1652, aged 69. See his Life, written by another great man, Henry de Valois, his intimate friend, with the funeral elogiums of the learned. Besides numerous other works, he printed, in 1613, xvi orations of Themistius, in Greek and Latin, with notes and conjectures of his own; and in 1634 [rather 1630], he published the works of the Emperor Julian, 4to. &c.

MORERI.

† SPANHEIM EZEKIEL, the eldest son of Frederick Spanheim, professor of divinity at Leyden, was born at Geneva,

in

PREFACE.

" and learned commentary, has inſtructed
" the moſt intelligent, without offending the
" moſt ignorant *."

Of all the remaining works of Julian, both
thoſe which are here tranſlated, and thoſe
which are not, M. de la Bleterie has given
the following very accurate account:

" Independently of thoſe faults of his
" age, which Julian has not ſufficiently
" avoided, I mean a taſte for declamation,
" and the malady of quoting inceſſantly the
" ancients, eſpecially the divine Homer,
" whether by way of ornament, or even of
" proof, I queſtion whether the two PANE-

---

in the year 1629. For proofs of his extenſive learning ſee his work *de præſtantiâ et uſu numiſmatum*, his Diſſertation on a medal of the Abderites, his five letters to Morell, a famous antiquary and medalliſt, which have been printed with the *Specimen univerſæ rei nummariæ antiquæ*, which the ſame Morell publiſhed at Leipſic, in 1695; his notes on Callimachus, and on the CÆSARS of the Emperor Julian, and ſome other treatiſes, whoſe title may be ſeen in Moreri, Paris edition, 1695. You may there alſo find a ſeries of all the employments to which he was ſucceſſively raiſed at the courts of various princes, till he was ſent for the fourth time to the court of France [by the Elector of Brandenburgh], after the peace of Ryſwick. He continued at Paris from that time to the beginning of the year 1701, when he was ſent ambaſſador to England by his maſter, the new king of Pruſſia [with the title and dignity of Baron]. He died there Oct. 28, 1710, aged 81.   BAYLE.

* *Preface à la Vie de Julien*, p. 1—3.

PREFACE

"GYRICS ON CONSTANTIUS * would afford
"much pleasure [to a modern]. Notwith-
"standing the beauties of narration, which
"Julian has the art of diffusing, they err
"essentially as to their subject. Equitable
"readers would blame the author for having
"been obliged to employ so much art and
"genius to erect into a hero a prince of
"moderate talents whom he hated and
"feared. But would they forgive a tranf-
"lator for fatiguing posterity by the irksome
"repetition of praises which fear and ne-
"cessity rendered excusable in the mouth of
"an orator who pronounced them on pain
"of death?

"THE PANEGYRIC ON THE EMPRESS
"EUSEBIA † is a memorial of the gratitude
"of Julian. He does not speak there, how-
"ever, sufficiently from the heart. It is a
"frigid, didactic, monotonous elogium. As
"the author quotes in it some particulars of
"antiquity, that are less known now than
"they were then, the generality of readers

---

* *Orat.* I. *Orat.* II. These two panegyrics contain many facts, and excellent principles of government. Julian wrote the second in Gaul. Some Pagan phrases occur in them, which would induce us to think that he retouched them after he had declared himself a Pagan. *Life of Julian.*
† *Orat.* III.

"would

PREFACE.

" would think the piece too learned, and
" would not fail to say, that Julian intended
" to convince his benefactress that he made
" use of the library which she had given him.

" THE DISCOURSE IN HONOUR OF THE
" SUN-KING *, *in Solem Regem*, is an elo-
" gium on the *Logos* of Plato. Julian has
" some remarkable expressions on the sub-
" ject of that intelligence, the eternal pro-
" duction of the Sovereign God, of whom
" it is the living image, which, from all
" eternity, according to Julian, arranged the
" universe, which preserves and will always
" preserve it, which, holding the same place
" in the intelligible world that the sun
" holds among corporeal beings, is the
" source, the centre, the light of the sub-
" altern Gods, and of all the spirits to which
" virtuous souls will be reunited after death;
" which manifests its power, and resides, in an
" especial manner, in the star whose rays
" enlighten the material world. This work
" is useful and curious to such as wish to
" know fundamentally the philosophical pa-
" ganism of the Platonists of that time, and
" the system of religion which Julian formed

* *Orat.* IV.

PREFACE.

" to himself. But this long discourse pre-
" sents such a confused mixture of meta-
" physics and physics; it has so much ver-
" bosity, so little justice and precision, that
" it can do no honour but to the fecundity
" of Julian, who composed it in the space
" of three nights.

" He employed only one in making the
" ELOGIUM ON THE MOTHER OF THE GODS*.
" It was composed at Pessinuntus in Phrygia,
" where was a temple of that Goddess, ap-
" parently to revive the zeal of the people.
" He tortures his genius and imagination to
" explain allegorically the fable of Cybele
" and Atys, with the ceremonies of their
" worship. All these efforts terminate merely
" in publishing, with the tone of an enthu-

* *Orat.* V. One of the orations of Julian is consecrated to the honour of Cybele, the Mother of the Gods, who required from her effeminate priests the bloody sacrifice so rashly performed by the madness of the Phrygian boy. The pious Emperor condescends to relate, without a blush, and without a smile, the voyage of the Goddess from the shores of Pergamus to the mouth of the Tyber; and the stupendous miracle, which convinced the senate and people of Rome that the lump of clay, which their ambassadors transported over the seas, was endowed with life, and sentiment, and divine power. For the truth of this prodigy he appeals to the public monuments of the city; and censures, with some acrimony, the sickly and affected taste of those men, who impertinently derided the sacred traditions of their ancestors. GIBBON.

" siast,

PREFACE.

" fiaft, a romance of very obfcure phyfics.
" If I perfectly underftood it, I fhould not
" have tranflated it, on account of the ob-
" fcenity of the poëtical fable, from which
" Julian, neverthelefs, endeavours to deduce
" even fome moralities.

" THE DISCOURSE entitled AGAINST IGNO-
" RANT CYNICS *, *contra imperitos canes*, is
" alfo an *impromptu* which he compofed in
" two days, at his leifure hours, indignant
" at the irreverence and audacioufnefs of a
" diffolute Cynic, who, not contented with
" leading a voluptuous life, ridiculed the
" fingularities of Diogenes, and treated him
" as a coxcomb. Julian undertakes the apo-
" logy of the mafter, and exerts himfelf
" againft the difciple, with all the warmth
" of a man, who, in order to be a new Dio-
" genes, wanted only the wallet and ftaff.
" I think that this piece, though inferior to
" thofe which I have tranflated, would not
" difpleafe in French.

" I will not fay the fame of THE DISCOURSE,
" which is addreffed TO another Cynic, na-
" med HERACLIUS †. This philofopher, ha-
" ranguing in the prefence of Julian, had de-

* *Orat.* VI.   † *Orat.* VII.
                            " livered

"livered an allegorical fable, in which he
"modestly took upon himself the part of
"Jupiter, and gave the Emperor that of the
"God Pan. Julian was still more hurt by
"the little respect with which the Cynic
"mentioned the Gods. He was very near
"imposing silence on this profane declaimer.
"But having then made an effort of patience,
"as well from regard for the audience, as
"for fear of being considered as he said, as
"a suspicious man; who is scared at every
"thing, he indemnifies himself by giving
"scope to his zeal in a long discourse; whose
"object is to prove that a Cynic, an enemy,
"by his profession, to all dissimulation and
"disguise, ought not to compose fables; or,
"if he will compose them, that they should
"at least be serious, instructive, religious.
"This discourse, which would be clearer,
"if the fiction which shocked Julian were
"known to us, contains some curious par-
"ticulars relating to the origin and nature
"of fable, on the ancient and modern
"Cynics, &c. But what seems there most
"worthy of attention is a fable by Julian,
"which I shall presently mention.

"Julian

PREFACE.

"Julian was only Cæsar when he com-
"posed the piece entitled, A CONSOLATORY
"DISCOURSE ON THE DEPARTURE OF SAL-
"LUST *. It is the same Sallust whom
"Julian afterwards made Præfect of Gaul,
"and who must not be confounded with the
"Præfect of the East. Under Constantius
"he had a considerable employment in Gaul.
"His talents and fidelity having rendered
"him the intimate and confidential friend
"of the Cæsar, the jealousy and intrigues of
"the court did not fail to displace and recall
"him. Julian, who was sensible of all the
"greatness of his loss, endeavours, in this
"discourse, to console himself, and to com-
"fort his friend, for such a cruel separation.
"He regrets not only the charms and de-
"lights of an union founded on the love of
"virtue and the public good, but also the
"assistance of another self, who partook his
"engagements, his pains, and his pleasures,
"of a true man, whose like he despairs to
"find, who loved him without interest, re-
"proved him without arrogance, and told

* *Orat.* VIII.

"him

" him the truth without difguife. He
" makes a very rare and moſt refpectable
" confeſſion, eſpecially in the mouth of a
" prince; he ſays, in exprefs terms, that he
" owes to Salluſt all his reputation. In this
" work are ſentiment and principles; but
" they are a little choaked by the quo-
" tations and examples of antiquity. The
" piece was compoſed to be publiſhed, though
" the author was apprehenſive that it would
" not. On that account he confines himſelf to
" generals. It is plain, that, full of vexation,
" and pierced with a grief which he conceals
" in the bottom of his foul, he chooſes to
" tell Salluſt any thing but what he tells
" him. If he ſpeaks to him of Scipio, Lælius,
" Cato, Pythagoras, Plato, Democritus, Pe-
" ricles, Anaxagoras, &c. it is becauſe he
" dares not ſpeak of what intereſts him moſt.
" Thoſe who cannot be ignorant are reduced
" by ſervitude and conſtraint to pedantry:
" witneſs moſt of the Greeks who wrote
" under the Roman empire. Julian, as a
" private man or the Cæſar, lived in a
" moſt dreadful conſtraint. This perhaps
" is one of the cauſes of that miſplaced
" erudition

PREFACE.

" erudition which disfigures many of his
" works.*

" He could, however, forego erudition
" when he pleased, as we may be convinced
" by reading his MANIFESTO against the Em-
" peror Constantius †. This work has no-
" thing pedantic, but the being addressed TO
" THE SENATE AND PEOPLE OF ATHENS,
" whom Julian treats as he would have
" done the Athenians in the time of Mil-
" tiades, Aristides, and Themistocles. The
" piece is written in a solid, noble, persuasive
" manner, without declamation, without di-
" gression, without a single quotation, even
" from Homer, and gives occasion to presume
" that the faults which are justly blamed
" would not have been found in the other
" works of Julian, if he had only exercised
" his pen on happy subjects ‡.

" A long FRAGMENT § of instruction was
" addressed by him, in quality of Sovereign
" Pontiff, to a Pagan priest. It seems at if

---

* This Oration is omitted by M. de la Bleterie, but is translated in the following work.
† *Epist. ad S. P. Q. A.*
‡ I have also translated this Epistle. M. de la Bleterie has omitted it from " motives of delicacy," having interwoven almost the whole of it into his " Life of Julian."
§ FRAGMENTUM ORAT. AUT EPIST.

" Julian

PREFACE.

"Julian there pretended to reduce Paganism
"into a system; and that the instruction was
"divided into two parts, the first of which
"concerned, if I may so express myself, the
"doctrine and the morals, and the second
"contained the rules of discipline. It is, in
"general, a valuable and a very honourable
"testimony to our religion, as, on one side,
"the reformer of Hellenism thinks nothing
"more proper to render it respectable than
"to borrow, if he could, from the Christian
"church, her discipline and manners; and,
"on the other, he substitutes to revealed
"facts some extravagant fables. He rejects
"what Moses informs us of the creation of
"Adam, in order gravely to utter a theurgic
"tradition, according to which, Jupiter,
"in arranging the universe, let fall some
"drops of blood, and, of that sacred liquor
"formed mankind. In truth, religion is
"well avenged of its enemies by the very
"absurdities which they prefer to its tenets;
"*and sending them strong delusion, they shall*
"*believe a lie.* Such a one, who ridicules
"the fable of Julian, if he does not believe
"our sacred scriptures any more than Julian,
"admits, as to the origin of man, and a mul-
"titude

"titude of other points, some hypotheses,
" which, by being invested with a meta-
" physical jargon, are not less irrational than
" his pretended tradition. In this same
" FRAGMENT the author avows, that he
" would have rebuilt the temple of Jeru-
" salem; and we are sensible of all the im-
" portance of that avowal. The account of
" the rules which he prescribes to his pontiffs
" is copied from the idea of what the church
" requires of her ministers. On the subject
" of public entertainments, obscene books,
" and romances, of that senseless philosophy
" which denies or calls in question the ex-
" istence of God, his providence, and the
" immortality of the soul, he explains him-
" self in so strong and Christian a manner,
" that nothing more would be wanting to
" ruin him in the opinion of some persons,
" if the hatred which he expresses for the
" religion itself, of which he has preserved
" those remains, did not make him find fa-
" vour in their sight. Nevertheless, how
" useful soever this FRAGMENT might be,
" my hand could not have a share in copy-
" ing

PREFACE.

" ing the blasphemies which Julian there
" utters against our inspired writers *.

" The BOOKS AGAINST THE CHRISTIAN
" RELIGION † which this prince composed
" during the long winter-nights, were an
" abstract of what unbelievers opposed to
" Christianity, and especially of the objec-
" tions of Celsus, Hierocles, and Porphyry.
" Though the work was weak and immetho-
" dical, the delicacy and agreeableness of the
" style, as well as the purple of the author,
" gave it a great reputation. The Pagans pre-
" ferred it to every thing, and with their Ju-
" lian in their hands went forth to attack the
" Christians. Superficial minds took, as usual,
" witticisms for reasons, trite sophistries for
" incontrovertible arguments, and the fre-
" quent quotations of scripture, with which
" the author paraded, as a proof that he was
" deeply versed in sacred literature, and that
" he had not ceased to believe it without
" knowledge of the cause. The Christians,
" distracted by domestic controversies, ne-
" glected to answer it; for infidelity is al-

---

* Omitting those " blasphemies," I have extracted the useful and instructive part of this Fragment, under the title of The Duties of a Priest.

† *S. Cyrilli contra Julian. libri X.*

" ways

"ways a gainer by our disputes. They had
"a specious pretext. Origen, Eusebius of
"Cæsarea, Methodius, and Apollinarius had
"answered it before. But the simple were
"scandalised; and not being able to discern
"of themselves whether the silence of one
"of the parties concerned proceeded from
"weakness or contempt, were tempted to
"ascribe the victory to him who was the
"last speaker. About the year 400, Philip,
"of Side in Pamphylia, deacon of the
"church of Constantinople, under St. Chry-
"sostom, endeavoured to avenge the honour
"of religion. The answer of Philip is lost;
"and the opinion, which Socrates gives of
"another work by the same author, affords
"us no reason to regret it. At length, fifty
"or sixty years after the death of Julian, St.
"Cyril of Alexandria, though very inferior
"to that prince in the art of writing, at-
"tacked the expiring refuge of Paganism,
"and destroyed it. This father has preserved
"us a part of the work which he refuted.
"These passages are less valuable to unbe-
"lievers than they perhaps imagine. They
"will find there some very mortifying con-
"fessions.

"fessions *. Divines observe there some un-
"suspected testimonies of the antiquity of
"some tenets †, of some customs and ex-
"pressions. The refutation by St. Cyril,
"which he dedicated to the Emperor Theo-
"dosius the Younger, is learned, profound,
"decisive against Julian and Paganism; but
"the perusal of it would be more agreeable,
"if his pen were as elegant as that of Julian.
"Besides, St. Cyril wrote for readers who
"were persuaded that, if Paganism was false,
"Christianity must necessarily be true. For
"this reason he applies himself less to answer
"directly the objections of Julian than to
"prove the weakness, or rather the nothing-
"ness, of Paganism. This method, which
"was then sufficient, would not be so well
"adapted to the necessities of our age, in
"which the same objections are unhappily
"too often repeated by men equally hostile
"to all religion. A direct refutation of
"these too famous books would be an em-

* *Cyrill. contr. Jul. l.* VI. 10.

† *Ibid. l.* x. These passages are quoted in *La Vie de Julien, pp.* 244, 245.

"ployment

PREFACE.

"ployment truly worthy of a philosophical
"divine *.

"It is useless here to mention some other
"works, which have not reached us. I will
"now give an account of those which I
"have translated.

"THE CÆSARS † are deemed unquestion-
"ably the master-piece of Julian. I express
"myself too freely, both as to his person
"and his writings, to be charged with that
"kind of idolatry which is too common in
"translators. I venture therefore to say, that
"profane antiquity does not afford any piece
"which is comparable to this for the merit
"of the subject, and very few which ought
"to be preferred to it for the merit of the
"execution.

"A Roman Emperor, who has had the
"advantage to be a private man, a mind
"filled, and perhaps a heart penetrated, with
"great maxims of government, a philoso-
"pher notwithstanding all impediments,
"born with much taste and genius for rail-
"lery, ready to seize the ridiculous, and never
"letting it escape, in others, not even in

---

* Mr. Gibbon is pleased to call this " a strange Centaur."
Vol. II. p. 369.

† *Cæsares, sive Convivium.*

" himself, knowing how to diftinguifh thofe
" light clouds which conftitute the difference
" between the middling and the good, the
" excellent and the perfect, between qualities
" which are eftimable and thofe which are
" only brilliant, nourifhed with the reading
" of Plato and Ariftotle, and fpeaking their
" language like themfelves, affembles in one
" piece all the Emperors who reigned before
" him for the fpace of about four hundred
" years,

" It is a moving picture, in which the
" fpectator fees rapidly paffing before his
" eyes, but without confufion, thofe mafters
" of the world defpoiled of their grandeur,
" and reduced to their vices and their virtues.
" By the aid of a fimple and ingenious fiction,
" Julian makes thofe who have difhonoured
" the purple difappear with ignominy; and
" among thofe who deferve to be placed
" in the number of fovereigns he choofes
" the moft illuftrious to make them contend
" for pre-eminence. Though he feems to
" leave the queftion undetermined, it is fuf-
" ficiently clear that Marcus Aurelius is the
" hero of the piece; that Julian gives him
" the preference, and means to announce to
                                          " the

" the univerſe that he has taken that philo-
" ſophical Emperor for his model.

" Such is the general plan of the Satire,
" or rather of the Judgment, of THE CÆSARS.
" I do not think that in any work ſo ſhort
" are to be found at once ſo many characters
" and manners, ſo much refinement and ſo-
" lidity, ſo much inſtruction, without the
" author ever aſſuming a dogmatical tone,
" ſo much wit and pleaſantry, without his
" ever ceaſing to inſtruct. In a word, it
" ſeems to me that THE CÆSARS ought to
" undeceive, or at leaſt to embarraſs, thoſe
" who have voted an excluſive eſteem to the
" productions of ancient Greece.

" The work, however, is not exempt from
" faults. Not to mention ſome railleries
" that are either frigid, or ſeem ſo to us,
" nor a few groundleſs and too ſevere ſen-
" tences which Julian pronounces on certain
" Emperors, in whoſe memory no one at
" preſent is much intereſted, the no leſs un-
" juſt than indecent manner in which he
" treats his uncle, Conſtantine the Great, is
" inexcuſable. In ſpite of his inclination,
" not being able to avoid making him enter
" into competition with the moſt diſtin-
" guiſhed.

"guished Emperors, he omits nothing that
"can ridicule and degrade him.

"This visible partiality, produced by his
"hatred of our religion, and by other causes
"which I have taken care to develope in
"the remarks, can injure only Julian.
"Neither his envenomed strokes, nor those
"of Zosimus, will prevent Constantine
"from being regarded as a prince of supe-
"rior merit, and highly worthy of the title
"of Great; any more than the extravagant
"elogiums of the Greeks, who give him the
"title of " equal to the apostles," will
"ever persuade us that all his actions were
"conformable to the sanctity of the gospel,
"of which he declared himself the pro-
"tector. Without dissembling either his
"faults or failings, I have detected the ca-
"lumnies by which a passionate enemy en-
"deavours to blacken him; and I have
"done it solely for the interest of the truth
"of history; for I am far from thinking,
"with this unjust censor, that the blows
"aimed at Constantine can fall upon re-
"ligion. If he has the glory to be the in-
"strument which God employed to rescue
"it from oppression, he is not, after all,
"either

PREFACE.

" either its founder or apostle. Without the
" Emperors, and in spite of their efforts,
" when Constantine embraced it, it had so
" much prevailed, that he has been suspected,
" though falsely, of having embraced it from
" policy. When we have the happiness to
" profess a religion so august, so divine,
" fixed on immoveable foundations, there
" would be pusillanimity, not to say cow-
" ardice, in thinking it dependent on, or
" reponsible for, the reputation of its first
" protectors. God, the supreme disposer of all
" events, and *who calls things that are not*
" *as though they were*, could, and yet he did
" not, have made Theodosius have reigned
" before Constantine, and have placed St.
" Lewis at the head of our Christian kings.

" I must observe, that in THE CÆSARS
" is a sort of contradiction. The author
" there supposes the Gods such as the poets
" represent them, yet he often recurs to the
" ideas of the philosophers. This is not
" a fault peculiar to him. It cannot be in-
" ferred from hence that he meant to ridi-
" cule religion, nor that he was a free-
" thinker. He considered the fables of the
" poets as fictions, which being taken lite-

" rally

" rally would have dishonoured the Deity;
" but persuaded that they must be turned
" into allegories, being a deist in speculation
" to a certain point, but a zealous pagan in
" practice, he conformed to the established
" language. This mixture of poetical and
" philosophical Paganism was not unusual.
" No one was hurt by it. We are justly
" shocked at it, and should be much more
" so, if reading the ancients had not fa-
" miliarised us to such absurdities.

" It is more than sixty years * since M.
" Spanheim, so well known in the republic
" of letters, undertook to translate THE
" CÆSARS into French. This learned fo-
" reigner was unacquainted with the refine-
" ments of our language; and his version
" no more resembles the original than a
" skeleton does a human body †. To the
" text he has added some remarks, has sup-
" ported his remarks by proofs, and en-
" riched them both with medals; the whole
" with so much profusion, that the small

---

* In 1683.
† In like manner, Mr. Gibbon styles this French version " coarse, languid, and correct." " The Abbé de la
" Bleterie," he adds, " has more happily expressed the
" spirit, as well as sense, of the original, which he has illus-
" trated with some concise and curious notes."

" work

" work of Julian is in a manner loſt in a
" quarto of above ſix hundred pages. It is
" a maſter-piece of typography, a treaſure
" of ancient literature ill-digeſted, and of
" numiſmatic erudition. This book is or-
" namental to libraries, but it alarms the
" generality of readers, whom the ſight of
" ſo prolix a commentary inſpires at leaſt
" with indifference for a text which, they
" ſuppoſe, requires ſo many illuſtrations.
" Every one is not obliged to know that
" commentators do not labour merely to
" give the meaning of their author; that
" they often chooſe him only for an oppor-
" tunity of emptying their common-place-
" books, and that they are generally as dif-
" fuſe on the moſt eaſy paſſages as they are
" ſuccinct, or even ſilent, on real difficulties.
" The Misopogon * is a ſatire leſs diver-
" ſified, but more ſingular, than the Cæsars.
" Julian, driven to extremities by the inha-
" bitants of Antioch, inſtead of avenging
" himſelf, or of pardoning them, like a
" prince, undertakes to avenge himſelf like
" an author; and no author, I fancy, ever
" conceived ſuch a project of revenge. He

* *Miſopogon, ſive Antiochus.*

" pretends

" pretends to turn his ill-humour againſt him-
" ſelf; he exaggerates his own imperfections,
" and repreſenting the good qualities that he
" may have as extravagances, he oppoſes them
" to the vices of Antioch, which he ironically
" exhibits as virtues.

" Julian draws himſelf more extraordi-
" nary than he really is, but he muſt have
" been very extraordinary to draw himſelf
" in ſuch a manner. If the work be defi-
" cient in dignity, it abounds with ſtrokes,
" ſallies, principles, and manners. Genius
" ſparkles throughout the whole; but the
" pleaſantry is too cauſtic and bitter. It is
" the laugh of a man in a paſſion, who acts
" the part of a philoſopher, and cannot ſup-
" port it to the end. He leaves at laſt the
" ironical tone, to aſſume that of invective
" and direct reproach. I think I may
" affirm that this ſatire flowed from the pen
" of Julian in a fit of chagrin and anger,
" and that he employed no more time in
" compoſing it than was neceſſary to write
" it. But ſuch as it is, it is an *unique*, and
" without having read it we cannot be ſuf-
" ficiently acquainted with Julian.

" A FABLE,

PREFACE.

" A FABLE *, which I have taken from
" the difcourfe to the Cynic Heraclius, will
" I doubt not be read with pleafure. Julian,
" in order to give him the model of an
" inftructive and religious fable, defcribes,
" in an allegorical fiction, but which it is
" impoffible to miftake, the misfortunes of
" his family, the dangers which he incurred
" in his childhood, his fyftem in religion
" and government. Though it is in profe,
" it is an excellent piece of poetry.

" The letters of celebrated men are ge-
" nerally the moft curious parts of their
" writings. Many of the EPISTLES † of
" Julian difplay his mind, his genius, his
" ideas on goverment and religion; others
" throw light on hiftory, facred and profane;
" and there are fome billets which prove
" that he was very capable of fucceeding in
" the laconic ftyle. Among his Epiftles are
" fome of his laws. Two or three more I
" have taken from the Theodofian Code.
" No Emperor made fo many laws in fo
" fhort a reign: excepting thofe which re-

---
* *Ex Orat.* VII.
† *Epiſtolæ.* Of the LXXI. Epiftles, thofe to Themiftius, Conftantius, and the Athenians, included; M. de la Bleterie has tranflated only XLVII.

" gard

"gard Christianity, his are esteemed by the
"lawyers; but unfortunately the Codes of
"Theodosius and Justinian scarce ever give
"more than the enacting part of the law,
"and not the preamble, in which the genius
"and eloquence of the legislator were dis-
"played.

"I have inserted in its place the EPISTLE
"TO THEMISTIUS *, which the editions
"place at the end of the Orations. It is in
"fact a treatise in the form of an Epistle, in
"which the author, seeing the rocks that
"surround the throne, expresses his anxieties
"and apprehensions, lays down excellent
"maxims concerning the duties of a sove-
"reign, and acknowleges his incapacity with
"a modesty highly laudable, if it be sincere.
"We perceive in this work a strain of de-
"clamation, and somewhat rather vague.
"It were to be wished that the author had
"applied a little more the principles which
"he draws from Aristotle and Plato. But
"it should be considered that Julian, when
"he composed this treatise, had just been
"declared Cæsar by Constantius, and that
"this new dignity had only increased his

* *Epistola ad Themistium.*

"slavery.

PREFACE.

"flavery. The piece is free enough for the
"time when it was written. Julian ven-
"tures to fpeak there as if he were inde-
"pendent, or at leaft as if he would one day
"be fo."

With a well-grounded confidence the learned writer adds, "Though the public is
"prejudiced againft notes, and regards them
"as fuperfluities which only ferve to en-
"large the volumes, I venture, however, to
"intreat them to caft their eyes on mine.
"They are extremely laboured, and, I pre-
"fume, nothing will be found in them ufe-
"lefs or trifling. I have entered into gram-
"matical difcuffions only when I thought
"them important, and to fhew that I could
"tire the reader by that kind of erudition
"as well as others. If fome fhould think
"that I ftop too often to parry the weak
"thrufts that Julian makes at Chriftianity,
"I will own, that, writing in a Chriftian
"nation, I am afhamed to be obliged to re-
"fute what deferves only contempt. But as
"for thofe who fhall think thefe precautions
"exceffive, I beg them to examine whether
"they do not contribute to make them ne-
"ceffary.

"ceſſary. *I am become a fool in glorying; ye
"have compelled me *."

The comment indeed of this learned foreigner is frequently ſuperior to the text; and the whole is ſuch a fund of critical, hiſtorical, and Chriſtian knowledge, that it cannot but be acceptable to an Engliſh reader. I muſt add, that I am alſo much indebted to the elegant (I am ſorry I cannot ſay, unexceptionable) *Hiſtory of the Decline and Fall of the Roman empire,* as will appear by the frequent quotations from that work in the notes. The Epiſtles of Libanius to Julian, which are alſo inſerted, and two Monodies on ſubjects mentioned in theſe works, will give ſome idea of the ſtyle of that ſophiſt.

Beſides the *Hiſtory of Jovian,* an abſtract of an Eſſay, by the Abbé de la Bleterie, "on "the rank and power of the Roman Em"perors in the Senate," which has not, to my knowledge, appeared in Engliſh, is annexed.

Chriſt-Church,
Canterbury, 1783.   J. DUNCOMBE.

The following ſhort Annals and Pedigree of Julian may ſerve to illuſtrate the hiſtorical events occaſionally mentioned in his writings.

* *Preface à l'Hiſtoire de Jovien,* p. x.—LXIII.

[xxxv]

ANNALS
OF THE
PRINCIPAL EVENTS
IN THE
LIFE of JULIAN.

FLAVIUS CLAUDIUS JULIAN was born at Constantinople. His mother, Basilina, died a few months after. — A.D. 331. Nov. 6.

His father, Julius Constantius, and most of his relations, were massacred by order of the Emperor Constantius. His half-brother, Gallus, is banished into Ionia; and he is sent to Nicomedia, where he is educated a Christian by the bishop Eusebius, and officiates as a lecturer in the church. He is put under the tuition of Mardonius, an eunuch. — 337.

He is taken from school, and confined six years with Gallus in a castle in Cappadocia. — 345.

Gallus is created Cæsar, and goes to reside at Antioch. — 351. Mar. 5.

Julian

A. D. 351.	Julian visits Edesius at Pergamus, and is perverted to Paganism by Maximus, who initiates him at Ephesus.
	He is sent to complete his education at Constantinople under Ecebolus and Nicocles.
354. Dec.	Gallus is deprived of the purple, and put to death in Dalmatia. Julian is conveyed to the court of Milan.
355. May.	He is sent to study at Athens, where he is initiated into the Eleusinian mysteries.
Oct.	He is recalled to Milan.
Nov. 6.	He is declared Cæsar, and soon after marries his cousin Helena, sister to Constantius. Writes his 1st panegyrical oration on Constantius.
Dec. 1.	Sets out for Gaul with 350 soldiers. Winters at Vienne, and there probably composes his Epistle to Themistius.
356 Jan. 1.	Enters on his 1st consulship with Constantius (the viiith). Writes his 2d panegyric on that prince.
June 24.	Arrives at Autun. Twice defeats the Alemanni, and retakes Cologne.
	Winters at Sens, where he repulses an attack of the enemy.
357 Jan. 1.	Enters on his iid consulship, with Constantius (the ixth.)

Defeats

THE LIFE OF JULIAN.

Defeats the Alemanni at Strafburgh, takes their king, Cnodomar, prifoner, &c.   A. D. 357. Aug.

Paffes the Rhine at Mentz.

Subdues the Franks. Winters at Paris.   Dec.

Defeats the Salians and Chamavians. Paffes the Rhine again. Two kings of the Alemanni furrender and fue for peace. Winters at Paris. Writes his confolatory oration on the departure of Salluft.   358. July.

Paffes the Rhine a third time, furprifes fix kings, who difputed his paffage, and refcues 20,000 prifoners. Reftores the ruined cities of Gaul.   359.

Winters again at Paris. Sends Lupicinus to Britain, to repulfe the Scots and Picts.

Enters on his IIId confulfhip with Conftantius (the Xth.)   360. Jan. 1.

The flower of the Gallic army being ordered by Conftantius to march into the Eaft, they mutiny at Paris, and proclaim Julian Emperor.   April.

He paffes the Rhine a fourth time (at Bonn) and fubdues the Attuarii. Declares himfelf a Pagan.   July.

Winters at Vienne, where he celebrates his fifth anniverfary, Nov. 6, 361. Lofes his wife.   Oct.

Paffes the Rhine a fifth time, and again defeats and reduces the Alemanni.

Marches

A.D. 361.	Marches against Constantius, and seizes the pass of Succi.
	Writes from Sirmium and Naissus to Athens, and the other cities of Greece.
Nov. 3. †	Constantius died at Mopsocrene in Cilicia, aged 45.
Dec. 11.	Julian enters Constantinople, and restores the Pagan worship. Winters there, and writes the Cæsars.
362. May 15.	Leaves Constantinople. In his way, visits the temple of Cybele at Pessinus in Phrygia, where he writes his vth oration.
June.	Arrives at Antioch, where he winters.
Dec.	Composes his books against the Christian religion.
363. Jan. 1.	Enters on his ivth and last consulship, with Sallust, præfect of Gaul. Attempts in vain to rebuild the temple of Jerusalem.
Feb.	Writes the Misopogon.
March 13.	Leaves Antioch, and marches against the Persians, joining his army at Hierapolis, where he passes the Euphrates.
April 7.	Passes the Chaboras, and enters the Persian territories.
	Besieges and takes by assault Perisabor and Maogamalcha in Assyria.

† Ammianus says, Oct. 3. But Idatius, Socrates, Cedrenus, the Alex. Chronicle, and others, say as above.

Transports

THE LIFE OF JULIAN.

Tranſports his fleet from the Euphrates to the Tigris. — A. D. 363.

Forces the paſſage of the Tigris, but, unable to reduce Cteſiphon, and deceived by a Perſian deſerter, burns his fleet and magazines, and advances into the inland country, where he is ſeverely diſtreſſed by famine. — June.

Retreats towards the Tigris. — 16.

Repulſes the Perſians at Maronga. — 22.

Receives a mortal wound in a ſkirmiſh, of which he died in the ſucceeding night, aged 32. — 26.

His remains, by his own deſire, were interred at Tarſus in Cilicia.

PEDIGREE

PEDIGREE OF JULIAN.

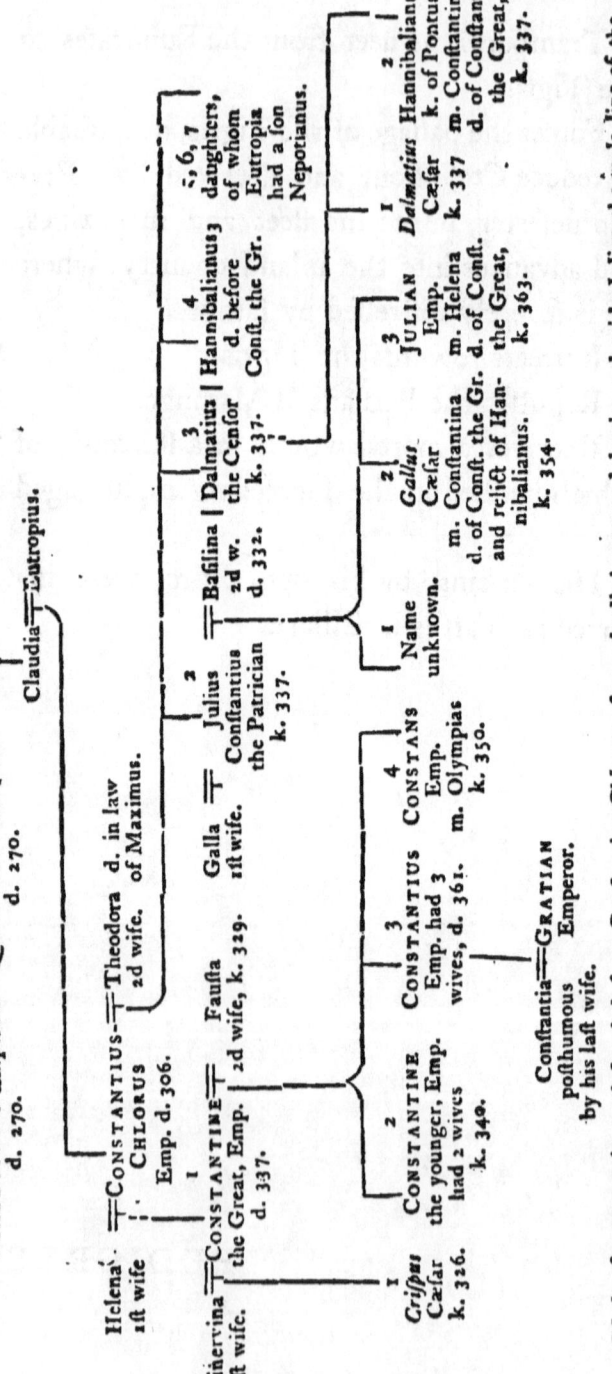

Of the fourteen princes descended from Constantius Chlorus, five only died a natural death; and with Julian the male line of the Flavian or Constantine family ended.

SELECT WORKS

OF

JULIAN.

Gallus * Cæsar to his Brother Julian Health †.

THE neighbourhood of Ionia has afforded me great joy, having dispelled the concern and indignation that I felt at a former report. What that was I will inform you. I heard that you

A. D. 351 or 352.

---

* Gallus was the elder brother of Julian, by a different mother, and having with him been secreted from the murderers of their relations in 337, they were banished by the Emperor Constantius into Ionia, from whence, in 345, they were conveyed to the castle of Macellum in Cappadocia. There they were not only educated Christians, but officiated as lecturers in the church of Nicomedia. Six years after, viz. on March 5, 351, Gallus was declared Cæsar by Constantius, and married to his sister Constantina. He then went to Antioch, to preside, with a delegated authority, over the three great dioceses of the Eastern Præfecture, and from that city this Epistle was probably

you had departed from your former religion transmitted to you by your anceſtor ‡, and, hurried away by mad and wicked advice, had embraced a vain ſuperſtition. How did I grieve at this information! For as I conſider your good actions, whenever they are celebrated, as advantageous to myſelf, ſo I eſteem your bad deeds (which Heaven avert!) as much or more detrimental. But the anxiety which this intelligence gave me, has been removed by the arrival of our father Ætius *, as he

---

probably written, Julian being then in Ionia, whither Gallus had diſpatched Ætius to ſtrengthen him in the Chriſtian Faith. Conſtantius, in the mean time, was marching towards the Weſt. The ſubſequent imprudence of Gallus, and his fatal cataſtrophe in 354, are related by Julian in his Epiſtle to the Athenians.

† The learned F. Petau ſuppoſes this Epiſtle to be ſpurious, without aſſigning a reaſon. Meſſrs de Tillemont and Spanheim think it genuine. In fact, we find nothing in it which does not agree with what we know from other hands.   La Bleterie.

‡ Gallus had ſome reaſon to ſuſpect the ſecret apoſtacy of Julian, and, in a letter to him, which may be received as genuine, he exhorts Julian to adhere to the religion of their anceſtors; an argument, which, as it ſhould ſeem, was not yet perfectly ripe.   Gibbon.

The grandfather of Gallus and Julian, Conſtantius Chlorus, the father of Conſtantine the Great and Julius Conſtantius, had been very favourable to the Chriſtians, and perhaps was a Chriſtian in his heart. Nothing more is neceſſary to authoriſe, in ſome degree, the expreſſion uſed by Gallus, his grandſon.   La Bleterie.

This conſtruction, it muſt be owned, is rather forced.

* Ætius, a Syrian by birth, a braſier, a goldſmith, an empiric, having ſtudied the categories of Ariſtotle, ſet up for a divine. He carried the principles of Arianiſm as far as

TO JULIAN.

he assures me, on the contrary, to my great joy, that you are zealously employed in houses of prayer †, and can hardly be removed from the tombs of the martyrs, but are totally attached to our worship. I must apply to you that expression of Homer: " Be this your aim ‡." Continue thus

as they would go; and, reviving the blasphemies of Arius, he plainly taught that the Word was only a creature. This occasioned his being styled *The Atheist*, not only by the Catholics, but even by the moderate Arians. Leontius, bishop of Antioch, did not scruple to ordain him a deacon; and Gallus took him for his oracle in divinity. Ætius was the dupe of Julian, who carried his dissimulation so far as to embrace a monastic life. Libanius speaks of this hypocrisy as if it were an innocent stratagem. " Though " Julian," says he, " had changed his religion, he still " professed the same, not being allowed to discover his " real sentiments. This was the reverse of the fable of " Æsop. The lion borrowed the skin of a vile animal. " Julian knew the better part, but he acted outwardly the " safest." *Liban. Orat. Parent.* We see that the panegyrist was no more scrupulous than the hero on the article of sincerity, even in the affair of religion. *Ibid.*

The death of Gallus was followed by the exile of Ætius. But he was recalled by Julian. See an Epistle from him to that prelate (as he was afterwards) the XXXIst.

† Σπουδαζειν σε ιφη εις οικους ευχων. In the Latin translation it is, *Te in domibus studiosè versari.* " That you are " studiously employed in houses ;" which, by omitting precum (ευχων) conveys no meaning.

‡ Βαλλ' ουτως, *Sic jaculare.* Iliad. VIII. 282.
Thus, always thus, thy early worth be try'd. *Pope*, 340.

These are the words of Agamemnon to Teucer, who was shooting his arrows with success against the Trojans. It should be remarked that the Greeks, and those who spoke Greek, whether Pagans or Christians, quoted Homer on every occasion, and made continual allusions to some passages of this poet. The Pagans, and Julian in particular, had the same respect for Homer that we have for the canonical books. LA BLETERIE.

to delight all who love you, remembering that nothing is preferable to religion. For the perfection of virtue instructs us to detest the fallacy of falsehood, and to adhere to truth; which is principally apparent in piety towards God. But a plurality of Gods is productive of endless dissensions and uncertainty. One only Deity by his sole power governs the universe*, not, like the sons of Saturn, by lot and partition, but because he is self-created and has almighty power, not acquired by force, but existing before all things. This is the true God, and to him all worship is due. Farewell.

Julian Cæsar to the Philosopher Themistius †.

A.D. 355 or 356.

I Earnestly wish to realise the expectations, which, you say, you have formed of me. But in this I fear I shall fail, as you promise much more for me than you ought to others, and especially to yourself.

---

* We read in the text, Το δε μοιον συν ενι υπαργον οι βασιλευσι τυ παντος, which gives no meaning. I think that we should read συν ενι υπαργω. Gallus will then speak like an Arian, like a faithful disciple of Ætius. The Christianity both of Julian and Gallus was in all appearance only Arianism.

La Bleterie.

† This philosophical Epistle " on the dangers of sovereign power" was written soon after Constantius had raised Julian to the dignity of Cæsar. It must not be forgotten that this was not only a designation to the empire, but also an actual

EPISTLE TO THEMISTIUS.

self. For long ago, on my suppoſing a competition between myſelf with Alexander and Marcus [Aurelius], I was wonderfully fearful and apprehenſive of falling far ſhort of the fortitude of the firſt, and of not making the leaſt approach to the perfect virtue of the other. On theſe conſiderations, an idle life ſeemed to me moſt deſirable; and recollecting with pleaſure the Attic fables, I wiſhed to ſing them to my friends, as porters in the ſtreets thus alleviate the weight of their bur-

actual aſſociation in a conſiderable part of the imperial power. The Greeks gave the Cæſar the title of βασιλευς δευτερος, or even, as they did the Emperor, ſimply that of βασιλευς. I ſhall preſently mention why I cannot adopt the conjecture of F. Petau, who imagines that Julian compoſed this treatiſe when the death of Conſtantius had made him maſter of the empire. And I ſhall examine, in the ſequel, whether the Themiſtius, to whom Julian writes, be the ſame whoſe works we have. LA BLETERIE.

Philoſophy had inſtructed Julian to compare the advantages of action and retirement; but the elevation of his birth, and the accidents of his life, never allowed him the freedom of choice. He might perhaps ſincerely have preferred the groves of the Academy, and the ſociety of Athens; but he was conſtrained at firſt by the will, and afterwards by the juſtice, of Conſtantius, to expoſe his perſon and fame to the dangers of Imperial greatneſs; and to make himſelf accountable to the world, and to poſterity, for the happineſs of millions.

Julian himſelf has expreſſed theſe philoſophical ideas with much eloquence, and ſome affectation, in a very elaborate Epiſtle to Themiſtius. The Abbé de la Bleterie, who has given an elegant tranſlation, is inclined to believe, that it was the celebrated Themiſtius whoſe Orations are ſtill extant. GIBBON.

Petau ſtyles this, "not an Oration, but an Epiſtle;" but "becauſe it is longer than an epiſtle," he places it among the Orations.

EPISTLE TO THEMISTIUS.

thens. But you, by your late epistle, have augmented my fears, and have proposed to me a much more arduous contention, by saying, that God has placed me in the same situation that Hercules and Bacchus were placed of old, who at the same time philosophised and reigned, and freed almost the whole earth and sea from the vices with which they were overwhelmed. You also advise me, banishing the thoughts of sloth and idleness, to consider how I shall act with propriety in this supposed contention. You then mention all the legislators, Solon *, Pittacus †, Lycurgus ‡; and you add, that the world may reasonably form greater expectations of me than it did of them.

On reading this passage I was struck with astonishment, knowing that you think it by no means allowable to flatter or falsify; and as to myself, being conscious of no superior talents, either natural or acquired, except my love of philosophy. Of the calamities, which have hitherto rendered this love imperfect, I say nothing. I knew not therefore what construction to put on these expressions, till this was suggested to me by Heaven, that you meant by thus praising to exhort me, and to display the magnitude of those trials to which every ruler must necessarily be exposed.

---

* One of the wise men of Greece, the lawgiver of Athens. See Plutarch and Diogenes Laërtius.
† Another of the wise men, contemporary with Crœsus, a philosopher of Mitylene. Some of his precepts are preserved in Ausonius *de Sapientia*.
‡ The lawgiver of Sparta. See Justin and Plutarch.

But

EPISTLE TO THEMISTIUS.

But this is rather a discouragement than a recommendation of such a state.

Suppose that a man navigating your strait *, and that not with ease or expedition, should be told by one skilled in divination, that he should traverse the Ægean, and afterwards the Ionian sea, and at last the main ocean. "Here," the prophet should say, "you see towns and harbours, but "there you shall discern neither watch-tower, nor "rock, happy if you discover some ship at a distance, "and can hail the crew. You shall often pray to "God for a safe return to land, even were your "life immediately to end; satisfied, if after having "reached the haven, and restored your ship to the "owners, and the mariners to their families, you "might commit your body to your native earth †." This might happen, but that it would must till the last moment remain uncertain. Do you think, that, after having heard this, such a man would even choose to dwell in a sea-port town? or rather, bidding adieu to riches and the profits attendant on commerce, to his domestic connections, to foreign friendships, and to the survey of distant cities and coun-

---

* It is difficult to conjecture what strait he means. I suspect it, however, to be the Bosphorus, and that Themistius was then at Constantinople.   PETAU.

If I were sure that this Epistle was addressed to the celebrated Themistius, I should affirm, that this strait was that of Constantinople.   LA BLETERIE.

† The ancients thought drowning the most dishonourable of deaths. Hence those passionate exclamations, under such an apprehension of Achilles in the Iliad, and Æneas in the Æneid.

EPISTLE TO THEMISTIUS.

tries, would he not think the advice of the son of Neocles *, "Live privately," the wisest that could be given?

Of this you seem so apprehensive, that you endeavour, by reproaching Epicurus, to prejudice me against him, and to eradicate that opinion. These are your words; "that he, a man of no business, "should praise idleness, and those Peripatetic "disputations, might well be expected." But that Epicurus was in this mistaken, I have been long and am firmly persuaded. Whether indeed it is proper to urge any one to public administration, who is naturally unqualified and of mean abilities, may deserve farther enquiry. For even Socrates is said to have withdrawn many from the forum who seemed not calculated for it; and he endeavoured, in particular, as Xenophon relates, to dissuade Glaucon, and the son of Clinias †, but could not restrain the impetuosity of that youth.

Shall we then compell those who are conscious of their own deficiencies, and urge them to be confident in such undertakings as depend not so much on virtue and a right disposition, as on fortune, who governs all things, and often forces us to follow her direction? Chrysippus ‡ in other things

seemed

---

* Epicurus.
† Alcibiades.
‡ Chrysippus is styled by Cicero "the most subtle inter- "preter of the Stoic dreams, and the support of the Por- "tico." His chief study was logic, which he carried to a trifling degree of subtlety. Of his works, which filled 705 volumes,

EPISTLE TO THEMISTIUS.

seemed wise, and was justly so esteemed; but his ignorance of fortune and chance, and other like causes, which happen independently of our actions, is not easily reconcileable with what time has evidently taught us by many examples. For in what particular shall we style Cato*, or Dion Siculus †, happy? Perhaps for their disregard of death, but certainly not for their leaving the works in which they at first engaged imperfect, works to which they had diligently attended, and for which they would willingly have suffered the severest calamities. When disappointed, they behaved, it is said, with moderation, not repining at fortune, and derived no small consolation from virtue; but they could by no means be styled happy, having failed in their greatest undertakings, unless in the sense of the Stoics. To which it may be answered, that to be praised and to be happy are not the same thing; and if all creatures naturally desire

---

volumes, some titles only remain. He died about 200 years before the Christian æra, and was honoured by the Athenians with a statue in the Ceramicus. His death is said to have been occasioned by an immoderate fit of laughter at seeing an ass eat figs. Chrysippus desired the ass might have a glass of wine to wash them down, and was so diverted with his own conceit, that it cost him his life. He is said to have been a very copious and learned writer, but obscure and immoral; though one would be inclined to think, from the respect with which he is mentioned by Epictetus, that this latter accusation is groundless.
Mrs. CARTER.

* Of Utica.
† A nobleman of Syracuse, attached to Plato, by whose counsel he freed his country from the tyranny of Dionysius. He was afterwards assassinated by one of his friends.

happiness, it is better for us to be declared happy than to be praised for virtue. Substantial happiness by no means depends on fortune. Those who are engaged in government cannot indeed breathe, as the saying is, without her * * * † as if philosophy could form a general, and place him above the reach of chance, like the pure, incorporeal, and intelligent world of ideas, whether they are produced in reality, or formed falsly. He indeed who is, according to Diogenes,

Of city, country, house depriv'd,

has nothing more to lose. But how can one whom custom has called forth, and as Homer, the first of writers, says,

—— Who mighty nations guides,

Directs in council, and in war, presides ‡, consistently place himself out of the reach of fortune? And if he be really subject to it, with what consideration and prudence must he act, so as

---

† Before this passage we have placed astericks, as something here is wanting. But in our MSS a fragment was inserted of another epistle, which, if I mistake not, Julian wrote to Arsacius, a High Priest, in which he gave some directions relating to religion and the worship of the gods. This we have extracted, and published separately, in another place; but what follows seems addressed to Themistius.   PETAU.

The above-mentioned Fragment of an oration, or epistle, (so styled) is characterised in the preface, and that unobjectible part of it, which contains "The Duties of a Priest," is detached and inserted, under that title, among these "Select Works."

‡Iliad, II. 25. Pope, 27.

to sustain with equanimity, like a sage pilot, the storms that assail him on every side?

If admiration be due to those who withstand her attacks with fortitude, much more is it deserved by those who receive her favours with moderation. By them the greatest of kings, the conqueror of Asia, was subdued, as in cruelty and insolence he far surpassed Darius and Xerxes, after he had conquered their dominions. By these weapons the Persians, Macedonians, Athenians, Syracusans, the Lacedæmonian magistrates, the Roman generals, and, lastly, many emperors, were attacked and totally destroyed. It would be endless to enumerate all who have fallen a prey to wealth, success, and luxury. And why should I mention those, who, overwhelmed by misfortunes, from freemen have become slaves, from noble mean, and from splendid abject? Would to Heaven, that human life afforded no such instances! But such there have been, and such there always will be, as long as the world exists.

But that I may not seem singular in thinking that Fortune has the chief sway in human affairs, I refer you, intelligent as you are and my instructor, to Plato, in his admirable book on Laws; and to convince you that I have not weakly imbibed this idea, I will transcribe the passage*: "God, and, with
"God,

---

* All this passage is taken from the fourth book of Plato *de Legibus*, which, in some places, we have corrected from

Plato

"God, Fortune, or Opportunity, govern all things human, but a third muſt be annexed; Art muſt attend them, as an aſſociate." He then proceeds to ſhew, that every king, every ſovereign artificer of great actions, ſhould be a kind of King-God. "Saturn," he ſays, "knowing (as we have before obſerved) that human nature is not of itſelf capable of governing mankind with ſupreme power and abſolute authority, without giving way to inſolence and injuſtice, then * placed at the head of our ſtates, as kings and magiſtrates, not men, but genii of a divine and more excellent nature; as we act with regard to our flocks and herds. For we never make an ox the ſuper-intendant of oxen, nor a goat of goats; but they are governed by us, a ſuperior race. In like manner †, the God, being a lover of mankind, has ſet over us a race of ſuperior beings, who, with great eaſe both to themſelves and us, undertake the care of us, and, diſpenſing peace, innocence ‡, and juſtice,

Plato himſelf. Others, which Julian ſeems to have expreſſed differently, we have remarked in the margin.
                                                          PETAU.
Petavius obſerves, that "this paſſage is taken from the fourth book *de Legibus*;" but either Julian quoted from memory, or his MSS. were different from ours. Xenophon opens the Cyropædia with a ſimilar reflection.   GIBBON.
The variations, which are ſpecified in the notes, are few and immaterial, being chiefly verbal.
* The word τοτε ("then") is not in Plato.
† Αρα, a kind of expletive, occurs here in Plato.
‡ Και ελευθεριαν και αφθον ("and freedom and plenty"), is added in Plato.

"preſerve

" preserve mankind in tranquillity and happiness.
" And this is agreeable to truth and reason; for
" those states * which are governed, not by a God
" but by some mortal, have no cessation from evils
" and oppressions. We should therefore exert our
" utmost efforts to imitate the life that was led in
" the reign of Saturn, and, with as much immor-
" tality as we have remaining, to govern, by his
" directions, both in public and private, our fami-
" lies and our states, considering † the law as the
" application of the divine mind. But whether
" one man, or a few, or a number of people ‡,
" govern any state, if their minds are enslaved by
" pleasure, and through a desire § of indulging it
" they trample on the laws, there is no chance
" of safety."

I have transcribed this whole passage of Plato on purpose to prevent your surmising, that I quote the words of the ancients fraudulently or erroneously, and without regard to the connection. But what says this passage really on the subject? You see, that, though a prince be by nature human, he should, in his conduct, be a divine and superior being, and entirely banish from his

---

* There is also a small difference here; ὅσων πολιῶν and ἀρχη in Julian, ὡς ὅσοι ἂν πολιων and ἀρχη in Plato.

† Ὀνομαζοντας in Julian, ἐπονομαζοντας in Plato.

‡ In other words, and nearer to the original, " a mo-
" narchy, an oligarchy, or a democracy."

§ There follows in Plato ῥιψασαι δε οὐδεν ἀλλ' ἀνοητω και ἀπληςω κακω νοσημαδι ξυνεχομενης αρξει δε, κ. τ. λ. which Julian perhaps, for the sake of brevity, omitted. Petau.

soul

EPISTLE TO THEMISTIUS

soul every thing that is mortal and brutish, except what must necessarily remain for corporeal uses. If any one, reflecting on this, should dread being engaged in such a state of life, would you rather recommend to him the Epicurean tranquillity, the gardens and suburbs of Athens, and the myrtles and cottage of Socrates? But I never preferred them to toils and dangers *. These labours I would willingly recount to you, and the hazards to which I was exposed from my friends and relations, when I was first instructed by your precepts, were you not well acquainted with them. To my conduct in Ionia, in opposition to one who was my relation by birth, but much nearer by friendship, and in favour of a man who was a foreigner, and little known to me, you are also no stranger. Did I not go abroad for the sake of my friends? In behalf of Carterius, I need not tell you, I went unsolicited, and intreated the assistance of my friend Araxius †. On account of the effects of the excellent Areta, and the injuries which she had suffered from her neighbours, did I not travel twice within two months into Phrygia, though my body

* The facts which Julian produces to prove that he never wanted courage fully convince me that this Epistle was prior to his residence in the Gauls. How many marks of firmness, how many valiant deeds, might he not have alleged, if it had been written after he was proclaimed Augustus? LA BLETERIE.
He might probably compose it at Vienne, where he passed the winter after his being appointed Cæsar.
† Ammianus mentions Araxius towards the end of b. xxvi, and relates, that, having espoused the party of Procopius, when he was killed he was banished to an island, and afterwards set at liberty. PETAU.

EPISTLE TO THEMISTIUS.

was infirm in consequence of a disorder contracted by former fatigues? Lastly, before my journey into Greece, while I continued with the army, many would say, with the utmost hazard, recollect what kind of letters I wrote to you, whether they were in a plaintive strain, or exhibited any marks of littleness, meanness, or servility. When I went again into Greece, did not I congratulate my good fortune, as if it had been a festival, affirming, that the change was most delightful to me, and that, according to the saying, I had gained

—Gold for brass, what cost a hundred beeves
For the low price of nine * ?

Such was my joy on being allowed to reside in Greece, though I had neither a house, nor any land, not so much as a field or a garden there. But perhaps you will say, that though I may seem to bear adversity with firmness, yet I am abject and pusillanimous in prosperity, as I prefer Athens to the splendor that now surrounds me †, regret that indolence, and, on account of my numerous avocations, detest my present state of life. But a better opinion of us should be

---
* Iliad. VI. 236. thus paraphrased by Pope, 292.
  For Diomed's brass arms, of mean device,
  For which nine oxen paid, a vulgar price,
  He gave his own, of gold divinely wrought,
  A hundred beeves the shining purchase bought.
† The Cæsars had all the marks of the Imperial power, excepting the diadem.   LA BLETERIE.

formed of us, not only with regard to idleness and employment, but according to that maxim, "Know thyself," and

That trade which he has learn'd let each man practise.

To govern seems to me more than human; and a king, as Plato says, "should be of a superior nature."

I will now quote a passage from Aristotle, to the same purpose; not " to carry owls to Athens *," as the saying is, but to shew that I have not entirely neglected his works. In his Political Discourses †, he thus expresses himself: " If any one
" should think it best for a nation to be governed
" by a king, what shall be determined in regard
" to his children ? Must his descendants also reign ?
" If they must, however incapable, much inconve-
" nience may ensue. But will not the sovereign
" in possession leave the government to his sons ‡ ?
" That he will not can scarce be supposed, as
" being a task too arduous, and requiring a grea-

---

* Γλαυκα Αθηναιοις αγων, *Noctuas Athenis ducens*. To the same purpose is out English proverb, "carrying coals to Newcastle." Equally needless was any information from Aristotle to Themistius.

† *Aristot. de Republica, lib.* III. *cap.* 15.

‡ In Aristotle it is Αλλ' ȣ καταλειψει τες υιεις διαδοχες ε βασιλευς, επ' εξουσιας ιχων τȣτο ποιησαι; " Will not the king leave his sons his successors, if he has it in his power ?" The instance of Marcus Aurelius and his degenerate son Commodus (see the Cæsars, p. 161.) seems a case in point. The "task" of disinheriting such a monster was too arduous, " the virtue" too exalted, even for that philosopher.

ter

EPISTLE TO THEMISTIUS.

"ter degree of virtue than is the lot of human nature."

Afterwards, speaking of a king who governs according to law, of which he is the minister and guardian, and styling him, "not a king," but ranking him in another class, he adds *, "As to absolute monarchy †, or arbitrary power, some think it inconsistent with nature for one to be lord of all ‡. For all men, being by nature equal, have the same natural rights §." And, a little after, he says, "Whoever therefore would have reason govern, would have God and the laws govern. But whoever would give the government to man, would give it to a wild beast ‖. For such is concupiscence, and anger also debases ** the best men. Law therefore is reason, exempt from passion."

The philosopher, you observe, seems here to distrust and reprobate human nature. For he says, in effect, that human nature is by no means equal to the eminence of such an exalted station. He thinks it difficult for a prince to prefer the general good of the state to that of his

---

* *De Republ. l.* III. *c.* 16.
† Παμβασιλεια.
‡ Both the prince and the philosopher choose, however, to involve this eternal truth in artful and laboured obscurity.
    GIBBON.
§ There follows in Aristotle, Και της αυτης αξιας κατα φυσιν ειναι ("And, according to nature, the same rank.")
‖ Ο δε ανθρωποσκελιυων, προσθησει και θηριον. The MS. of Vossius, unsatisfied with "a single beast," affords the stronger reading of θηρια ("beasts"), which the experience of despotism may warrant.
    GIBBON.
** Αρχοντας και ("magistrates and") is inserted in Aristotle.

children, He says, that " it is unjust for one to
" govern many of his equals." And at last, in
the close of his discourse, he adds, that " law is
" reason, exempt from passion;" and that " go-
" vernment should be entrusted to law alone, and
" not to any man. For the reason that men pos-
" sess, even if they are virtuous, is debased by
" anger and lust, most savage beasts."

This doctrine of Aristotle seems perfectly agreeable to that of Plato. First, he thinks that the governor ought to excell the governed, not only in
virtue, but in nature; which is not easy to find
among men. And also, that he should, to the utmost of his power, obey the laws, not those which
were enacted on a sudden emergency, or compiled
by men who were not entirely governed by reason;
but by such, as, having pure minds and souls, had
a view not only to present offences and contingen-
cies, but from the nature of government, and also
the nature of justice and of guilt, after obtaining
all possible instruction, framed laws for all the people in general, without respect to friend or foe, to
neighbour or relation. And this is much preferable, as they meant to promulge and transmit
their laws, not to their contemporaries only, but
to posterity and foreigners, with whom they never had, nor expected to have, any connection or
intercourse. I have heard that the wise Solon,
though by his civil institutions he made the people
free, incurred much reproach by consulting with
his

EPISTLE TO THEMISTIUS.

his friends as to cancelling of debts*, and thus giving them an opportunity of improving their fortunes. So difficult it is to avoid such fatalities, even though a man were to enter into the public service unimpassioned.

As such are my apprehensions, I often regret my former state of life, and, in deference to you, I reflect that you have said, not only that those great legislators, Solon, Lycurgus, and Pittacus, were proposed for my emulation †, but also that I must quit the shade of philosophy for the open sunshine. As if you should say to a man, who, for the sake of his health, had used moderate exercise at home, "You must now repair to Olympia ‡, and "exchange your domestic recreation for the games "of Jupiter; where your spectators will be the "Greeks resorting from all parts; and, in parti- "cular, your fellow citizens, for whom you must "enter the lists; and also some Barbarians, whom "you must astonish, in order to render your country "as formidable to them as you can." This would immediately alarm him, and make him enter the lists with terror. Suppose me now affected in the same manner by your epistle. Whether my opinion on the subject be just or not, whether I am a little

---

* Before the resolution which Solon had taken to extin- guish debts transpired in public, some of his friends bor- rowed large sums, well knowing that they should be excused from paying them.   LA BLETERIE.

† See p. 7.

‡ A town of Peloponnesus, where was a temple of Jupi- ter, in honour of whom the Olympic games were celebrated there every fifth year.

EPISTLE TO THEMISTIUS.

miftaken, or totally err, I expect to learn from you.

The matters in your epiftle as to which I am doubtful, and therefore wifh you to explain, my deareft and moft refpectable friend, fhall now be mentioned. You " prefer," you fay, " an active " to a philofophical life;" and you appeal to the teftimony of the wife Ariftotle, who makes happinefs confift in acting well; but " whether a po-" litical or a contemplative life fhould be preferred, " he was," you fay, " rather undetermined." For, in fome places, he gives the preference to contemplation; in others, he commends the " architects," as he ftyles them, " of illuftrious deeds." " Among " thefe," you fay, " are kings." But Ariftotle never ufes the word which you have introduced. And the contrary may rather be inferred from the paffage that you have quoted. For inftance: " We think thofe acquit themfelves moft properly " in all external actions, who are, as it were, men-" tal architects." This may be fuppofed to mean law-givers, or political philofophers, and all who act merely by thought and reafon, rather than the artificers of civil tranfactions; for whom it is not fufficient to confider, and devife, and inftruct others in their duty; but every thing that the laws direct, or circumftances may require, they muft undertake and execute themfelves; unlefs we call him n architect, who is

——— in m hty actions fkill'd *,

* Μεγαλων επιφορα εργων. Odyff. xxi. 26.

EPISTLE TO THEMISTIUS.

as Homer poetically styles Hercules, the greatest of such artificers.

But if we admit this to be true, and think those only happy who have administered public affairs, such as have ruled or reigned over many, what then shall we say of Socrates? As to Pythagoras *, and Democritus †, and Anaxagoras ‡ the Clazomenian, they, perhaps you will say, were in another respect happy, on account of their contemplations. But Socrates, rejecting a speculative, and preferring an active life, could not govern his own wife, nor his son, nor indeed restrain two or three disorderly citizens. Will you say, that he was not active, as he was not a ruler? On the contrary, I maintain, that the son § of Sophroniscus performed greater actions than Alexander ‖; for to him I ascribe

---

* A philosopher of Samos, who travelled as far as India, through Ægypt, in search of knowledge; and on returning opened a school in a remote part of Italy (Magna Græcia), in the reign of Tarquin the Proud. See Cic. *Tusc. Quæst.* IV. 1. He held the transmigration of souls, and was thought by his scholars infallible.

† Of Abdera, from his ridiculing the eager pursuit of welath and honour, known by the name of the laughing philosopher. Yet his own father was so rich, that at one time he feasted Xerxes and his army. He died at the age of 99 years. See Cic. *de Fin.* v. 29. and *Acad.* IV. 17.

‡ A man of high birth, and a higher mind, the preceptor of Pericles. See the Consolatory oration on the deprture of Sallust.

§ Socrates. His father was a stone-cutter of mean fortune, and his mother (Phænarete) a midwife.

‖ Julian is right in preferring Socrates to the conqueror of Asia, the wisest and most enlightened of philosophers to the scourge of mankind. But whatever he may say of pretended philosophical conversions, as rare as defective, men derived very little advantage from the instructions of Socrates: witness the deplorable state in which the nations by whom philosophy was most cultivated were with regard both to religion and manners before the publication of the gospel. It was reserved for twelve men, of the dregs of the people, and of a nation which Athens and Rome considered as barbarous, to effect in the world a reformation which philosophy had never attempted and deemed impossible. If men had had for apostles only Socrates, and the philosophers of different sects proceeding from his school, the world would still have been what it was formerly. In the midst of the profoundest darkness, some men, a little less blind than the vulgar, and often more vicious, had a glimpse of a small number of truths, which served as food for their pride, and exercise for their tongues, rather than as a rule for their conduct. Some considered every thing as problematical, even the existence of God, and the principles of morality. Others, raving at vice, dishonoured virtue, and affronted public decency. Some performed virtuous actions, but from fanaticism and self-love. Many concealed, and badly concealed, under the philosophical cloak, some abominations which now we dare not name. The most enlightened, through want of zeal for the truths with which they were best acquainted, and besides not being able to support them but by subtle and far from popular arguments, held them in captivity. They had not the courage merely to propose to the multitude the fundamental tenet of the unity of God. The people, without instruction, without principles, without manners, without an idea of the duties of man, rushed headlong into all the horrors of idolatry; and the pretended sages, such as Socrates, Plato, Cicero, Seneca, &c. had the meanness to worship in the temples the same Gods whom they ridiculed in their schools and in their writings: or at the most, like Julian, and the Platonists of his time, by the aid of some arbitrary system they formed a monstrous mixture of the tenets of the divine unity together with the speculative and practical follies of polytheism. It is even more than probable, that the general corruption and the various revolutions that happened in the world would have absolutely extinguished the weak lights of philosophy if Christianity had not come to strengthen, purify, and extend them, and to place within the reach of the dullest minds both what the philosophers could not, and what they dared not, teach. Probably the nations which dismembered

EPISTLE TO THEMISTIUS.

the military skill of Xenophon *, the fortitude of Antisthenes †, the Eretrian ‡ and Megarean § philosophy; a Cebes ‖, a Simmias **, a Phædon ††, and innumerable others; not to mention the colonies that we have received from Athens; from the Lyceum, the Porch, and the Academies ‡‡. Who is now preserved by the victories of Alexander?

bered the Roman empire would again have plunged us into barbarism, if the Christian religion had not civilised them. Will those who oppose it never have the equity to consider, that without it they would certainly have been abandoned to the most foolish superstitions, and perhaps have been in a state similar to that of the savages of America? LA BLETERIE.

* Of the "military skill" of Xenophon there needs no other proof than the retreat of the ten thousand Greeks, which he conducted.

† The founder of the sect of the *Cynics*, which Diogenes, one of his principal hearers, rendered so considerable. *Patientiam*, says Cicero (*de Orat.* III. 17.) *et duritiam in Socratico sermone maximè adamarat.* He styles him also (*ad Attic.* XII. 38.) *hominis acuti magis quàm eruditi.*

‡ From Menedemus, because he was of Eretria [in Euboea] the Eretrians were so called; all whose good was placed in the mind, and the quickness of its apprehension, by which truth is discerned. *Cic. Acad.* IV. 42.

§ From Euclid, a disciple of Socrates, who was of Megara [in Achaia], his followers were styled Megareans, who maintained that only to be good which was single, and always the same. *Ibid.*

‖ Of Thebes. He wrote three dialogues, whose titles are preserved by Diogenes Laertius (*Vit. Philos.*) The first of them, his *Table*, is still extant.

** Of Thebes also. Laertius enumerates twenty-three of his dialogues.

†† Phædon of Elis was first a slave, but being emancipated he studied philosophy, and became the chief of the sect called Elean.

‡‡ The schools of Aristotle, Zeno (or the Stoics) and the Academics.

What nation is more wisely governed, what individual is improved, by them? Many you may find whom they have enriched, but none whom they have made wiser, or more temperate, either in themselves, or towards others: on the contrary, they have fomented pride and insolence; while all who are now reformed by philosophy, are reformed by Socrates. In this opinion I am supported by Aristotle, who seems to mean the same, by saying, that " the theological work *, which he was com-
" posing, required as great abilities as those which
" subverted the Persian empire." In this I think he reasoned right. For victories are principally owing to courage and fortune, and, if you please, a kind of prudential cunning. But he who conceives true ideas of God is not only endued with perfect virtue, but it may justly be doubted whether such a one should be styled a man or a God. For if it be true, that all things are so constituted as to be best known by those who are connected with them, he who is acquainted with the divine nature may, in like manner, be deemed a pure intelligence.

But since I am returned to the comparison between a contemplative and an active life, from which I had digressed, and which, at the beginning of your epistle, you wished to decline; I will

---

* Τῃ Θεολογικῃ συγγραφῃ. " On the nature of God." The sequel shews, that it should be thus translated. I know not what this work of Aristotle is; and Julian, if I mistake not, is the only one who has mentioned it. LA BLETERIE.

EPISTLE TO THEMISTIUS.

mention the fame philofophers that you did, Areus *, Nicolaus †, Thrafyllus ‡, and Mufonius ‖. Not one of thefe had the government of his country; though Areus, it is faid, refufed the præfecture of Ægypt, which was offered him. But Thrafyllus, being the intimate friend of that cruel tyrant Ti-

---

* A philofopher and a man of learning, who, with his two fons, Dionyfius and Nicanor, was attached to the perfon of Auguftus, whofe confidence he poffeffed. Seneca fays, that he was the comforter of Livia, when fhe feemed inconfolable for the lofs of Drufus. *Senec. Confolat. ad Marciam.* LA BLETERIE.

† A friend of Auguftus, M. Agrippa, and Herod the Great, who learned of him philofophy. At the defire of that king of the Jews, he wrote an univerfal hiftory. He did honour to philofophy by his difintereftednefs and generofity. He anticipated in every thing the wants of his friends, and faid, that " money, like inftruments of mufic, " was only ufeful to thofe who employed it." He compofed the Life of Auguftus, or rather the hiftory of his education. We have only fome fragments of his works, which are in the extracts of Conftantine Porphyrogenetus, publifhed by M. de Valois. *Ibid.*

‡ A Platonic philofopher and a celebrated aftrologer. It appears in Tacitus, *Annal.* VI. with what addrefs and prefence of mind he contrived to efcape the cruelty of Tiberius, and to gain his confidence. *Ibid.*

‖ C. Caius Mufonius Rufus, a Roman knight. Not contented with profeffing the Stoic philofophy, he endeavoured to diffufe it among the young nobility of Rome, and fpeaking freely of the conduct of Nero, that tyrant committed him to a dreadful prifon, from whence he fent him firft into the ifland of Gyaros, and afterwards to the ifthmus of Corinth, there to work in chains. A friend commiferating his fituation, " I had rather be here," faid Mufonius, " than act on a ftage like Nero." After the death of his perfecutor, he returned to Rome, and was the only philofopher whom Vefpafian did not expell. As Julian fays, that Mufonius fuftained the cruelty " of tyrants," he was again perfecuted by fome other befides Nero; no doub by Domitian. *Ibid.*

berius,

berius, unless he had exculpated himself by the discourses that he has left, would have contracted a perpetual and indelible stain. Thus civil government was of no service to him. Nicolaus was the artificer of no great deeds, and he is better known by his writings concerning them. Musonius also, by supporting with fortitude and subduing by firmness the cruelty of tyrants, became distinguished, and was no less happy than those who governed the greatest kingdoms. As for Areus, when he refused the præfecture of Ægypt, he willingly deprived himself of the greatest happiness, if he thought an active life the greatest. You yourself too are inactive, as you neither command an army *, nor harangue the people, nor govern any nation

---

* Indeed the Themistius, with whom we are acquainted, was not a warrior. Nor did he harangue the people; no one, I imagine, had then that privilege, except the Emperors and Cæsars. He was not Præfect of Constantinople till the reign of Theodosius. Nevertheless, the manner in which Julian here mentions the Themistius, to whom he is writing, would make one think, that he was rather a mere philosopher, concentered in his school, than the celebrated Themistius, who had been made senator of Constantinople two months before Julian was named Cæsar, and who had always the ambition to be at once a philosopher and a statesman. Besides, the Themistius to whom the epistle is addressed, appears to have been one of the most intimate friends of Julian; and Themistius the senator, in an oration pronounced in the reign of Theodosius, in which he boasts of the regard which the Emperors had had for him, intimates that Julian did not love him, because, he says, that prince had been forced (by truth, no doubt) to acknowledge him for the first of philosophers. In short, what is still of more consequence,

Julian

EPISTLE TO THEMISTIUS.

nation or city: but does it follow, that you are not wife? And if you should form several philosophers, or only three or four, you would contribute more essentially to the happiness of mankind than many kings united. A philosopher acts no inconsiderable part; he is not, as you have said, the director only of public counsels, nor is his action confined to thinking. But if he confirm his words by his deeds, and appear such as he would have others to be, he will urge to action

---

Julian was not Cæsar when Themistius was made senator; yet Themistius, in the discourse where he thanks Constantius for his new dignity, congratulates the Emperor on having taken Julian for his colleague. These difficulties are very strong; but may it not be said in answer, 1. That Themistius was perhaps one of the senators who were styled *alletti* or *immunes*, and who enjoyed all the privileges of senators, without being obliged to exercise the functions? 2. Themistius was at least as good a courtier as philosopher. Policy therefore did not allow him to boast, in the reign of Theodosius, of having been the friend of Julian. He rather chose to have it then believed, that, if that prince had given him great marks of esteem, it was not so much from inclination and choice, as because he could not refuse them. The vanity of Themistius, which is very apparent in the oration in question, concurred with policy to make him speak this language. 3. It is true, that the letters by which Constantius made Themistius senator were read in the senate of Constantinople on the first of September, 355, and that Julian was not declared Cæsar till the sixth of November following; but the acknowledgement in which the new senator mentions the association of Julian was, as appears by the discourse itself, pronounced some time after the letters of Constantius had been read at Constantinople, and when it was just known that Julian was Cæsar. Nothing hinders our supposing that two months and a half, or three months, intervened between the reading of those letters and the discourse in question.   LA BLETERIE.

with

with more perfuafion and effect than thofe who excite to it by command.

But I muft now return to the fubject with which I began, and conclude an epiftle already perhaps too long. This is the fum of it; that it is not for the fake of avoiding fatigue, nor of purfuing pleafure, nor from a love of floth and idlenefs, that I am averfe to public bufinefs; but, as I faid at the beginning, from a confcioufnefs of my not having fufficient knowledge or genius, and alfo from an apprehenfion of throwing a reproach on philofophy (whom though I love I have not won, and who by the men of this age is already too much flighted), having written fomething formerly, and now being corrected by your admonitions.

May God grant me fuccefs, and prudence to deferve it! I have now the utmoft occafion for the affiftance principally of the Supreme Being, and alfo of you philofophers, for whofe credit I have expofed myfelf to danger. If God fhall by my means grant to mankind a bleffing * beyond my abilities alone to procure, you will have no reafon to be offended at my difcourfes. For as I am confcious of nothing good, this only excepted, that having nothing, I do not think that I abound †, I con-

---

* This bleffing was particularly the re-eftablifhment of Paganifm.   LA BLETERIE.

† Οτι μηδε οιομαι τα μεγιϛα εχειν, εχων γε ουδεν. As both Julian and his correfpondent were, no doubt, well acquainted with the writings of the Apoftles, I will hazard a conjecture that this was intended as a fneer on an expreffion

EPISTLE TO THEMISTIUS.

continue to act, as you observe, in the same manner; and I intreat you not to form high expectations of me, but to submit every thing to God. So if any faults should be committed, I shall be blameless; but if all things should succeed to my wishes, I shall be grateful and moderate, not arrogating to myself the deeds of others, but ascribing, as is just, every thing to God *, and knowing that my acknowledgements are due to him, let me exhort you to return him yours also.

---

of St. Paul, in 2 Cor. vi. 10. Ὡς μηδεν εχοιλες, και παντα κατεχοντες, *As having nothing, and yet possessing all things.* The expressions at least are very similar.

* That piety of spirit, that true magnanimity, which Julian here professes, has been nobly exemplified, while I am writing this, by a modern commander, the retriever of the glory of the British flag, whom we find, in the midst of the most brilliant success, " giving God the glory," and not scrupling to declare, that " It has pleased God, " out of his Divine Providence, to grant to his Majesty's " arms a most complete victory," &c. See Sir George Rodney's Letter in the London Gazette of May 18, 1782.

A CONSOLATORY ORATION ON THE
DEPARTURE OF * SALLUST †.

A. D. 358.

UNLESS, my dear friend, I communicate to you what has occurred to me in private, since I heard of your approaching departure, I shall

---

* One MS. adds, τυ αγαθωτατυ, (" the excellent.")

† This is a farewell encomium on Salluſt, who was going into Illyricum and Thrace, he being one of the few who was dear to Julian, and his confidential friend. He wrote this Oration when he governed the Gauls with the title of Cæſar, during the life of Conſtantius. The time when Julian celebrated the departure of Salluſt with this Oration may be aſcertained from a paſſage in the Epiſtle to the Athenians, where he mentions, that Conſtantius removed Salluſt from the Gauls, becauſe he was his friend.

PETAU.

This Oration exhibits to us a picture of an excellent temper, on the eminence to which Julian was now exalted, in not being able to be ſeparated from the deareſt and moſt uſeful guide and companion of his life without the utmoſt regret.   SPANHEIM.

Salluſt was an officer of great merit, by birth a Gaul. What employment Conſtantius had given him in the Gauls is not known, but it was certainly one that was conſiderable. He was a Pagan, a man of learning, of great ability in buſineſs, and of diſtinguiſhed probity; ſufficient recommendations to the friendſhip of Julian. Salluſt had the rare talent of giving advice without petulance, and without that air of confidence, which too often renders the truth, and always thoſe who ſpeak it, diſguſting. The freedom with which he reproved the prince was ſoftened

by

shall think myself deprived of some consolation; or by respect, cordiality, and tenderness. Julian revered him as a father, and all the good that Julian did was attributed to Sallust, without exciting any jealousy in Julian. The intrigues of Florentius and some other officers induced the Emperor to recall Sallust, on a pretext that was honourable to him; but, in reality, to mortify Julian, who was left at the discretion of persons unworthy of their posts, and his professed enemies. He was extremely concerned at the loss of Sallust. To assuage his grief, he addressed this discourse to him, in which he takes leave of him in an affecting manner, with testimonies of the sincerest friendship and esteem. Afterwards, when he was Emperor, he made him Præfect of the Gauls. LA BLETERIE.

On his entering the Persian territories [April 13, 363], Julian received a letter from his old friend Sallust [then in Gaul], conjuring him not to take the field till he had appeased the Gods, who seemed, by various prodigies, to declare against the Persian war. But the die was cast. *Ibid.*

See also Epistle XVII, and what M. de la Bleterie says farther of this discourse in the Preface.

The measures of policy, and the operations of war, must submit to the various operations of circumstance and character, and the unpractised student will often be perplexed in the application of the most perfect theory. But in the acquisition of this important science Julian was assisted by the active vigour of his own genius, as well as by the wisdom and experience of Sallust, an officer of rank, who soon conceived a sincere attachment for a prince so worthy of his friendship; and whose incorruptible integrity was adorned by the talent of insinuating the harshest truths, without wounding the delicacy of a royal ear. GIBBON.

This excellent minister was speedily recalled by the jealousy of the Emperor; and we may still read a sensible but pedantic discourse, in which Julian deplores the loss of so valuable a friend, to whom he acknowledges himself indebted for his reputation. *Ibib.*

This Sallust must be carefully distinguished from the venerable Præfect of the East, who had the singular honour of twice refusing the empire, once after the death

A CONSOLATORY ORATION

or rather I shall imagine that my dignity * affords me no advantage unshared by you. For having participated with each other in much joy, and in much grief, both in words and deeds, in public and in private, at home and in the field, for the present evils, be they what they may, we must both have recourse to the same remedy. But who will supply us with a lyre like that of Orpheus, or with songs like those of the Sirens, or with the drug Nepenthes †? Whether this was a fiction derived

---

of Julian, and again on the death of Jovian. Julian honoured the consulship with the name of the Præfect of Gaul (A. D. 363.) *Ibid.*

The fourth Oration of Julian, *In Solem Regem*, composed in three nights, is addressed to the same Sallust, and towards the conclusion he mentions a former work (now lost) "on the Κρονια," or *Saturnalia*, which was also inscribed to him, and of which one paragraph (quoted in the first note on the Cæsars, p. 145.), is preserved by Suidas.

* Of Cæsar, which Constantius had conferred on him at Milan, Nov. 6, 355. See the Epistle to the Athenians, p. 77.

† Odys. IV. 221. On the arrival of Telemachus at the court of Menelaus at Sparta,

> ——— With genial joy to warm the soul,
> Bright Helen mix'd a mirth-inspiring bowl;
> 'Temper'd with drugs of sovereign use t'asswage
> The boiling bosom of tumultuous rage,
> To clear the clouded front of wrinkled care,
> And dry the fearful sluices of despair.
> . . . .
> These drugs, so friendly to the joys of life,
> Bright Helen learn'd from Thone's imperial wife,
> Who sway'd the sceptre, where prolific Nile
> With various simples cloaths the fruitful soil, &c.
>
> FENTON.

Julian

derived from Ægyptian lore, or was invented by the poet himfelf, and 'interwoven in his fequel of the Trojan calamities, as if Helen had learned it in Ægypt, it expreffes what ought to be the language of thofe who wifh to difpel, not the miferies which the Greeks and Trojans mutually inflicted, but mental fufferings, and to reftore chearfulnefs and tranquillity. For pleafure and pain feem to flow from the fame fource, and in their turns fucceed each other. And thofe events which occafion great labour and trouble, in the opinion of the wife, give a mind, that is rightly difpofed, not more pain than pleafure. Thus from the bittereft herb that grows on Hymettus * the bee extracts fweet juice, and works it into honey. Such bodies, as are healthy and robuft, are nourifhed by any kind of food, and that which is generally deemed unwholefome, far from impairing, increafes their ftrength. But on thofe, whofe conftitutions, by nature, education, or ftudy, are weak, and through their whole life, valetudinary, the flighteft attacks make violent impreffions. So, in regard to the mind, thofe who are thus [fufceptible, muft be

---

Julian refers to the fame paffage in his xxxviith Epiftle. And Milton thus alludes to it, in his Mafk of Comus:
Not that Nepenthes which the wife of Thone,
In Ægypt, gave to Jove-born Helena,
Is of fuch power to ftir up joy as this,
To life fo friendly, or fo cool to thirft.

* A mountain of Attica, famous for excellent honey.
Ubi non Hymetto mella decedunt.   Hor.

contented *] with being moderately well, and though they are not endued with the strength of Antisthenes † or Socrates, or the fortitude of Callisthenes ‡, or the temperance of Polemo ‖, yet if they can be serene in such trials, perhaps in greater difficulties they may be chearful.

As to myself, sensible how much I suffer and shall suffer from your journey, my concern was equal to that which I felt on first leaving my preceptor §. For I immediately recollected the labours which we have shared, our pure and unfeigned affection, our innocent and unreserved

* Imperfect. The translator has supplied the chasm by conjecture.

† A philosopher and teacher of rhetoric at Rhodes, who, on hearing Socrates, bade his scholars seek a new master, for he had found one. He was the founder of the Cynic sect, and the master of Diogenes.

‡ A philosopher and disciple of Aristotle, who frequented the court of Alexander the Great. On his opposing that prince being worshipped in the Persian manner, he was accused of a pretended conspiracy, and cruelly exposed to lions.

‖ Polemo was a profligate young rake of Athens, and even distinguished by the dissoluteness of his manners. One day, after a riotous entertainment, he came reeling, with a chaplet on his head, into the school of Xenocrates. The audience were greatly offended at his scandalous appearance; but the philosopher went on, without any emotion, in a discourse on temperance and sobriety. Polemo was so struck by his arguments, that he soon threw away his chaplet; and from that time became a disciple of Xenocrates; and profited so well by his instructions, that he afterwards succeeded him in the Socratic school.

Mrs. CARTER.

§ The eunuch Mardonius. See the Misopogon.

con-

conversation, our concurrence in all things laudable, the alacrity and resolution with which we uniformly opposed the wicked, and the firmness with which we constantly maintained our purpose, having one and the same mind, similar manners, and being united by the strictest friendship. Besides, I recollected that expression,

—— On the field Ulysses stands alone *.

For I now much resemble him, since God has removed you, like Hector †, far from the darts which have been launched at you by sycophants; or rather at me, endeavouring to wound me through you; as thinking no method so certain as that of depriving me, if possible, of the society of a faithful friend, an alert defender, and a sharer, with the utmost alacrity, in all my dangers. You, I think, at being denied a participation in my cares and labours, are no less affected than I am; but on

---

* Il. xi. 401. Οιωθη δ' Οδυσσευς. Pope, 509. It has before been remarked, (p. 5. note.) that it was fashionable for the Greeks in general, and Julian, their admirer and imitator, in particular, to quote Homer at random on every occasion. The above expression is applied by the poet to Ulysses, when Diomed had been wounded by Paris, and obliged to quit the field.

† Il. xi. 164. This passage is again quoted and applied, with more propriety, by Julian to himself in his Allegorical Fable. That Hector was removed from the battle was a desirable circumstance to Ulysses; not so the desertion of his friend Diomed. To this therefore the removal of Sallust from Julian seems more applicable.

my account, and for my safety, are rather more anxious than myself. For as I never preferred my own interest to yours, I have always experienced from you the same attention. I am therefore justly and deeply concerned, that to you, who, with respect to others, can say,

> "I heed them not, for my affairs are prosperous,"

I alone should occasion grief and anxiety. But in this, it seems, we are equal sufferers; you, however, lamenting only on my account, but I constantly regretting the loss of your society, and recollecting the friendship which we mutually pledged to each other, cemented first and principally by virtue, and afterwards by the obligations, not from you to me, but those which were largely conferred on me by you. This friendship we bound not by oaths, or other such ties, like Theseus and Pirithous*, but by a perpetual concurrence in opinion, in being so far from uniting to injure any one, as never to converse on the subject. But if any thing happened advantageous to an individual, or the common good was in view, this engaged our private discourse.

That I have abundant cause to lament, on being separated, for ever so short a time, not only from a friend, but, God knows, a faithful assistant,

---

* The sworn friendship of these two heroes was proverbial. See the Life of Theseus in Plutarch.

Socrates,

Socrates, I doubt not, the great herald and teacher of virtue, would allow; as far as his sentiments may be conjectured from Plato. For these are his words: " Rightly to govern a state, I deem a most " difficult task; for it cannot be governed without " faithful friends and counsellors; and such can- " not easily be found." And if Plato thought this more arduous than digging through Athos, what can we expect, who in wisdom and knowledge are more unequal to him than he was to God? But I not only regret the mutual assistance which we gave to each other, in civil administration, and which enabled us more easily to support whatever happened unexpectedly either by accident, or by the machinations of our enemies; but the approaching loss of my chief solace and delight rends and afflicts my heart. For what friend equally benevolent have I now remaining? Whose sincere and innocent confidence shall I be able now to endure? Who will advise me prudently, reprove me mildly, confirm me in virtue without pride and arrogance, and use freedom of speech without asperity; like those, who from medicines extract the nauseous, and leave the useful? These advantages * I have derived from your friendship. Destitute of

---

* In the original, Αλλα τυτο μεν εκ της σης φιλιας το ονειδος εκαρπωσαμην; literally, " But I have reaped this *disgrace* from " your friendship." Perhaps we should read το ονειαρ (*utile*). The Latin translator renders it by *famam hanc* (which may be taken either in a good or bad sense); and Mr. Gibbon (see his second note; p. 31.) by " reputation."

that, how shall I compose numerous orations? Who, when, in despair, I am hazarding my life, from regret of you, of your counsels and benevolence, will persuade me to be resigned, and to submit with fortitude to whatever God decrees? For this, in concurrence with him, the great Emperor * seems to have determined. By what method, by what charms, can the mind be enabled to support such anxiety and distress with moderation? Shall we imitate the discourses of Zamolxis †, and mutter his incantations, which, when Socrates had introduced them at Athens, he obliged beautiful Charmides ‡ to sing, before he would cure him of his head-ach? Or if these, as being too vast, and intended for greater trials, like large machines in a small theatre, are unmanageable, yet, from former occurrences, collecting, as it were, from a variegated meadow, some choice and beautiful flowers, shall we solace our minds with narrations, interspersing with them some strictures from philosophy? As draughts that are too luscious are ren-

---

* Constantius.

† A Gete, and servant of Pythagoras; who, at his return, civilised his countrymen, and by them was reputed a God.

‡ An Athenian, the son of Glaucon, famous for his beauty. See the Dialogue of Plato so named, in which Charmides is an interlocutor. "If," says Socrates, "what Critics here say be true, if you are extremely temperate, you have no more occasion for Zamolxis, or the incantations of Abaris the Hyperborean; that alone will be a sufficient remedy for your head." Charmides is also mentioned by Plato in his Theages, Protagoras, and Banquet.

dered

dered more palatable by the infusion of certain drugs, so when such narrations are seasoned with some apt maxims of philosophy, those parts of ancient history which seem tedious are stripped of their redundant loquacity.

What first? What next? What last shall I relate *?

Was not Scipio, loving Lælius, and being equally loved by him, so closely connected with him, that he undertook nothing without having previously consulted and advised with him? which occasioned the envious traducers of his actions to say, that Lælius was the author of them, and Africanus only the performer. The same report prevails in regard to us, and I hear it, I confess, with great satisfaction. For to adopt the good advice of another seemed to Zeno † a proof of greater virtue than

---

* Odyss. IX. 14.

† Zeno, the founder of the Stoic sect, was born at Citium, a sea-port town in the island of Cyprus. He was originally a merchant, and very rich. On a voyage from Tyre, where he had been trading in purple, he was shipwrecked near the Piræum. During his stay at Athens, he happened to meet, in a bookseller's shop, with the second book of Xenophon's *Memorabilia*; with which he was extremely delighted; and asked the bookseller where such kind of persons, as the author mentioned, were to be found. The bookseller answered, pointing to Crates, the Cynic, who was luckily passing by, "Follow him;" which Zeno did, and became his disciple. But his disposition was too modest to approve of the Cynic indecency; and forsaking Crates, he applied himself to the Academics, whom he attended for ten years, and then formed a school of his own. There was a constant severity, or perhaps austerity, in his manners, his dress, and his discourse; except at an

than originally to conceive what is juſt and right thus altering a line of Heſiod:

That man is beſt who follows good advice *,

from

―――― who counſels wiſely for himſelf.

Yet I do not approve the alteration, as I think the ſaying of Heſiod much more true. But better than either is that of Pythagoras, from whom that proverb originated, "With friends all things are "common." This indeed does not refer to money only, but includes a communion of minds and underſtandings. So that what you ſuggeſt is no leſs the property of him who adopts it; and in ſuch parts of yours as I performed, you are juſtly entitled to a ſhare. But let thoſe actions be aſcribed to whom they will, they belong to another; and

entertainment, when he uſed to appear with chearfulneſs and eaſe. His morals were irreproachable; and he was preſented by the Athenians with a golden crown, becauſe his life was a public example of virtue, by its conformity with his words and doctrines. He lived ninety-eight years, and then ſtrangled himſelf, becauſe, in going out of his ſchool, he happened to fall down, and break his finger.

DIOGENES LAERTIUS.

* Ουτος μεν παναριςος, ος ευ ειποντι πιθηται.

In the Works and Days of Heſiod, ver. 291. we read,

Ουτος μεν παναριςος, ος αυτω παντα νοηση.

(In Julian, ποιθ' ιαυτω) to which latter hemiſtich, it ſeems, Zeno ſubſtituted part of ver. 293, viz.

Εσθλος δ' αυ κακεινος, ος ευ, κ. τ. λ.

He too is good, *who follows good advice.*

Heſiod and Livy thought, that he who counſelled wiſely for himſelf, was the firſt of men, and that he who followed the good advice of others was the ſecond. But Zeno preferred the latter.

of their suggestions the invidious can make no advantage.

I now return to Africanus and Lælius. After Carthage * was destroyed, and all Libya was subjected to Rome, Africanus dispatched Lælius with the intelligence of his success. Scipio was concerned at being thus separated from his friend; yet he did not think his grief inconsolable. Lælius too, it is probable, was afflicted at departing alone; yet this calamity did not seem to him insupportable. Cato also took a voyage, leaving his intimate friends at home. Pythagoras too travelled into Ægypt, and so did Plato and Democritus, without any companion, leaving behind them many whom they highly esteemed. Pericles made war against Samos †, unaccompanied by Anaxagoras, and conquered Eubœa ‡; by his counsels indeed, for he was his

---

* By mentioning Libya afterwards, Julian seems to mean Old Carthage; but C. Lælius, as we learn from Livy (xxvii. 7.), was dispatched to Rome by Scipio Africanus the elder, with the account of " the conquest," not destruction, " of New Carthage, the capital of Spain, in one " day."' He was indeed dispatched, many years after, by the younger Scipio, from Africa, with Syphax and other prisoners, and with the intelligence of the victory of Zama: but it does not appear that he was sent with the account of the destruction of Old Carthage. Julian trusted much to his memory, which sometimes deceived him.

† Making war with the Samians, Pericles gained a naval victory, and at last took their city.

‡ Eubœa having rebelled against the Athenians, he invaded it with a fleet and army, and reduced it to their obedience. See his Life in Plutarch.

A CONSOLATORY ORATION

"As some way-faring man, who wanders o'er
"In thought —*.

", Assisted by this, you may easily discern from
"Athens one who is in Ionia; from the Gauls
"those who are in Illyricum and Thrace; and
"him who is in the Gauls from Thrace or
"Illyricum. For, though plants, when removed
"from their native soil in an improper season,
"cannot be preserved, yet men, when they travel
"from place to place, do not, in like manner,
"soon decay, or change their disposition, or de-
"viate from the right principles which they had
"previously imbibed. Therefore if we do not
"love with more ardour, we certainly should not
"abate in our benevolence. Luxury is attended
"by lasciviousness, but poverty by virtuous love.
"Thus we shall be happier by the increase of
"our mutual affection; and shall see ourselves
"fixed, like statues in their niches, in the mind
"of each other. Now I shall behold Anaxagoras,
"and then Anaxagoras will behold me; for no-
"thing prohibits our seeing each other; not the
"flesh and nerves, the face and form, or a bodily
"representation, (though nothing perhaps will
"prevent even these appearing to our minds), but
"the virtue, the actions, the discourses, the con-
"versations, the meetings that frequently oc-
"curred between us; when we not unskilfully

* Il. xv. 80. Pope, 86. Homer here compares the flight of Juno, from Ida to Olympus, to a man travelling in idea.

"joined

" joined in the praise of education, and justice,
" and of that understanding which directs all
" things human and divine; and also on civil
" government, and laws, on virtuous conduct, and
" ingenuous studies; we made such observations
" as our memories suggested. Reflecting on these
" things, and ruminating on such representations,
" we shall disregard the delusions of nightly
" dreams; nor will the senses, affected by a bad
" habit of body, present to the mind vain and
" empty visions. For, instead of employing the
" assistance and ministration of the senses, the
" mind will meditate on these subjects, and thus
" inure itself to the contemplation and compre-
" hension of incorporeal objects. For by the
" mind we associate even with the Almighty, and
" are naturally enabled to behold and investigate
" things that escape our senses, that are in place
" far distant, and even things that have no place *.
" And such a vision all whose lives have rendered
" them worthy of it, conceive in their minds and
" perfectly enjoy."

* Thus Shakespeare:
The poet's eye, in a fine frenzy rolling,
Doth glance from heaven to earth, from earth to heaven,
And, as imagination bodies forth
The forms of things unknown, the poet's pen
Turns them to shape, and gives to airy nothing
A local habitation, and a name.
   Midsummer Night's Dream, Act V. Sc. I.

Pericles

A CONSOLATORY ORATION

Pericles, being endued with true magnanimity, and educated free in a free city, might solace himself with such sublime meditations. But I, born " in these degenerate days *," console and beguile my mind, and asswage the bitterness of my sorrow, by arguments more human; thus endeavouring to apply some remedy to the many anxious and distressing ideas which on that subject perpetually assail me; like a charm against the bite of a wild beast, deeply wounding my heart and vitals. Of all my afflictions this is the principal; I am now left alone, deprived of a sincere, social intercourse, and an unreserved communication. For I have none remaining whom I can consult with equal confidence. But cannot I easily converse with my self? Or cannot some other engage my thoughts, and oblige me to regard and attend to subjects not of my own choosing? Is not this similar to writing on water, or boiling a stone, or investigating the traces of the flight of birds? Our conversing on such subjects none can hinder. And perhaps God will suggest something better. For it is impossible that a man who gives himself up to the Almighty should be entirely neglected and deserted by him. But God with his own arm defends him, endues him with strength, inspires him with courage, instills into his mind what he should do, and deters him from what he should forbear. A divine voice

* Οἷοι νῦν βροτοί εἰσ'. Il. v. 304. An expression often quoted by our author.

accompanied Socrates *, forbidding him to do

* The notion of Socrates having a supernatural attendant, either an evil spirit, as some of the Fathers imagined, or a good one, as others have conceived, has been lately discussed, in " an Essay on the Dæmon or Divination of " Socrates," by Mr. Nares, who maintains, " that the " divinations of Socrates were perfectly analogous to those " in common use at the time in which he lived; but that " he, from a scrupulous exactness in his expressions, (and " probably also with a desire to inculcate, as frequently " as possible, the notion of a constantly active and super- " intending providence) chose rather to refer his divi- " nation always to its primary and original cause, the " Gods, than to their secondary and unconscious instru- " ments, the omens by which it was conveyed. In con- " sequence of these ideas, he appropriated to the subject " an expression, which first the malice of his enemies, and " since the mistaken zeal of his friends, have wrested to " his disadvantage, as if he had pretended to a communi- " cation with some attendant Dæmon; than which nothing " could be more remote from his ideas. It appears, in- " deed, that he conceived the particular signal, or omen, " by which he was directed, to be something in a manner " appropriated; or at least more accurately observed and " attended to by him than by others. But in this there is " nothing repugnant to the common notions of prophetic " warnings in his and every age, nor in the least subversive " of what has been here advanced. From this represen- " tation of the matter it will appear, that there is, in " the history of this extraordinary man, nothing which " can countenance the vague and romantic notion of " attendant tutelar dæmons; nor any thing which can " in the least invalidate our conceptions of his strict in- " tegrity and open disposition: a conclusion, which every " lover of philosophy will doubtless embrace with pleasure, " if the arguments and authorities which form the foun- " dation of it be deemed of sufficient strength." The author supports this ingenious hypothesis by passages to the same purpose from Plato, Xenophon, and Plutarch.

If Julian had not been more a Greek than a Roman, he would have mentioned also, on this occasion, Numa and his nymph Egeria.

whatever was improper. And Homer says of Achilles, "His mind was inspired *," intimating, that our thoughts are suggested by God, when the mind, by reflection, converses first with itself, and then privately with God, without interruption; for the mind requires not ears to learn, nor God a voice to teach, what is necessary, but, without sensation, a participation of the Almighty is given to the mind. How, and in what manner, I have not leisure now to examine; but that this is effected there are sure and faithful witnesses, not such as are ignoble, and to be classed with the Megareansians, but those who have had the first reputation in wisdom. Therefore, as we expect that God will be for ever present with us, and that we shall again have a mutual intercourse, the violence of our affliction ought to abate. Even Ulysses, who so much lamented his confinement in an island for seven whole years, though I praise him for his bravery on other occasions, I admire not for his grief on this. For what availed his gazing on the sea, and shedding tears †? Not to be dejected and dispirited by misfortunes, but to act with intrepidity in the midst of danger and destruction, seems indeed more than can be expected from man. But it

---

* By Juno. Il. I. 55. Thus also Virgil, *Hic mentem Æneæ genitrix pulcherrima misit.* Æn. xii. 554.

† Odyss. v. 82. All on the lonely shore he sat to weep,
And roll'd his eyes around the restless deep;
Tow'rd his lov'd coast he roll'd his eyes in vain,
Till dimm'd with rising grief, they stream'd again.
 Pope, 105.

is unjust to praise, and not to imitate, the ancients, or to think that God readily assisted them; but will overlook those of this age whom he sees attached to virtue, since on that account he was pleased with them. It was not for personal beauty; or Nireus * would have been more beloved by him. Nor was it for strength; as the Læstrygons † and Cyclops ‡ were greatly superior in strength to Ulysses. Nor was it for riches; for then Troy would have remained in safety. But why should we labour to investigate the reason of the poet's saying that Ulysses was beloved by God §, when we may hear it from himself?

Because, in every useful art refin'd,
His words were eloquent, and wise his mind ‖.

It is plain therefore, that, if we have these endowments, the Almighty will not deny us his support, but, according to the oracle given of

---

* Il. ii. 671. Nireus is here mentioned as the most beautiful of the Greeks, Achilles only excepted; but his name never occurs again; for
— few his troops, and small his strength in war.
It is remarkable, that Nireus is introduced by Euripides [Iphigenia in Aulis] as accompanying Ulysses, though their manners were unsuitable, and their dominions [Syma and Ithaca] far distant. In the vith book of Quintus Calaber, Nireus falls by the spear of Eurypylus. WODHULL.
† Odyss. x. 119, &c.
‡ Ibid. ix. 125, &c.
§ Θεοφιλη Διι φιλος (beloved by Jupiter) in Il. xi. 419, 473.
‖ Odyss. xiii. 332. [Minerva] by saying to Ulysses, that she would never overlook nor desert him, " Because, &c." shews that of all we have, virtue only is esteemed by God and divine. *Plutarch. de audiendis Poetis.*

whatever was improper. And Homer says of Achilles, " His mind was inspired *," intimating, that our thoughts are suggested by God, when the mind, by reflection, converses first with itself, and then privately with God, without interruption; for the mind requires not ears to learn, nor God a voice to teach, what is necessary, but, without sensation, a participation of the Almighty is given to the mind. How, and in what manner, I have not leisure now to examine; but that this is effected there are sure and faithful witnesses, not such as are ignoble, and to be classed with the Megarensians, but those who have had the first reputation in wisdom. Therefore, as we expect that God will be for ever present with us, and that we shall again have a mutual intercourse, the violence of our affliction ought to abate. Even Ulysses, who so much lamented his confinement in an island for seven whole years, though I praise him for his bravery on other occasions, I admire not for his grief on this. For what availed his gazing on the sea, and shedding tears †? Not to be dejected and dispirited by misfortunes, but to act with intrepidity in the midst of danger and destruction, seems indeed more than can be expected from man. But it

---

* By Juno. Il. I. 55. Thus also Virgil, *His mentem Æneæ genitrix pulcherrima misit.* Æn. xii. 554.

† Odyss. v. 82. All on the lonely shore he sat to weep,
 And roll'd his eyes around the restless deep;
 Tow'rd his lov'd coast he roll'd his eyes in vain,
 Till dimm'd with rising grief, they stream'd again.
  Pope, 105.

is

is unjuft to praife, and not to imitate, the ancients, or to think that God readily affifted them; but will overlook thofe of this age whom he fees attached to virtue, fince on that account he was pleafed with them. It was not for perfonal beauty; or Nireus * would have been more beloved by him. Nor was it for ftrength; as the Læftrygons † and Cyclops ‡ were greatly fuperior in ftrength to Ulyffes. Nor was it for riches; for then Troy would have remained in fafety. But why fhould we labour to inveftigate the reafon of the poet's faying that Ulyffes was beloved by God §, when we may hear it from himfelf?

Becaufe, in every ufeful art refin'd,
His words were eloquent, and wife his mind ‖.

It is plain therefore, that, if we have thefe endowments, the Almighty will not deny us his fupport, but, according to the oracle given of

---

* Il. ii. 671. Nireus is here mentioned as the moft beautiful of the Greeks, Achilles only excepted; but his name never occurs again; for

— few his troops, and fmall his ftrength in war.

It is remarkable, that Nireus is introduced by Euripides [Iphigenia in Aulis] as accompanying Ulyffes, though their manners were unfuitable, and their dominions [Syma and Ithaca] far diftant. In the vith book of Quintus Calaber, Nireus falls by the fpear of Eurypylus.   WODHULL.

† Odyff. x. 119, &c.
‡ Ibid. ix. 125, &c.
§ Θεοφιλη Διι φιλος (beloved by Jupiter) in Il. xi. 419, 473.
‖ Odyff. xiii. 332. [Minerva] by faying to Ulyffes, that fhe would never overlook nor defert him, " Becaufe, &c." fhews that of all we have, virtue only is efteemed by God and divine.   *Plutarch. de audiendis Poetis.*

old to the Lacedæmonians, invoked, or not invoked, God will be present with us.

Having thus sought consolation, I now return to that circumstance, which, though at first it seems trivial, is generally thought of no small importance. Alexander is said to have wished for Homer, not as a friend indeed, but as a herald, as he was to Achilles, and Patroclus, and the two Ajaces, and Antilochus. But he, always despising what he had, and coveting what he had not, slighted his contemporaries, and was never satisfied with what was granted him. If he had been indulged with Homer, he would probably have requested the lyre of Apollo, on which he played at the nuptials of Peleus *, thinking it not a fiction of the genius of Homer, but a true fact related in verse, like these.

Aurora now, fair daughter of the dawn,
Sprinkled with rosy light the dewy lawn †.
And, The Sun arose ‡.
And, Crete, a fruitful soil §.

---

* Il. xxiv. 62. Juno says to the Gods,
To grace those nuptials, from the bright abode,
Yourselves were present; where this minstrel-god
(Well pleas'd to share the feast) amid the choir,
Stood proud to hymn, and tune his youthful lyre. Pope.
This harmonious banquet is also celebrated by Euripides, in one of the chorusses of his Iphigenia in Aulis. Apollo is there introduced foretelling the glory of Achilles.
† Il. viii. 1. Pope.
‡ Odyss. iii. 1.
§ Ibid. xix. 172. Fenton.

And other similar passages of the poets, which are plain and obvious, as some of the objects still remain, and some of the facts are still transacted.

But whether the excellence of his virtue, and a wisdom, by no means inferior to his great superfluity of worldly happiness, inflamed his mind with such ambition, that he coveted more than any one else; or whether the excess of his valour and intrepidity tended to arrogance, and bordered on ostentation; must be left to the discussion of those who would compose his panegyric or satire; if any share of the latter can be thought his due. I, on the contrary, always satisfied with what is present, and not in the least desirous of what is absent, contentedly acquiesce in having my merits proclaimed by a herald who has been a spectator and a fellow-combatant with me in all *, but whose judgement partiality never biasses, nor prejudice perverts. Sufficient is it for me to profess my friendship; in other respects I shall be more silent than those who are initiated by Pythagoras †.

But here I must advert to the general report, namely, that you are going not only among the Illyrians, but also to the Thracians, and those

* Sallust himself, no doubt, on whose representation of his conduct Julian might indeed safely rely.

† The scholars of this philosopher in their probation were enjoined silence, and were only to hear; which time was called ἐχεμυθία. Gell. 1. 9. See the Epistle to Themistius, p. 21. note *.

Greeks who dwell near that sea*. This, being the place of my birth and education, has inspired me with a great regard for those people, and their country, and cities; and an equal regard perhaps they retain for me. To them, I am confident, your arrival will be most acceptable, and that they will think it a happy exchange, as you have left me here. By saying this, I mean not to infinuate that I wish it; on the contrary, if you could return hither immediately, by the same road, I should be much more gratified. But as it must happen, I am confidering how to support it with firmness and equanimity, while I congratulate them on seeing you just come from us. On your account, I reconcile myself to the Gauls; deeming you worthy of being ranked among the first of the Greeks, in justice and other virtues; as being also an adept in oratory, and far from a novice in philosophy, in which the Greeks alone are perfect; investigating truth, as its nature requires, by reason, and not suffering us to be deluded by idle inventions, and incredible fables, like many of the Barbarians.

And now (to dismiss you with auspicious omens) where-ever you go, may the benevolent God be your guide, and Jupiter the friendly and hospitable receive you, conducting you safely by land, and, if you embark, smoothing the waves! May you be loved and honoured by all men; so that they may rejoice at your arrival, and lament at your

---

* The Propontis, which laves Conftantinople, where Julian was born. It divides the Hellespont and the Thracian Bosphorus.

ON THE DEPARTURE OF SALLUST.

departure! Still retaining your affection for us, may you never want the society of a friend equally faithful! May God also conciliate to you the favour of the Emperor; may he regulate every other circumstance to your complete satisfaction; and grant you a safe and speedy return to your own country and to us! In these prayers for you I unite with the good and virtuous. Let me add,

With health, with joy, to his lov'd native shore
May the kind Gods my honour'd friend restore *!

---

* Ουλι τι, και μιγα χαιρι· Θιοι δι τοι ολϐια δοιιν,
Νοϛησαι οικον δι φιλην ις πατριδα γαιαν.

The first line is taken from ver. 401, and the second is an alteration of Νοϛησαντα in ver. 404, of Odyss. xxiv. with the addition of most part of ver. 562 of Odyss. x.

Besides the warmth of affection that breathes through this whole composition, several parts of it, especially the conclusion, in the original, are poetical without being turgid.

Julian Cæsar to the Emperor Constantius *.

A. D. 360.

EVER retaining one and the same opinion, I have adhered to what I faithfully purposed, not less from principle than by the covenant of treaties, as has evidently appeared in various instances. As soon as I was created Cæsar, you exposed me to all the tumults and horrors of battle; yet, contented with a delegated authority, like a faithful apparitor, I filled your ears with frequent accounts of successes answerable to your wishes; never dwelling on my own dangers, though by continual proofs it may appear, the Germans being every where scattered and disordered, that I was always the first in labours, but the last in refreshment.

---

* The Gallic legions being ordered by Constantius to march into the East, a tumult arose (as Julian himself relates more particularly in the succeeding epistle to the Athenians); and from the subordinate dignity of Cæsar he was exalted by the army to the supreme rank of Augustus. This epistle, written soon after that event, is preserved by Ammianus.

He composed, in his own name, and in that of the army, a specious and moderate epistle, which was delivered to Pentadius, his master of the offices, and to his chamberlain Eutherius; two ambassadors, whom he appointed to receive the answer, and observe the dispositions, of Constantius.

GIBBON.

But,

EPISTLE TO CONSTANTIUS.

But, with your leave, I will inform you whether any innovations have now been made, as you imagine. The foldiers, wafting their lives in many and fevere wars, without advantage, have formerly held confultations, raging and impatient of a ruler in the fecond place, being fenfible that no recompence can be made them by the Cæfar for their daily fatigues and frequent victories; their refentment has been appeafed by no increafe of honours, not even by a year's pay now due, to which this alfo has been unexpectedly added; their being ordered to the moft diftant parts of the Eaftern world, men accuftomed to frozen climates were to be feparated from their wives and children, and were dragged forth indigent and naked. Being therefore more bitterly enraged than ufual, affembling in the night, they befieged the palace, exclaiming JULIAN AUGUSTUS with loud and repeated cries. I trembled, I confefs, and withdrew; and while I could, fought fafety by filence * and retirement. But no refpite being allowed, guarded, as I may fay, by the free fortrefs of my breaft, I went forth and prefented myfelf to them, thinking that my authority or mild words might allay the difturbance. Their fury was wonderful, and it went fo far, that, on my endeavouring by intreaties to conquer their obftinacy, rufhing clofe up to me, they threatened inftant death. At length fubdued, and conjec-

* In the original, *fimulatione*. I prefer the correction of Gelenius, *muffatione*.

turing *, that, when I was killed, another perhaps would be declared prince, I assented, thus hoping to appease the tumult.

This is the substance of what has happened, which I request you to accept with complacence. And think not that any thing is misrepresented, or credit the evil reports of the malicious, who are accustomed to promote the revolts of princes for their own advantage; but banishing flattery, the nurse of vice, cultivate the most excellent of all virtues, justice; and receive with good faith the equitable terms which I offer, considering them as beneficial both to the Roman state and to us, who are allied by consanguinity, and by the eminence of superior rank. These requests, (excuse me) as they are founded in reason, I am less anxious for your granting than for your approving and thinking them just and proper. I am ready also with chearfulness to obey your commands. What may be necessary I will reduce into a short compass.

I will furnish Spanish horses † for your chariots, and some Letian ‡ youths, sprung from Barbarians on

---

* In the original, *Mecúmque ipse contestans.* In the margin of the Royal MS. *conjectans* is written in the same hand.
VALOIS.
The translator has adopted the latter.

† Zonaras says the same thing. And he adds, that Julian inscribed his letter with the name of Cæsar, not Augustus, lest Constantius, offended at it, should immediately disdain it: which Julian also confirms in his Epistle to the Athenians. *Ibid.*

‡ The Leti, or Læti, were some half-barbarians, who dwelt in the Gauls; or (as our Ammianus subjoins) *cis Rhenum edita barbarorum progenies. Ibid.*

this side the Rhine, or, at least, from vassals who have revolted to us, to be incorporated with your provincials and targeteers. And these, as long as I live, I promise to supply, not only with gratitude but delight. Prætorian præfects, of distinguished equity and merit, shall be given us by your clemency *. As for the other usual magistrates, and the directors of the war, it is proper that they should be left to my nomination, and also the guards. For, when they can previously be learned, it is absurd for the manners and tempers of those who are stationed by the Emperor's side to be unknown to him. The following rule, without the least hesitation, I would establish: Gallic recruits, just enlisted, should not be sent, either voluntarily, or by force, to foreign and far distant countries, and oppressed with daily fatigues or vexatious accidents, lest the youth should be totally exhausted, being afflicted with the recollection of past, and sinking under impending, dangers. Nor can it be proper to oppose the Parthians with auxiliaries drawn from hence, since the barbaric fury is not yet quelled, and (if you will permit me to speak the truth) these provinces, harrassed by continual misfortunes, require external and powerful assistance. In giving this advice I study, I am convinced, the public good, requesting and intreating; for I know, not to arrogate more than my station warrants, what embarrassed and desperate

---

* A term of respect, like "majesty," &c.

EPISTLE TO CONSTANTIUS.

affairs have been retrieved by the agreement of princes mutually complying with each other; and the example of our ancestors will shew, that rulers, thinking in this and the like manner, have, as it were, discovered the method of living happily, and of endearing their memory to the latest times *.

* In this negociation Julian claimed no more than he already possessed. The delegated authority which he had long exercised over the provinces of Gaul, Spain, and Britain, was still obeyed under a name more independent and august. The soldiers and the people rejoiced in a revolution, which was not stained with blood. Florentius was a fugitive; Lupicinus a prisoner. The persons who were disaffected to the new government were disarmed and secured; and the vacant offices were distributed according to the recommendation of merit, by a prince who despised the intrigues of the palace, and the clamours of the soldiers.
GIBBON.

" To this ostensible epistle he added," says Ammianus, " private letters, *objurgatorias et mordaces*," which the historian had not seen, and would not have published. Perhaps they never existed. *Ibid.*

These " stinging" letters, Zonaras says, were not sent by Julian at that time, but afterwards, when Leonas, who had been ambassador to Julian, returned unsuccessful to Constantius. " Leonas therefore, despairing of being able to " execute any part of his commission, returned with the " letters of Julian, in which he impudently upbraided the " Emperor, as having been very criminal towards his re- " lations, and threatened that he would revenge their in- " juries."
VALOIS.

The ambassadors found Constantius at Cæsarea in Cappadocia. On reading the letters with which they were charged, this prince flew into a dreadful passion; and viewing them with a look that seemed to threaten their lives, he commanded them to withdraw, without condescending to give them any further audience, or to ask them any questions. He was very near quitting the Persian war to march directly against Julian. However, he only dispatched a Quæstor, named Leonas, to him, with a menacing letter, and recalled his principal officers. LA BLETERIE.

THE

The Emperor Julian to the Senate and People of Athens *.

THOUGH many actions have been performed by your ancestors, for which you, as well as they, are justly renowned, and though many trophies have been erected by all Greece in general, and

A. D. 361.

---

* Julian wrote this epistle soon after his being proclaimed Emperor in the Gauls; and while he was marching with his army against Constantius. For Libanius affirms, that he then wrote letters to several cities of Greece, in order to exculpate his assuming the empire to other nations. "He was so much more solicitous," says that orator, in his Panegyric on the consulship of Julian, " to
" exculpate himself than to gain a victory, that, while he
" was exposed to the greatest dangers, he apologised for him-
" self by the Greeks; to all mankind, writing epistles to
" them, according to the several dispositions of each city,
" some longer, and some shorter, as might suit those to
" whom they were addressed."
 This epistle therefore explains the motives of his conduct, and fully describes the patience with which he had hitherto borne the repeated injuries and provocations of Constantius, and the great reluctance with which, by the concurrence of the army, he was exalted to the empire. Indeed, of all the remains of that apostate, none seems to me more worthy of publication and the perusal of the learned, especially of those who study history. For it accurately relates that whole transaction, throws light on many parts of this subject transmitted to us by Ammianus and others, and also contains several historical facts and circumstances not to be found elsewhere. The great regard which Julian had for Athens and the Athenians, and the

reasons

EPISTLE TO THE ATHENIANS.

and by your city in particular, when she contended singly either with the neighbouring states, or with the Barbarians, none of her deeds are so distinguished, no acts of her heroism so illustrious, as not to be rivalled by the other cities. In some, they have co-operated with you; others they have performed unaided and alone. But lest, by mentioning particulars, I should seem to draw an odious comparison, or to give an invidious preference, in order to serve my cause, as is usual with orators, who by faintly praising, really de-

---

reasons why he resorted thither, Gregory of Nazianzus declares in his second oration *ςηλητ.*   PETAU.

After having made himself master of the pass of the Succi, in his march against Constantius, while Julian resided at Naissus in Illyricum, waiting for his troops, and making new levies, he wrote to several cities of Greece, among others to Athens, Lacedæmon, and Corinth, not only to engage them in his interest, but also to justify his proceedings.

In particular, he made it a point of honour and religion to take for judges the Athenians, so celebrated in antiquity for their love of justice, by carrying his cause to the tribunal of Areopagus, where the Gods had formerly appeared. Of all his manifestoes we have only that which was addressed to them. It is an eloquent and perfectly well-written piece.   LA BLETERIE.

The most authentic account of the education and adventures of Julian is contained in this epistle, or manifesto. It deserves the praises of the Abbé de la Bleterie, and is one of the best manifestoes to be found in any language.
  GIBBON.

His epistle to the Senate and people of Athens, seems to have been dictated by an elegant enthusiasm, which prompted him to submit his actions and motives to the degenerate Athenians of his own times, with the same humble deference, as if he had been pleading, in the days of Aristides, before the tribunal of the Areopagus. *Ibid.*

preciate

EPISTLE TO THE ATHENIANS.

preciate and decry the merit of their opponents, this only I will fay of you, to which, of all that tradition has tranfmitted the other Greeks can produce nothing parallel. You obtained the dominion over the Lacedæmonians, not by the force of your arms, but by the fame of your juftice. Ariftides * the Juft was formed by your laws. And thefe proofs of your virtue, fplendid as they are, you have confirmed by ftill more fplendid facts. For in mere matters of opinion we are liable to miftake, nor is it unufual to find, among many wicked men, one who is virtuous. Is not Deioces † celebrated among the Medes, Abaris ‡ among the Hyperboreans, and Anacharfis § among the Scythians; of whom it was remarkable, that, though they lived in nations notoriouſly unjuſt, they nevertheleſs cultivated juſtice? The two laſt ſincerely; the firſt was prompted by intereſt to diſ-

* See his Life in Cornelius Nepos.

† He determined with ſo much prudence the differences of the Medes, that he deſerved to be choſen their king. He built, according to Herodotus, the city of Ecbatana, and reigned forty years, from the year of the world 3358 to 3398.   MORERI.

‡ A Scythian, who wrote Apollo's Northern Journey in verſe, oracles, predictions, &c. Jamblichus ſays, he was a ſcholar of Pythagoras, which does not agree with what the ancients affirm of Abaris being prior even to Solon. *Ibid.*

§ Another Scythian, contemporary with Solon, of whom he learned philofophy at Athens.

He was the only philofopher of his nation, whence the proverb, *Anacharſis inter Scythas.* At length he was killed by his brother the king of Scythia, for endeavouring to introduce the Athenian laws. See Diogenes Laërtius, in his life, *l.* 1.

ſemble

semble it. But it is difficult to produce a whole city and nation, who practise justice, both in word and deed, except yourselves. Of many instances that have occurred among you it may be sufficient to mention one. When Themistocles *, after the Persian war, had formed a plan of privately setting fire to the naval arsenals of the Greeks, and dared not publickly to propose it, but said, he would communicate the secret to any one whom the people by their suffrages would elect, they named Aristides. He, on hearing the proposal, concealed the particulars, and only informed the people, that " nothing could be more advan-
" tageous, but at the same time more unjust, than
" the advice of Themistocles." Upon which, the city immediately disclaimed and declined it; a signal instance of magnanimity, and highly becoming a people educated under the eye of the wisest Goddess!

If these things happened among you in ancient times, and a small spark, as it were, of the virtue of your ancestors has ever since been preserved, you ought, when you hear of any great action, to consider, not the surprising singularity of it, like that of a man walking with as much strength and agility as if he had wings, but whether its motives were just and right. And if so, both in public and private it will receive your deserved applause; if not, it will with reason be disregarded and condemned. Nothing is so nearly allied to wisdom as

* See his Life in Plutarch.

EPISTLE TO THE ATHENIANS.

justice. Those therefore who despise it you should banish as profaners of your Goddess. Though you are not strangers to my affairs, this is the occasion of my present address. If any thing should chance to have escaped your knowledge (and some particulars probably may, even of those in which you all are interested), it may thus be communicated to you, and by you to the other Greeks. And let me not be charged with trifling, if I endeavour to comprise in my discourse those scenes which have lately been presented to the eyes of all men, as well as former transactions, as I wish to have every thing that relates to me generally known. I will begin with my ancestors.

That the family of my father, and that of Constantius, had the same origin, you need not be informed. Our fathers were brothers, having the same father. How that most humane Emperor acted afterwards towards me, who was so nearly related to him, and how he unjustly put to death six of his own and my cousins, as well as my father, his own uncle, together with another uncle of us both, and also my elder brother *; and after having

---

* He says, that " six cousins and two uncles" were slain by Constantius. The latter, I find in the history of those times, were [Julius] Constantius, the father of Julian, and Dalmatius, both sons of [Constantius] Chlorus, by Theodora, the daughter-in-law of Maximian-Herculius, and brothers of Constantine. [See the " Pedigree of Julian."] But the historians mention only " three" cousin-germans, viz. Dalmatianus and Hannibalianus, the sons of Dalmatius, and Nepotianus, the son of Eutropia, the sister of Constantine. The others were killed, soon after the death

EPISTLE TO THE ATHENIANS.

ing intended to deſtroy me * and another brother †, changed our ſentence into baniſhment, from which he afterwards releaſed me, but deprived him, juſt before he was killed, of the name of Cæſar; all theſe dreadful tragical events why ſhould I relate? eſpecially, as he is ſaid to have repented, and to have been much afflicted, attributing to them his want of children, and alſo his ill ſucceſs in the

of Conſtantine, by a conſpiracy of the ſoldiers. Nepotianus was ſlain after the death of Conſtans, not, however, by Conſtantius, but by the tyrant Magnentius. So ſay Socrates, Zoſimus, Eutropius, and Victor. I read therefore of but "two" couſins ſlain by Conſtantius. The reſt let the diligent and learned inveſtigate.   PETAU.

* We learn, from this paſſage, what is mentioned, as I recollect, by no other writer, that Julian had, beſides Gallus Cæſar, another, and that an elder brother, whom he here plainly diſtinguiſhes from Gallus, and mentions to have been killed, before Gallus was Cæſar, by Conſtantius. Who he was, or what was his name, I profeſs myſelf to be ignorant. But ſo was Socrates.   *Ibid.*

Julian here charges his couſin Conſtantius with the whole guilt of a maſſacre, from which he himſelf ſo narrowly eſcaped. His aſſertion is confirmed by Athanaſius, who, for reaſons of a very different nature, was not leſs an enemy to Conſtantius. (tom. 1. p. 856.) Zoſimus joins in the ſame accuſation. But the three abbreviators, Eutropius and the Victors, uſe very qualifying expreſſions, "*ſinente potius quam jubente;*" "*incertum quo ſuaſore,*" "*vi militum.*"   GIBBON.

† Socrates (III. 1.) ſays, that " Gallus was ſuffered to " live, becauſe, on account of his weak conſtitution, it was " thought that he could not live long; and Julian, becauſe " he was only eight years old." But in this, Socrates is not quite accurate. For Julian was not " eight," but only " five" years old: as he died in the 31ſt year of his age, in that of our Lord 363. But Conſtantine died in 337.
  PETAU.

Perſian

EPISTLE TO THE ATHENIANS.

Persian war &c. Such rumours, at least, were circulated among the courtiers, in the hearing of me and my late brother Cæsar Gallus; for so he was then styled. Having put him also to death, in defiance of all laws, he neither suffered him to be entombed with his ancestors, nor his memory to be honoured. But, as I said before, * we were informed and convinced, that some of these crimes originated from misapprehension and misinformation, and others from the overbearing insolence and compulsion of a turbulent and mutinous army. Such reports often reached us in our confinement in a certain Cappadocian farm †, to which no one was allowed access: there we were both placed; my brother, recalled from exile; and I, almost a child, removed from school. Why should I mention those six years ‡, in which we were educated in a kind of foreign country, and as strictly guarded as if we had been in Persia, no stranger, nor

---

* In the reign of Constantius, Sapor vanquished the Romans in three battles, invaded Mesopotamia, took Amida, Singard, &c.

† Ammianus (xv. 2.) relates, that "Julian was accused of "going from the farm of Macellum, in Cappadocia, into "Asia, for the sake of liberal studies, and, in his way "through Constantinople, of seeing his brother." This χωρα, or farm, he afterwards calls ἀγρος, and thus the Latins term a farm *possessio*, PRÆDIUM.

Mr. Gibbon, in different places, styles this Farm " an " ancient palace," " a strong castle," " the residence of " the kings of Cappadocia;" " the situation," he adds, " was pleasant; the buildings stately, the inclosures spa- " cious." It was at the foot of Mount Argæus, not far from Cæsarea, the capital of the province.

‡ From 345 to 351.

any

any of our friends, being admitted to us; where, secluded from all liberal studies, and debarred all intercourse with families of rank, we were forced to associate only with our domestics? From thence, by the assistance of the Gods, I was at length happily released; but my brother was most unfortunately inveigled to court. If there was any thing rustic and uncivilised in his deportment *, it was owing to that mountainous education. He therefore who doomed us to it is justly chargeable with the blame. Thanks be to the Gods, philosophy has purified me; but this blessing was denied to my brother. For after he had exchanged the country for the court, and had been invested with the purple, he immediately became an object of envy; nor did that envy cease, till, not contented with stripping him of the purple, it had accomplished his destruction. Yet though he might be

* This opinion of Julian concerning his brother is expressed by Libanius, in his panegyric on the consulship of Julian, p. 234, where he mentions some letters, in which he, a private man, admonished Gallus, then Cæsar, of his duty: " If his brother had attended to his letters, we " should now have had two princes. For he who did " not reign dared to admonish him who did. But when " he, who might have alleged something in his own de- " fence, had been put to death unheard, an inclination " appeared of preferring some charges against the other, " as if he had killed him; but that not being practicable, " his life was spared to be harrassed by fatiguing journeys, " thus suffering, though innocent, the punishment due to " guilt." The disposition of Gallus is also mentioned by Nazianzen, in his *Steliteut*. I. " Though of a passionate " temper, he was unaffectedly pious." PETAU.

· deemed

EPISTLE TO THE ATHENIANS.

deemed unfit to govern, surely he was not unworthy to live. And even allowing the expedience of depriving him of life, he should not have been denied the usual privilege of criminals, that of being heard in his own defence. The law does not forbid him who has the right of imprisoning robbers to put them also to death; deprived of all their honours, and reduced from a princely to a plebeian rank, it says, that they shall be executed without a trial. What if he could have produced the persons who impeached these traitors *? For in some of their letters that were shewn him, heaven knows what charges were contained! Thus, incensed by an unbecoming weakness, he was rashly betrayed into passion. He did nothing, however, that deserved death; but, you may say, that it is a rule universal, both among Greeks and Barbarians, that he who has received may revenge an insult. True—yet Constantins revenged it too severely. But he did nothing more than is usual. " It is usual," he once said, " for an enemy, when " enraged, to go any lengths." But to gratify an

---

* See in Ammianus (xiv. 1. 7.) a very ample detail of the cruelties of Gallus. His brother Julian insinuates that a conspiracy had been formed against him; and Zosimus names the persons engaged in it; a minister of considerable rank, and two obscure agents, who were resolved to make their fortunes.   GIBBON.

Julian perhaps here refers to the massacre at Antioch of the Imperial ministers, Domitian and Montius, by the command of Gallus.

eunuch *, his chamberlain †, and also his master-
cook, Constantius sacrificed to his most inveterate
enemies ‡ his cousin-german, the Cæsar; the huſ-
band of his ſiſter §, the father of his niece, whoſe
sister

* Eusebius, who ruled the monarch and the palace with
such absolute sway, that Constantius, according to the
ſarcaſm of an impartial hiſtorian, poſſeſſed ſome credit
with his haughty favourite: *Apud quem (ſi vere dici debeat)
multa Conſtantius potuit.* Amm. xviii. 4. Gibbon.

† A favourite eunuch, who, in the language of that age, was
styled the *præpoſitus*, or prefect, of the ſacred bed-chamber.
His duty was to attend the Emperor in his hours of ſtate,
or in thoſe of amuſement, and to perform about his perſon
all thoſe menial services which can only derive their splendor from the influence of royalty. Under a prince who
deſerved to reign, the great chamberlain (for ſuch we may
call him) was an uſeful and humble domeſtic; but an artful domeſtic, who improves every occaſion of unguarded
confidence, will inſenſibly acquire over a feeble mind that
aſcendant which harſh wiſdom and uncomplying virtue can
ſeldom obtain. *Ibid.*

‡ The Emperor was easily convinced that his own safety
was incompatible with the life of his cousin; the ſentence
of death was ſigned, diſpatched, and executed; and the
nephew of Conſtantine, with his hands tied behind his
back, was beheaded in priſon, like the vileſt malefactor.
Ibid.

This event happened "near Pola in Iſtria," ſays Ammianus, "where Criſpus, the ſon of Conſtantine, was for-
"merly killed." Near Flanona, or Flavona, in Dalmatia,
(not far from Pola) ſay Socrates and Sozomen.

§ Gallus had married Conſtantia [rather Conſtantina],
the daughter of Conſtantine, and ſiſter of Conſtantius.
Julian mentions his having a daughter by her; and alſo
that Conſtantius had before married the ſiſter of Gallus.
Theſe two circumſtances, related, as far as I know, by him
only, were before unknown. The firſt of theſe is deduced
from this paſſage a little corrected. For αδελφιδης ("niece")
ſhould evidently have been written, inſtead of αδελφιδους
("nephew.")

after he himself had married, and who was connected to him by so many domestic ties." Me, not without difficulty, he dismissed, after removing me to various places, and keeping me in confinement, seven months. And if some God, to insure my safety, had not ingratiated me with his beautiful and excellent wife, Eusebia *, I could not have escaped his resentment. Though the Gods will attest that my brother, when he pursued those measures, was never seen by me, even in a dream; for neither was I with him, nor did I visit him, nor was I in his neighbourhood. And when

("nephew.") Gallus had the same father as Julian; his mother was Galla, the sister of Rufinus and Cerealis, whom the Consulship, says Ammianus (l. xiv.) had ennobled. Constantius seems to have married the daughter of this Galla before Eusebia, and I know not whether it was she with whom Constantius celebrated his nuptials in the life-time, and by the management of his father, as related by Eusebius, in his Life of Constantine. That Constantius had more wives, is affirmed by Ammianus. And Victor says, in his Epitome, " of his wives, of whom he had " many, he loved Eusebia most." Eusebia is generally mentioned as the first; and Faustina [or Fausta] as the second and last, by whom he had a posthumous daughter, Constantia, who was married to the Emperor Gratian. PETAU.

* A woman of beauty and merit, who, by the ascendant she had gained over the mind of her husband, counterbalanced, in some measure, the powerful conspiracy of the eunuchs. She was a native of Thessalonica in Macedonia, of a noble family, and the daughter, as well as sister, of Consuls. Her marriage with the Emperor may be placed in the year 352. In a divided age, the historians of all parties agree in her praises. GIBBON.

In sulmine tam celso humana, is her panegyric by Ammianus. "In such an exalted station not inhuman," gives an imperfect idea of it in English.

I wrote

I wrote to him, which was seldom, my letters were short. I therefore gladly took refuge in the house of my mother. For as to the estate of my father, of none of his possessions had I the least share, no land, nor a house, not a slave, the worthy Constantius having seized all my paternal inheritance, without giving me the merest trifle. Having despoiled Gallus of the effects of his mother, he gave him a few of his father's.

Most part, at least, if not the whole, of his behaviour to me, before he conferred on me that most respectable name *, but in fact imposed on me a severe and laborious slavery, you shall now hear. Having thus with great difficulty, and beyond my expectation, escaped, and being happily sheltered under the roof of my mother, a sycophant, from the neighbourhood of Sirmium †, falsely reported, that new commotions might be expected there. You have heard, no doubt, of Africanus and Marinus; nor can the name of Felix have escaped you, and what was their fate ‡.

As

---

* Of Cæsar.

† The capital of Illyricum, at present Sirmisch or Sirmick, a small town, almost ruined, in the Lower Hungary.
LA BLETERIE.

‡ Ammianus (xv. 3.) mentions a drunken and treasonable entertainment at Sirmium, given by Africanus, governor of the second Pannonia (A. D. 354), in consequence of which, on the information of Gaudentius, the sycophant here meant, all the company were arrested. Marinus, a tribune, and the principal delinquent, stabbed himself in a tavern, on the road, at Aquileia. And the rest were put to the torture at Milan, and afterwards imprisoned. This, doubtless, is the incident to which Julian alludes. A person named

As soon as Constantius received this intelligence, and had also been assured by Dynamius, another informer from the Gauls, that Sylvanus * would soon revolt against him; alarmed and terrified he sent for me, and after ordering me to retire for a short time into Greece, he suddenly recalled me. He had never seen me before, except once in Cappadocia, and once in Italy, at the earnest intreaty of Eusebia, that I might be assured of safety. Yet I was six months in the same city † with him, and he promised to see me again. But that heaven-detested eunuch ‡, his trusty chamberlain, was ignorantly and undesignedly my friend, by preventing my frequent access. Constantius himself perhaps might not wish to see me; nevertheless, all my misfortunes were owing to that favourite, as he was apprehensive, that, if we

---

named Felix was made master of the offices by Constantius, but rejected by Julian. And there was another who was Count of the sacred largesses. But probably this Felix was one of the riotous company abovementioned.

* For an account of this revolt see a note in the succeeding page.

Οσοι υπω τυ Νηλυ, και εν αυτω πολεμον αναφανισθαι. This I cannot understand. What follows is related more at large by Ammianus and Zosimus. See also *Orat.* III. " on Eusebia." Petav.

These words may be thus corrected: Οσοι υπω τον Σιλβανον αυτω πολεμιον αναφαινισθαι. Zosimus mentions the same Dynamius at the end of l. ii. But he is mistaken in ascribing to him the death of Gallus Cæsar; as Dynamius calumniated Sylvanus, not Gallus. Valois.

This correction is adopted by the translator.

† Mediolanum, or Milan.

‡ Eusebius above-mentioned, whom Julian, when he was Emperor, put to death.

should be acquainted, a friendship might ensue; and if my fidelity had been approved, I might have been invested with some place of trust.

As soon as I returned from Greece, the blessed Eusebia, by the eunuchs of her houshold, shewed me many acts of kindness. And soon after, on his arrival, after terminating the war with Sylvanus*, I

* In the summer which preceded the elevation of Julian (Sept. A. D. 355.) this general had been chosen to deliver Gaul from the tyranny of the Barbarians; but Sylvanus soon discovered that he had left his most dangerous enemies in the Imperial court. A dexterous informer, countenanced by several of the principal ministers, procured from him some recommendatory letters; and erasing the whole of the contents, except the signature, filled up the vacant parchment with matters of high and treasonable import. By the industry and courage of his friends, the fraud was, however, detected, and, in a great council of the civil and military officers, held in the presence of the Emperor himself, the innocence of Sylvanus was publickly acknowledged. But the discovery came too late; the report of the calumny, and the hasty seizure of his estate, had already provoked the indignant chief to the rebellion of which he was so unjustly accused. He assumed the purple at his head-quarters of Cologne; and his active powers appeared to menace Italy with an invasion, and Milan with a siege. In this emergency, Ursicinus, a general of equal rank, regained, by an act of treachery, the favour which he had lost by his eminent services in the East. Exasperated, as he might speciously allege, by injuries of a similar nature, he hastened, with a few followers, to join the standard, and to betray the confidence, of his too credulous friend. After a reign of only twenty-eight days, Sylvanus was assassinated. The soldiers, who, without any criminal intention, had blindly followed the example of their leader, immediately returned to their allegiance; and the flatterers of Constantius celebrated the wisdom and felicity of the monarch who had extinguished a civil war without the hazard of a battle. GIBBON.

was

was allowed to go to court, induced by what is called a Theffalian perfuafion upon force *. For on my refolutely declining all intercourfe with the palace, the courtiers convening, as if they had been in a barber's-fhop, fhaved my chin, and throwing over me a military mantle, transformed me, as they thought, into a very ridiculous foldier. For none of the finical ornaments of thofe wretches were fuitable to my tafte. I walked about therefore, not like them, ftaring on every fide, and with a haughty gait, but poring on the ground, as I had been taught by my preceptor †. This was at firft the fubject of their laughter, but foon after of their fufpicion, which at length gave place to envy. But I muft not omit, that I refided among them, and that I did not difdain even to lodge

* This proverb, Θιτταλικη πιθαναγκη, is alfo quoted by Julian, in his firft Oration, and by Eunapius. But, as to its origin, the collectors of proverbs are filent. Petau. Spanheim fuppofes it to originate from the impoftures, perfidy, and magic of the Theffalians, which were alfo proverbial. Our Englifh proverb, which is not unlike it, "Patience on force," has an addition, which may perhaps afford a clue; "is a medicine for a mad horfe;" the inhabitants of Theffaly being anciently famous for their horfemanfhip. Πιθαναγκη is applied by Cicero to Cæfar, ad Attic. IX. 13.

† Mardonius, an eunuch, mentioned afterwards more particularly in the Mifopogon.

Julian himfelf relates, with fome humour, the circumftances of his own metamorphofis, his down-caft looks, and his perplexity at being thus fuddenly tranfported into a new world, where every object appeared ftrange and hoftile.
GIBBON.

with

with those whom I knew to have been the assassins of all my relations, and whom I had reason to suspect of meditating also my destruction. What floods of tears I shed *, and what lamentations I uttered, when, extending my hands towards your citadel †, I intreated and implored Minerva to protect her servant, and not to deliver him up to his enemies, many of you, who were present, can attest; and, above all, the Goddess herself knows, that I petitioned death of her at Athens in preference to that journey. That the Goddess did not abandon me, nor deliver me up, the event has shewn. On the contrary, she has every where been my guide, and was constantly with me,

---

* Libanius, in his panegyrical Oration on the consulship of Julian, p. 235, has taken this, and some other passages, almost in the same words, from this Epistle. PETAV.

† This was the temple of Minerva at Athens. The Emperor assigned Athens for the place of his honorable exile, which is implied in what Julian says above of his "short retirement into Greece." He was sent thither in May, 355, and there "spent six months amidst the "groves of the Academy (as Mr. Gibbon expresses it) "far from the tumult of arms, and the treachery of "courts, in a free intercourse with the philosophers of "the age, who studied to cultivate the genius, to en- "courage the vanity, and to inflame the devotion of their "royal pupil. Gregory Nazianzen was his fellow-student; "and the symptoms, which he so tragically describes, of "the future wickedness of the apostate, amount only to "some bodily imperfections, and to some peculiarities in "his speech and manner. He protests, however, that "he then foresaw and foretold the calamities of the "church and state." St. Basil was another of his fellow-students.

borrowing

borrowing guardian-angels * from the Sun and Moon †.

What follows may be also worth relating. On my return to Milan, where I resided in one of the suburbs, Eusebia frequently sent me friendly messages, and urged me to write to her, on any subject, with the utmost confidence. This induced me to compose this letter, or rather petition, with an adjuration: " So may you have children and heirs, " so may God bless you with both, as you send " me home ‡ immediately §!" After this, I was apprehensive of not being able to convey it safely

---

* Julian did not yield till the Gods had signified their will by repeated visions and omens. His piety then forbade him to resist. GIBBON.

He here declares himself a Pagan, which may serve to correct the hasty assertion of Ammianus, who supposes Constantinople to have been the place where he first discovered it. *Ibid.*

† Julian, however, seems to have " borrowed" these angels from the Christian Scriptures, with which he was well acquainted. On the angels of the Sun he descants at large in his ivth Oration *ad Solem Regem*, and they are also mentioned by Iamblichus, in his Life of Pythagoras, and by Proclus on the 2d book of Hesiod.

‡ So he styles Asia Minor, where he had been educated.

§ Julian animated his army, not only by presents, but by constantly swearing by the importance of the enterprize in which they were engaged. " So may we subdue the " Persians!" " So may we repair the shattered Roman " world!" As Trajan is reported frequently to have confirmed what he said by swearing, " So may I see Dacia re- " duced to a province!" " So may I master the Danube " and Euphrates with bridges!" and the like.
AMMIANUS.

EPISTLE TO THE ATHENIANS.

into the palace. And therefore I befought the Gods to inform me by night whether I fhould fend it to the Emprefs, or not. They threatened me, if I fent it, with the moft ignominious death. I appeal to all the Gods for the truth of what I affert. In obedience to them, I fuppreffed it. But from that night I imbibed an idea which it may not be improper to mention. "Now," faid I to myfelf, "I undertake to oppofe the Gods, and
" imagine that I can judge for myfelf better than
" they who know all things. Human wifdom,
" confining its view to the prefent, may think
" that it judges well, when, in fome inftances,
" which rarely happen, it commits no miftake.
" But no one deliberates on events that will hap-
" pen three hundred years hence, as that is im-
" poffible, or on occurrences that are long paft,
" that being needlefs; but only concerning objects
" that are prefent, and of which the beginnings
" and feeds, as it were, now exift. But the wif-
" dom of the Gods, obferving the moft diftant
" events, or rather all things, always directs what
" is right, and does what is beft. As they are no
" lefs the caufe of the prefent than of the future,
" muft they not neceffarily be acquainted with the
" prefent?" Thus far then the laft advice feemed to me much the moft prudent; and viewing it in the light of juftice, I added, " Would you not be
" provoked at being defrauded of any part of your
" property, or, on your requiring its attendance,

" if

EPISTLE TO THE ATHENIANS.

"If any one of your domestic animals * should
"abscond? And will you, who pretend to be a
"man, and that not of the common, vulgar herd,
"but of the rational and temperate, defraud the
"Gods of your service, and not suffer them to dis-
"pose of you as they please? Beware lest you act
"not only foolishly, but contemptuously, with re-
"gard to the divine laws. What occasion is here
"for fortitude? The pretence is ridiculous.—Will
"you then condescend to cringe and flatter, in
"order to preserve your life, instead of removing
"every obstacle, and allowing the Gods to act as
"they please; dividing your solicitude for yourself
"with them †, as was the wish of Socrates; com-
"mitting every thing to them, possessing and
"usurping nothing, but chearfully accepting
"whatever they bestow?" Thinking this advice
most safe and prudent, as it was suggested by the
Gods (for by avoiding present evils to expose myself
to future dangers seemed the utmost rashness), I
desisted and obeyed. Immediately I was honoured
with the title, and invested with the robe ‡, of
Cæsar.

---

* In the original, και ιππος, και προβατον, καν βοιδιον, ("a
"horse, a sheep, or a heifer.")

† Διαλομενον προς αυτας [τας Θεας] την επιμελειαν την εαυτε.
This language Julian perhaps rather learned from Christianity: Πασαν την μεριμναν υμων επιρριψαντες επ' αυτον [τον Θεον]
κ. τ. λ. *Casting all your care upon him*, &c. 1 Peter. v. 7.

‡ Ammianus, xv. 8. "Saying this, he thus accosts Julian,
"soon after he had been arrayed with the purple, and de-
"clared Cæsar, to the great joy of the army, but some-
"what dejected, and with his brow contracted." He means
there-

Cæsar. Of this slavery was the consequence, and every day, how great, O Hercules, was my apprehension, how imminent my danger! Barred gates, guards, servants searched, left they should convey letters from my friends, and a strange houshold! I was with difficulty allowed to bring with me to court, as my personal attendants, four domestics; two of whom were boys; and of the two others one only, my librarian *, from conscientious motives, was privately, to the utmost of his power, my assistant. The other, who of my many friends and companions alone was faithful, was my physician †. Not being known to be also my friend, he was

therefore the purple which was common both to the Cæsar and the Augustus.   PETAU.

After the investiture of the Cæsar had been performed, the two princes returned to the palace in the same chariot; and during the slow procession, Julian repeated to himself a verse of his favourite Homer, which he might equally apply to his fortune and to his fears:

Ελλαβε πορφυρεος θανατος, και μοιρα κραταιη. Il. v. 83.
——— the *purple* hand of death
Clos'd his dim eyes, and fate suppress'd his breath.
        POPE, 108.

The word "purple," which Homer had used as a vague but common epithet for death, was applied by Julian to express, very aptly, the nature and object of his own apprehensions.   GIBBON.

* Euemerus. He was employed in the care of a valuable collection of books, the gift of the Empress, who studied the inclinations, as well as the interest, of her friend.
        Ibid.

† Oribasius. See the first note on Epistle XVII. which is addressed to him in confidence. The elogium of "singular fidelity" is applied by the Latin translator to the librarian. The original, I think, warrants my applying it, as is more probable, to the physician.

EPISTLE TO THE ATHENIANS.

my fellow-traveller. Such were my fears and apprehensions, that the visits which were offered me by many of my friends, whom I much wished to see, I chose to decline, lest I should involve them in my misfortunes *. But this, though connected with my subject, is rather foreign to it.

With three hundred and sixty soldiers Constantius sent me into Gaul, which was then in confusion, in the middle of winter †, not so much to command his armies there, as to be subordinate to his generals. For they had express orders to be as much on their guard against me as against the enemy, lest I should attempt any innovations. Every thing being thus settled, about the summer solstice ‡ he allowed me to join the army, bearing his

---

* Julian represents, in the most pathetic terms, the distress of his new situation. The provision of his table was, however, so elegant and sumptuous, that the young philosopher rejected it with disdain. Amm. xvi. 5. GIBBON.

† Libanius, in his panegyric on the consulship of Julian, says the same, viz. that "less than four hundred soldiers "were given him, in the depth of winter;" and what follows he has transcribed, as has before been observed, from this Epistle. Ammianus (xv. 8.) says, that "Julian was "declared Cæsar on the 6th of November [355]; soon after "Helena was given him in marriage; and on December 1, he set out for Gaul." Marcellus and Sallust were sent with him, and to them all the management of the province and of the war was entrusted, lest Julian should attempt any innovations. PETAU.

‡ I cannot agree with the learned [Latin] translator, who, for " summer," affirms we should read " winter solstice." For this passage is not to be understood of that year, towards the end of which Julian was sent into the Gauls; but of the subsequent year, when he entered on his first consulship
with

EPISTLE TO THE ATHENIANS.

his robe and image." For he had both said and written, that "he did not mean to give the Gauls a king, but one who should exhibit to them his dress,* and image." ⌊ ... ⌋ ⌈ ... ⌉ The first campaign, as you have heard, having been ill-conducted †, and no advantage gained, at my return into winter-quarters, I was exposed to the utmost danger. For I had not the power of assembling the troops; this was entrusted to another, and a few only were quartered with me. My assistance being requested by the neighbouring towns, after sending them most of my forces, I ⌊ ... tell ... you ... every ... thing ... itself ... I ... first ... had ... ⌋

... with Constantius; which was the year of Christ 356. At the summer solstice the Gallic soldiers used to set out on expeditions.   VALOIS.

* Σχημα not οχημα ("carriage") the common reading.   Ib∥.

† Julian was made Cæsar in the consulship of Arbetio and Lollian, A. D. 355. Towards the end of that year, [as above mentioned], he was sent into Gaul, and wintered at Vienne, where he entered on his first consulship, with Constantius (the 8th time) for his colleague, at the beginning of the year 356, which was the first year of his Gallic government. This campaign, Julian complains, was unsuccessful, and that no advantages were gained. But if we refer to Ammianus, we shall find that less indeed than accorded with the inclination and impetuosity of Julian, yet much, nevertheless, was done against the Barbarians. While he was at Vienne, hearing that the Germans were making incursions in order to ravage Gaul, and had with difficulty been repulsed at Augustodunum, [Autun] he determined to pursue them. After defeating and dispersing them, he recovered Colonia Agrippina, [Cologne]. And he so terrified the kings of the Franks, that he compelled them to make peace. " Rejoicing" (adds Ammianus) " at these first fruits of conquest, he went into " winter-quarters at Treves, a then convenient town of
                                                                     " the

had scarce any left *. So affairs were circumstanced. But the general in chief †, having in-

" the Senones." I suspect therefore that Julian wrote [ου] κακως δε, ως ακηκοαλι, [" not] ill conducted, as you have " heard;") and, soon after, πραχθεντος [τινο;] σπυδαιν, (" and " [some] advantage gained.") But wintering at Sens, with a few soldiers, the enemy assembled on a sudden, and besieged the town; and Marcellus, master-general of the cavalry, who commanded in the next cantonment, neglected and refused to assist him. Yet in twenty days the Barbarians raised the siege, and retired. This we collect from Ammianus XVI. 4. PETAU.

Ammianus appears much better satisfied with the success of this first campaign than Julian himself; who very frankly owns that he did nothing of consequence, and that he fled before the enemy. GIBBON.

* In the original, αυτος απελειφθην μονος, " I was left " alone."

† As soon as Constantius heard how perfidiously Marcellus had acted at Sens, " absolving him from his military " oath" (these are the words of Ammianus) " he ordered " him to retire to his own house; and he, as if he had been " grievously injured, plotted something against Julian, " trusting that the ears of Augustus would be open to every " charge." But the eunuch Eutherius, the most faithful præfect of his chamber, being dispatched by Julian, refuted this calumny. This Marcellus was a native of Serdica, whither, when he was displaced, he retired. So says Ammianus, as I have corrected him. The common reading is neither perfect, nor conveys that sense. For, after a long digression, arising from the eunuch Eutherius, on the wickedness of the eunuchs, Ammianus, returning to Marcellus, expresses himself thus: *Nunc redeam unde diverti. Superato, ut dixi, Marcello,* everfaque Serdicâ, *unde oriebatur,* &c. Read *reverſoque Serdicam.* PETAU.

The son of this Marcellus aspiring to the empire was put to death by Julian in 361. Libanius speaks rather more advantageously of the military talents of Marcellus. And Julian intimates [above] that he would not so easily have been recalled, unless he had given other reasons of offence to the court. GIBBON.

curred the displeasure of the Emperor, was superseded and dismissed, for inability; and, because I had acted with clemency and moderation, my talents and abilities were not deemed equal to the command. For I thought it by no means right to struggle with my yoke, or officiously to assume the general *, by obtruding my advice, unless when I saw something hazardous attempted, that I thought should have been omitted, or neglected, that should have been done. But having more than once received some [im]proper † treatment, I determined for the future to be silent, and contented myself with the pageantry of the robe and image. For to that I thought I had a right.

Constantius imagining that the Gallic affairs would soon wear a better aspect, not indeed that the alteration would be so great, gave me the command of the armies ‡ in the beginning of spring. As
soon

---

* Ζυγομαχην, ὐδὲ παρατρώπητιν.

† Καθηκοντως ("properly") in the original. Ου ("not") seems necessary to be prefixed, implying, that he afterwards was quiet, because he had once or twice been treated ill. PETAU.

‡ When Julian was appointed general, and what was the nature of his commission, deserves enquiry. He himself says, that it happened after Marcellus was dismissed, and sent to Serdica. But he also mentions, that, after he obtained this command, he rebuilt Colonia Agrippina (Cologne) and another town, Tabernæ, with some other towns of Gaul, to the number of forty-five, recovered from the Barbarians. Very different is the account given by Ammianus. For he affirms, that Julian recovered Colonia before the end of the first year of his being in Gaul, that is, in the consulship of Constantius (the 8th time) and
Julian,

soon as the corn was ripe, I took the field, many of the Germans dwelling securely near the towns that they had destroyed in the Gauls. There were forty-

Julian, of our Lord 356, before Marcellus was commissioned by Constantius, which happened towards the end of the same, or the commencement of the ensuing year. Marcellus was succeeded by Severus, a man well versed in the art of war, good-natured, and unassuming; at the acquisition of whom Julian expressed much pleasure, and declared "that he would obey his able directions," (says Ammianus) "as a soldier should an [obliging] leader." The sense requires *morigerus*. Barbatio also was sent with him, who was to attack the Barbarians in another quarter with twenty-five thousand men. He was master-general of the foot, and Severus of the horse, as Ammianus informs us, l. xvi. But if we compare the words of Julian with the history of Ammianus, we shall find, that the command of the army was given him in the second year of his being in the Gauls, viz. A. D. 357, when he engaged the Alemanni and king Cnodomar," after the corn was ripe." For in that year he acted as general, at least, of that army which Severus had commanded. And so far was Barbatio, who commanded the other, from obeying him, that he neglected and refused to assist him, when he was in danger. Therefore his saying, " he gave me the command " of the armies," I do not think true of them all. Nor should it be omitted, that, even in the first year, when Marcellus was still in Gaul, the Cæsar Julian was not so obnoxious to the generals as not to be entrusted with some command. For Ammianus relates (xvi.) that, in that year, which was 356 of Christ, when Julian went to Rheims, " he ordered the army to be collected in one body," in order to disguise his force; " which army was then commanded by Marcellus, the successor of Ursicinus;" and also that Ursicinus himself was ordered to wait in the same place the event of that expedition. But though he had the title of governing the province, and managing the war, yet the masters-general of the forces, as Constantius had ordered, did not implicitly obey him, but in general, were refractory. Add, that Julian here oratorically depresses

G 2   his

forty-five such towns that were dismantled *, besides villages and smaller fortifications. The Barbarians then possessed all the territory on this side of the Rhine, from its sources to the ocean. Those who were the nearest to us were three hundred stadia † distant from its banks. A district thrice as extensive was left a desert by their devastations, where the Gauls could not pasture their cattle. Some towns were also deserted by their inhabitants, though the Barbarians had not yet approached them. Finding Gaul thus distressed, I recovered the city of Agrippina [Cologne] on the Rhine, which had been taken about ten months before, and also the neighbouring castle of Argentoratum [Strasburgh] near the foot of Vosegus ‡; and we

his situation below the truth, as if he had then no other employment than carrying about the Imperial image. Zosimus says, (l. III.) that " Constantius permitted Julian, " at his departure, to regulate the Gauls as he should " think expedient." This Constantius seems to have done openly; but privately he ordered his præfects to watch all his words and actions, and sometimes to obey perversely. See the Oration of Libanius on the consulship of Julian.
              PETAU.

* Zosimus (l. III.) says, that " forty towns in Gaul, " which the Barbarians had destroyed, were rebuilt by " Julian." And he also mentions, how much they had overrun Gaul. Libanius enumerates as many as Julian, taking all that history from this Epistle.   *Ibid.*

† Near forty miles.

‡ One of the principal mountains in Gaul, now Mount Vauge, which separates Burgundy from Lorrain, and also divides Lorrain from Alsace, stretching towards the north. It gives rise to the rivers Maese, Moselle, and Sar.
              CLUVIER.

fought not ingloriously *. Of this battle, no doubt, you have heard †. The Gods then giving me the captive king of the enemy ‡, I did not envy Constantius the glory of the action. Though I was not allowed to triumph, I had it in my power to have slain my enemy, nor could I have been prevented leading him through Gaul, exposing him in the towns, and thus insulting the misfortunes of Cnodomar. None of these measures, however, I approved, but immediately sent him to Constantius, who was then just returned from the Quadian and Sarmatian war §. While I was fighting, he was travelling alone, and holding an ami-

* Και εμαχισαμην ουκ' αχλεως. The very words of Horace, on a different and less glorious warfare, l. III. ode 26, *Et militavi non sine gloriâ.*

† Julian himself speaks of the battle of Strasburgh with the modesty of conscious merit. Zosimus compares it with the victory of Alexander over Darius; and yet we are at a loss to discover any of those strokes of military genius which fix the attention of ages on the conduct and success of a single day. GIBBON.

‡ Meaning Cnodomar, who, in his flight, falling from his horse into a morass, and being taken prisoner, was sent to Constantius. See Ammianus (l. XVI. 12.) "Six thousand of the Germans," he says, "were killed in this battle, besides those that were drowned, and only two hundred and forty-three of the Romans." PETAU.

§ The events of this war are related by Ammianus, (XVI. 10. XVII. 12, 13. XIX. 11.) The Quadi, a fierce and powerful nation, were reduced to sue for peace; and the Sarmatian exiles, who had been expelled from the country by the rebellion of their slaves, were reinstated. Constantius, after this success, received the name of Sarmaticus. GIBBON.

G 3 cable

EPISTLE TO THE ATHENIANS.

cable intercourse with the nations that border on the Danube. Yet not I, but he, triumphed *.

Another year succeeded, and a third, in which all the Barbarians were driven out of Gaul, most of the towns were rebuilt, and many loaded vessels arrived from Britain. Having collected a fleet of six hundred ships †, four hundred of which I had caused to be built in less than ten months, I brought them all into the Rhine; no easy task, on account of the irruptions and neighbourhood of the Barbarians. This had seemed so

---

* Constantius, though he was forty days journey distant, arrogated to himself the glory of this victory, describing the battle, as if he had been present, in letters crowned with laurel, which he sent to the provinces, and never mentioning the name of Julian. AMMIANUS.

† Zosimus reckons eight hundred, which, he says, were built of materials found on the banks of the Rhine; that they might sail to Britain, and bring back corn and provisions to supply the garrisons. I know not that Ammianus mentions so many ships being built. He says, indeed, in his XVIIIth book, that Julian fortified the towns that had been destroyed by the Barbarians, and built granaries in the room of those which were burnt, where the provisions accustomed to be brought from Britain might be lodged. PETAU.

If we compute the six hundred corn-ships at only seventy tons each, they were capable of exporting a hundred and twenty thousand quarters (see Arbuthnot's "Weights and Measures"); and the country, which could bear so large an exportation, must already have attained an improved state of agriculture. These barks were framed in the forest of the Ardennes. GIBBON.

Some of these vessels, as appears from Ammianus, must have been freighted with provisions, as well as with corn, which would reduce the quantity of the latter.

imprac-

EPISTLE TO THE ATHENIANS.

impracticable to Florentius *, that he had agreed to give two thousand pounds weight of silver † to permit a free passage. Constantius, on being informed of this (for they corresponded concerning this proposed present), expressly ordered me to agree to it, unless I thought it absolutely disgraceful. But how could I possibly think otherwise, when it seemed so to Constantius himself, though he was always very obsequious to the Barbarians? No payment therefore was made; but marching against them, the Gods being present and propitious, I surprised part of the Salians ‡, I reduced the Chamavians ‡, and took great numbers of cattle,

---

* Prætorian Præfect of Gaul, an effeminate tyrant, a crafty and corrupt statesman, incapable of pity or remorse.   GIBBON.

† Five *aurei* (somewhat more than eleven shillings each) were the legal tender for a pound of silver.   GREAVES.
Consequently two thousand pounds of silver would amount to 5500l. sterling.

‡ Ammianus (XVII. 8.) relates, that, in the year when Datianus and Cerealis were consuls, Julian undertook an expedition against the Salian Franks, who had formerly settled near Toxandria [from the neighbourhood of Tongres to the conflux of the Vahal and the Rhine] whom, terrified at his sudden approach, he forced to surrender. Afterwards, he subdued the Chamavians [a people near Munster]. Treating the Salians with lenity, he marched against the Quadi, whom, on account of their notorious robberies, he justly destroyed. And then happened that remarkable story of the king of the Chamavians, which is related by Eunapius, and more briefly by Zosimus. PETAU.
See it also in the Abbé de la Bleterie's *Vie de Julien*, p. 82—4. and in Mr. Gibbon's Roman History, II. p. 171.

EPISTLE to the ATHENIANS.

cattle, with many women and children. This irruption so much alarmed the Barbarians, that hostages were immediately sent me, and the free importation of corn was secured.

To relate every circumstance would be tedious. In short, thrice, while I was Cæsar *, I passed the

---

, This difference of treatment confirms the opinion, that the Salian Franks were permitted to retain the settlements in Toxandria. GIBBON.

It is pretended, that the name of Toxandria is still preserved in a village, in the territory of Liege, called Tessender-loo. LA BLETERIE.

* In the years 356, 358, and 359. Ammianus treats eloquently of the two latter. The first he does not mention; but it may be inferred from what he says in his xvith book, where, relating the actions of the year 357, he says, that what chiefly induced Julian to give battle to the Germans and Cnodomar was, that " in the year just " ended, the Romans making large incursions beyond the " Rhine, no one appeared in defence of his own home, " nor stood his ground; but the Barbarians, removing to " a distance, subsisted with difficulty, blockading all the " roads with trunks of trees, during the inclemency of " winter." Which words mean, that Julian made war on the Germans beyond the Rhine in the year above-mentioned, and therefore at the approach of winter. And this happened at the time when he recovered Agrippina [Cologne]. PETAU.

It was not enough for Julian to have delivered the provinces of Gaul from the Barbarians of Germany. He aspired to emulate the glory of the first and most illustrious of the Emperors; after whose example, he composed his own Commentaries of the Gallic war. Cæsar has related, with conscious pride, the manner in which he twice passed the Rhine. Julian could boast, that, before he assumed the title of Augustus, he had carried the Roman eagles beyond that great river in three successful expeditions.
GIBBON.

Rhine.

EPISTLE TO THE ATHENIANS.

Rhine. Twenty thousand captives * I rescued from the enemy on the other side of that river. In two battles and one siege, I took a thousand prisoners, and those not of a useless age, but men in the prime of life. Four bands of the most chosen † foot I sent to Constantius, with three others, not inferior, of horse, and two most distinguished cohorts. I now, such was the will of the Gods! took all the towns: before, I had taken near forty. I invoke Jupiter, and all the tutelar Gods of cities and of nations, to attest my attachment and fidelity to him. I have acted towards him as I would wish a son of my own to act towards me. The respect that I shewed him exceeded that of any former Cæsar to any other Emperor. I may boldly dare him therefore to allege any thing against me, even to the present moment, on that head. Some ridiculous pretences he has invented. " He has de-" tained," says my adversary, " Lupicinus ‡, and

---

* He meant, no doubt, in different campaigns.
LA BLETERIE.

Zosimus relates the whole transaction at large. See *Legatiouum excerpta ex Eunapio.* PETAU.

† What one of our modern generals calls " the *elite* of " the army." But why " the *flower* of the army" should not sound as well, or why our brave garrison of Gibraltar should not make "*sallies*" as well as " *forties*," &c. is difficult to conceive. These military Gallicisms were ridiculed long ago with great humour in the Tatler.

‡ This Lupicinus, master-general of the cavalry, on the death of Severus, was gone to Britain at the time when Julian was made Emperor by the army; but as he was of a haughty and enterprising spirit, lest he should take any steps against the new Emperor, a notary was dispatched to Bononia [Boulogne] to observe that coast. AMMIANUS.

" three

"three * others." And supposing I had even put them to death, traitors and conspirators as they were, it still would have become him to have smothered the resentment which their sufferings might have excited, for the sake of friendship and union. These men, not in the least hurt, I secured as dangerous disturbers of the public peace, and though I expended upon them much of the public treasure, I plundered them of nothing. But what would have been their punishment, if Constantius had been injured, and inflicted it? And does not he, by his resentment against me, on account of these men, who bear not the least relation to him, arraign and deride my folly, in having been so obsequiously attentive to the assassin of my father, of my cousins, and, in a word, the executioner of my whole family and kindred? Consider also the deference that I have paid him ever since I became Emperor; as appears from my letters.

How I behaved to him before that time, I will now inform you. Being sensible that I should incur the whole danger and disgrace of every fault, though committed by others, I intreated him, that, if he had determined to declare me Cæsar, he would give me the best and ablest counsellors. Instead of which, he gave me at first the vilest. When one of them, the most abandoned of all,

* Of the other three nothing certain can be affirmed. Florentius seems to have been one of them, who, Ammianus

all *, * * * * † he listened indeed very readily, and gave me with reluctance an excellent officer in Salluſt ‡. On account of his virtue, he ſoon became invidious. But not being ſatisfied with him alone, and obſerving the different manner in which Conſtantius treated the others, confiding in them, and not regarding him, embracing his right hand and his knees, " Though I am not acquainted," ſaid I, " or ever was, with any one of theſe, yet " knowing them by report, and in deference to " you, I will conſider them as my friends, and " eſteem them as old acquaintance. It is not " proper, however, that my affairs ſhould be con- " fided to them, or that theirs ſhould be embroiled " by mine. I requeſt you, therefore, to direct me, " by ſome written rules §, what you would wiſh

anus ſays, at the very beginning of Julian's government fled from Vienne, where he then was, to Conſtantius. Julian " leaving his family and effects untouched, and al- " lowing him the uſe of a public carriage, ordered him to " return in ſafety into the Eaſt." PETAU.

If Florentius fled to Conſtantius, how could he be one that was " detained by Julian?"

* Meaning Marcellus, of whom above. *Ibid.*

† Imperfect.

‡ We are ignorant of the actual office of this excellent miniſter, whom Julian afterwards created Præfect of Gaul.
GIBBON.

§ When Julian was ſetting out, Conſtantius gave him a letter, in which he not only preſcribed rules for his conduct, but alſo limited his diet, and the amount of his daily expences. Ammianus, l. xvi. 5. " Laſtly, as he conſtantly " peruſed the letter, which Conſtantius, as if he had been " ſending a ſon-in-law to ſchool, had written with his own " hand, regulating, with too much freedom, what ſhould " be expended on the Cæſar's table," &c. PETAU.

" me

" me to avoid, and what to do. Then, with the
" utmost reason, you will praise me if I obey,
" and punish me if I transgress. But I am firmly
" of opinion, that I shall in no instance controvert
" your commands."

The innovations that Pentadius immediately attempted *, it is needless to mention. I opposed them all, consequently he became my enemy. Soon after, by perverting another, and then a second, and a third, and by bribing against me Paul † and Gaudentius ‡, notorious slanderers, he succeeded in having Sallust, who was my friend §, recalled, and Lucian immediately appointed to succeed him. Florentius also was irritated by my opposing his in-

---

* At his complaining of Pentadius I am much surprised. For Ammianus mentions Pentadius (l. xx.) and says, that " he was master of the offices to Julian, and " was sent by him, when he was made Emperor, to Con-" stantius, with Eutherius, his chief chamberlain." He cannot therefore be the same, who, Julian here says, was his enemy while he was Cæsar. PETAU.

† Paul was a notary, born in Spain, famous for cruel informations under Constantius, who was burnt alive, with Apodemus, when Julian was Emperor. See Ammianus, (l. xix. and xxii.) *Ibid.*

‡ Gaudentius also was a notary, and having been sent into the Gauls as a spy on the actions of Julian, was afterwards put to death by him at Antioch. Ammianus, (l. xxii.) *Ibid.*

Their executions [those of the two former] were accepted as an inadequate atonement by the widows and orphans of so many hundred Romans, whom those legal tyrants had betrayed and murdered. GIBBON.

As to Gaudentius, see the third note on Epistle X.

§ See the Consolatory Oration on his departure, p. 30, &c.

satiable

EPISTLE TO THE ATHENIANS.

fatiable avarice *. They therefore perfuaded Conftantius, already perhaps jealous of my actions, to remove me from the command of the forces. And he wrote letters filled with invectives againft me, and threatening deftruction to the Gauls. Soon after, it appeared that he had ordered all the flower of the army, without exception, to be withdrawn from Gaul, charging Lupicinus and Gintonius † with this commiffion, and commanding me in no refpect to oppofe them.

In what words fhall I now relate the works of the Gods? It was my intention, they can witnefs, divefting myfelf of all regal ftate and magnificence, to reft in peace, and never more to act in public. I only waited the return of Florentius and Lupi-

---

* See Epiftle XVII.

† " Sintula, then tribune of the ftables to the Cæfar," fays Ammianus, (l. xx. 4.) " was joined in commiffion " with Decentius, a tribune and notary, to conduct the " troops out of the Gauls." Of Gintonius I do not remember to have read. But of this hiftory fee more in Ammianus and Zofimus, and alfo in the Oration of Libanius on the confulfhip of Julian. PETAU.

Julian was furprifed by the hafty arrival of a tribune and a notary, with pofitive orders from the Emperor, which they were directed to execute, and he was commanded not to oppofe; that four entire legions, the Celtæ, the Petulants, the Heruli, and the Batavians, fhould be feparated from the ftandard of Julian; that, in each of the remaining bands, three hundred of the braveft youths fhould be felected; and that this numerous detachment, the ftrength of the Gallic army, fhould inftantly begin their march, and exert their utmoft diligence to arrive, before the opening the campaign, on the frontiers of Perfia. GIBBON.

cinus,

cinus, the one being in Britain *, and the other at Vienne. In the mean time, a great disturbance was raised among the natives and soldiers, an anonymous libel being dispersed in a neighbouring town, among the Petulants and the Celts (the legions so named) filled with invectives against Constantius, and with complaints of his having betrayed the Gauls. And the author of that paper no less lamented my disgrace. This being circulated, a general disaffection ensued, and those who were most in the interest of Constantius used their utmost endeavours to persuade me to detach the troops as soon as possible, before the like libels were dispersed among the rest of the army. (Not one of my friends was then present). They were Nebridius †, Pentadius, and Decentius ‡, the latter

---

* Ammianus (l. xx. 1.) The valour of Lupicinus, and his military skill, are acknowledged by the historian, who, in his affected language, accuses the general of exalting the horns of his pride, bellowing in a tragic tone, and exciting a doubt whether he was more cruel or avaricious. The danger from the Scots and Picts was so serious, that Julian himself had some thoughts of passing over into the island.

GIBBON.

† Prætorian Præfect. This faithful minister singly opposed the solemn engagement of the troops to devote themselves to the service of Julian. Alone and unassisted, he asserted the rights of Constantius in the midst of an armed and angry multitude, to whose fury he had almost fallen an honourable, but useless, sacrifice. After losing one of his hands by the stroke of a sword, he embraced the knees of the prince whom he had offended. Julian covered the Præfect with his imperial mantle, and protecting him from the zeal of his followers, dismissed him to his own house,

with

latter of whom Constantius had dispatched for that purpose. My reply, that " we ought to " wait for Lupicinus and Florentius," was totally disregarded, they all insisting that the opposite plan should be pursued, unless I meant to confirm and corroborate former suspicions. " Besides," they added, " the detaching the troops will now be " deemed your measure; but when those ministers " return, Constantius will impute it not to you, " but to them, and consequently will reprobate " your conduct." Thus I was persuaded, or rather compelled, to write to him. For he may be said to act by persuasion, who has the liberty of refusing; but those who can be compelled it is needless to persuade; as they act not by choice, but necessity. There being two roads, it was next debated which should be taken. I proposed one;

---

with less respect than was perhaps due to the virtue of an enemy. The high office of Nebridius was bestowed on Sallust. *Ibid.*

Nebridius had before been Count of the East, and, from being quæstor to Julian, was made by Constantius præfect of the Gauls, in the room of Florentius, who had been removed to the præfecture of Illyricum. Florentius refused to return from Vienne, dreading the resentment of the army. Nebridius retired in a private station into his native country, Tuscany. Pentadius is mentioned above.

‡ There is some corruption in this passage, for neither were they absent, nor friends to Julian. On the contrary, they adhered to Constantius. PETAU.

The present reading may be supported either by omitting the preceding paragraph, or by putting it (as in the translation) into a parenthesis. " Nebridius, &c." will then refer to the friends before mentioned, of Constantius, as they certainly were.

EPISTLE TO THE ATHENIANS.

but they compelled me to adopt * the other; left my opposition should excite some tumult and disorder in the army; and when a disturbance was once begun, a general confusion might ensue. An apprehension this, which seemed by no means groundless. The legions approached. I, as usual †, went out of the city to meet them, and urged them to pursue their march. They halted one day; till when I was a stranger to what they had been concerting. Jupiter, the Sun, Mars, Minerva, and all the Gods know ‡, that I had not the least suspicion of their intentions till the evening of that day, when at sun-set they were disclosed to me §. [At midnight] on a sudden the pa-

* Through Paris. Julian honestly and judiciously suggested the danger and temptation of a last interview of the soldiers with their wives and children. GIBBON.

† Even the Emperors themselves used to meet the legions by way of honour. VALOIS.

‡ Such an oath would be decisive in the mouth of a Pagan, convinced of his false religion even to fanaticism and enthusiasm, as Julian was, if Julian had not given some proofs of duplicity. But when a man is capable of being of two religions at the same time, of believing one and professing the other, he may well allow himself in perjury. Be that as it may, it must be owned, that if that prince moved the springs which raised him to the supreme power, he concealed his play so well, as to seem to owe all to chance, and nothing to intrigue. LA BLETERIE.

It may seem ungenerous to distrust the honour of a hero, and the truth of a philosopher. The devout Abbé de la Bleterie is almost inclined to respect the devout protestations of a Pagan. GIBBON.

§ He then resigned himself to a short slumber; and afterwards related to his friends, that he had seen the Genius of the empire waiting with some impatience at his door, pressing for admittance, and reproaching his want of spirit and ambition. Ibid.

lace

EPISTLE TO THE ATHENIANS.

late * was invested, and an universal shout was raised, while in the mean time I was deliberating what measures to pursue, but without forming any determination. Though my wife was then living †, I happened to sleep alone, in an adjoining upper chamber ‡, from which, there being an opening in the wall, I paid my adoration to Jupiter. The clamour increasing, and a general tumult prevailing throughout the palace, I intreated that God to give

---

* Most probably the palace of the baths (*thermarum*), of which a solid and lofty hall still subsists in the *rue de la Harpe*. The buildings covered a considerable space of the modern quarter of the university; and the gardens, under the Merovingian kings, communicated with the abbey of St. Germain des Prez. By the injuries of time and the Normans, this ancient palace was reduced, in the twelfth century, to a maze of ruins, whose dark recesses were the scene of licentious love.   GIBBON.

These remains, which have all the marks of antiquity, are the greatest curiosity in Paris. They are inclosed in a house, whose sign is the iron cross. Our kings of the first race resided in that palace. The daughters of Charlemagne were confined there after his death, when Lewis the Debonnair, a friend to full chant, but an enemy to gallantry, had caused their lovers to be put to death. "He "thought, without doubt," says F. Daniel, with great simplicity, "that the example would intimidate, and that "they would have no more. He was, it seems, mistaken; "they were never without them." *Tableau de Paris*, ch. Antiquities.

† Helena died soon after, at Vienne, says Ammianus, (l. xxi.); others say, in the palace of Julian, and was buried near her sister Constantina, at Rome.

Her pregnancy had been several times fruitless, and was at last fatal to herself.   GIBBON.

‡ From Mr. King's very ingenious "Observations on "Ancient Castles," p. 5, &c. we learn, that " the state- "apartments (which Julian, no doubt, then occupied) were
  " always

give me a sign. This he immediately shewed me, commanding me firmly to confide in it, and not oppose the resolution of the army *. Though I had received these omens, I did not, however, yield without reluctance, but resisted as much as possible, nor would I admit of the salutation, or the diadem. But not being able singly to oppose so many, and the Gods, whose will it was, strongly animating them, and at the same time, composing my spirits, at length, about the third hour, some soldier, I know not whom, giving me a collar †, I put it on, and then re-entered the palace, groaning, as the Gods can witness, from the bottom of my heart; for though the confidence which the former sign had given me in God could not but inspire

" always in the third story, an habitation both stately and airy, free from the annoyance of the enemy's instruments of war."

The windows also of these rooms, even in our cold climate, though highly ornamented, " appear to have had no glass, and to have been fenced only with iron bars and wooden shutters, as is known to have been the usage in early times." *Sequel to the Observations on Ancient Castles*, p. 108.

That the Jews, as well as Pagans, prayed " with their windows open," appears from this passage of Daniel, vi. 10. *He went into his house, and* his windows being open *in his chamber toward Jerusalem, he kneeled upon his knees,* &c.

* The conduct, which disclaims the ordinary maxims of reason, excites suspicion, and eludes our enquiry. Whenever the spirit of fanaticism, at once so credulous and so crafty, has insinuated itself into a noble mind, it insensibly corrodes the vital principles of virtue and veracity.

GIBBON.

† Even in this tumultuous moment, Julian attended to the forms of superstitious ceremony, and obstinately refused the

EPISTLE TO THE ATHENIANS.

inspire me with fortitude, I was ashamed and abashed at not seeming to obey Constantius faithfully to the last.

A great dejection prevailing in the palace, the friends of Constantius endeavoured to improve that opportunity of forming a conspiracy against me, and distributed money among the soldiers, hoping to alienate some of them, so at least as to make a division between us, if not to persuade them openly to attack me. One of the officers who attended my wife in public *, hearing what they were clandestinely transacting, disclosed it to me. But finding that I disregarded it, with the frenzy of an enthusiast, he loudly exclaimed in the marketplace, " Soldiers, foreigners, and natives, do not " betray the Emperor." The minds of the troops being thus inflamed, they all ran armed to the palace. Finding me there alive and unhurt, and rejoicing like friends who meet unexpectedly, they embraced me, clasped me in their arms, and bore me on their shoulders. It was indeed a most pleasing sight, seeming like inspiration. Surrounding me on all sides, they then insisted that every friend of Constantius should be put to death. The strenu-

---

the inauspicious use of a female necklace, or a horse's collar (*equi phaleræ*), which the impatient soldiers would have employed instead of a diadem.   GIBBON.

The collar which he put on, enriched with jewels, belonged, says Ammianus, to " one Maurus, afterwards a " Count, then a spearman of the Petulants." This event happened in April, 360.

* Ammianus styles him *aliquis palatii decurio*, a kind of lictor.

ous endeavours that I used to save them, all the Gods know. After this, what was my conduct towards Conſtantius? In my letters * to him, even to the preſent hour, I have never aſſumed the title which the Gods have given me, only ſtyling myſelf Cæſar; and I prevailed on the ſoldiers to ſwear to me, that they would attempt nothing farther, if he would ſuffer me to dwell peaceably in the Gauls, and ratify all that had been done. Add to this, the legions that were with me ſent him an united letter, urging a reconciliation between us. In return, he ſpirited the Barbarians againſt us, proclaimed me to them as a public enemy, and bribed them to ravage the Gallic provinces. He wrote alſo to them who were in Italy, and warned them to guard againſt thoſe who came from the Gauls. In the towns bordering on the Gallic frontier, he ordered magazines to be formed; in particular, one of ſix hundred thouſand quarters † of flour at Brigantia ‡, and another of as many more at the foot of the Cottian Alps §; that he might be enabled to march an army againſt me. All theſe things were not only ſaid but done. For the letters which he ſent ‖ to ſpirit the Barbarians I intercepted, and all

---

* The Epiſtle to which Julian principally alludes has been inſerted, p. 54.

† Three hundred myriads, or three millions of *medimni*, a corn meaſure familiar to the Athenians, and which contained ſix Roman *modii*.　　　　　　　　　GIBBON.

‡ Now Bregentz, on the banks of the Lake of Conſtance.

§ The mountains that divide Dauphiny from Piedmont.

‖ Meaning the letters which Ammianus mentions in his xxiſt book. Yet he expreſſes himſelf with cool and candid heſitation, *ſi famæ ſoli admittenda eſt fides*.　　GIBBON.

EPISTLE TO THE ATHENIANS.

the provisions, which he had ordered to be collected, I seized, and also the letters of Taurus *. Besides this, he addressed me still as Cæsar, and declared, that he would never be reconciled to me. He sent, however, one Epictetus †, a Gallic bishop, to assure me of my safety; and in all his letters he intimates, that he will spare my life; but as to my honour, he is silent. In regard to his oaths, I think, as the proverb says, they should be written in ashes, so little do they deserve belief. My own honour, not only for the sake of what is just and right, but for that of the safety of my friends, I am determined to maintain; not to mention the cruelties exercised throughout all the world.

These arguments are to me conclusive; these measures appear to me just; and I adopted them at first in the sight and hearing of the Gods. Afterwards, on the very day in which I was going to

---

* Præfect of Italy, and Consul, with Florentius, in 361, when this Epistle was written. He was banished by Julian, soon after, during his præfecture and consulship, to Vercellæ, in Italy.

† There was a bishop of that name, a remarkable favourer of the Arian sect, who, to gratify Constantius, used great severity towards the Catholics. But he was bishop of Centum-cellæ [now Civita-Vecchia] in Thuscia [Tuscany] not in Gaul. Perhaps Julian wrote Κιντυμκιλλων (" of Centum-cellæ,") instead of των Γαλλιων (" of the Gauls".) Yet Ammianus relates, that the person, who was sent into the Gauls with these orders to Julian, was the quæstor Leonas.. PETAU.

harangue

harangue the army concerning our march hither *, sacrificing for the event, for my own safety, and much more for the public welfare, and the general freedom of the world, especially of the Gallic nation, whom he has twice abandoned to her enemies, not sparing the sepulchres of their ancestors, though he pays the utmost attention to those of foreigners †, the omens were auspicious. I thought it therefore necessary to reduce our formidable enemies ‡, and to coin lawful money of gold and silver; and if even now he should be disposed to treat with me, will be satisfied with what I at present possess. But if he should pre-

---

* Illyricum, where this Epistle was written.

† The primitive Christians called the temples of the Heathens "sepulchres," in contempt, because temples began to be built where their Gods were buried. But this the Gentiles afterwards retorted on the Christians, on account of the relics of the martyrs, preserved and worshiped in the churches. And hence they styled the Christian churches nothing but ταφος ("tombs.") VALOIS.

‡ After Julian had dismissed Leonas, and sent a new embassy to the Eastern court, that he might keep his troops in exercise, and preserve the reputation they had gained, he passed the Rhine for the fourth time, subdued the Attuarii, a nation of the Franks, who still made incursions into Gaul; and, repassing the Rhine, reviewed and strengthened all the garrisons in the frontier towns, as far as the country of the Rauraci (now the canton of Basil); from whence he repaired to Besançon, and then to Vienne, where he kept his winter-quarters. Before the conclusion of the winter, the Germans under king Vadomar, having revolted and pillaged Rhoetia (now the country of the Grisons), he seized and banished that prince, and passing the Rhine for the fifth and last time, surprised the Barbarians, and forced them to swear to a peace, which they never presumed to violate again during his life.

LA BLETERIE.

EPISTLE TO THE ATHENIANS.

fer engaging in a war, and will in no respect recede from his former determination, I am ready to do or suffer whatever the Gods may decree. It is more disgraceful to be conquered by ignorance and pusillanimity, than by strength and numbers. If he excells me in numbers, that is owing, not to himself, but to his armies. If he had surprised me still loitering in the Gauls, and tenacious of life, and had surrounded me, declining danger, on the flanks and in the rear by the Barbarians, and in front by his own troops, I must have submitted, not only to the utmost extremity, but, which to the wise is the greatest of evils, to disgrace *.

Such are the reflections, men of Athens, which I have communicated to my fellow-soldiers, and now transmit to you and the other cities of Grece †. May the Gods, the Lords of all, afford me the assistance, which they have promised, to the last, and grant to Athens, that I may, as much as possible, deserve her favour, and that she may for ever have such Emperors as may intimately

---

* Julian explains, like a soldier and a statesman, the danger of his situation, and the necessity and advantages of an offensive war. GIBBON.

† Lacedæmon and Corinth, Zosimus says, were two of the other cities that Julian addressed, but all that remains of either, or any, of those Epistles, is two short paragraphs of that to the Corinthians, preserved by Sozomen; in one of which he says, " Having reluctantly commenced this " war, but having now, in great measure, succeeded, " though not yet arrived at the conclusion ;" and in the other, he claims their favour, " on account of the friend- " ship of his father, who had dwelt among them."

know, and with a diftinguifhed preference efteem, her *!

* The humanity of Julian was preferved from the cruel alternative, which he pathetically laments, of deftroying, or of being himfelf deftroyed; and the feafonable death of Conftantius delivered the Roman empire from the calamities of civil war. The approach of winter could not detain the monarch at Antioch; and his favourites durft not oppofe his impatient defire of revenge. A flight fever, which was perhaps occafioned by the agitation of his fpirits, was increafed by the fatigues of the journey; and Conftantius was obliged to halt at the little town of Mopfucrene, twelve miles beyond Tarfus, where he expired, after a fhort illnefs, in the forty-fifth year of his age, and the twenty-fourth of his reign. GIBBON.

This event happened on Sept. 3, 361. It is pretended that, upon his death-bed, he named Julian his fucceffor, willing, no doubt, to make a merit of what he could no longer with-hold from him, and by that to engage him to protect Fauftina, whom he had married after the death of Eufebia, and whom he left pregnant of a princefs [Conftantia], who was afterwards married to the Emperor Gratian. Julian immediately haftened towards Conftantinople, which he entered, accompanied by the fenate, foldiers, and people, on Dec. 11. LA BLETERIE.

AN ALLEGORICAL FABLE *.

A CERTAIN rich man † had numerous flocks and herds, and many horses ‡, grazing in his meadows. He had also many shepherds, as well slaves as freed-men, and hired servants, herdsmen, goat-herds, grooms, with many estates, some of which were bequeathed to him by his father §; but most of them he had acquired, being desirous to enrich himself by right or wrong, and having little regard for the Gods. He had several wives, by whom he had sons and daughters ‖, among

A. D. 362.

---

* Julian has worked the crimes and misfortunes of the family of Constantine into an allegorical Fable, which is happily conceived and agreeably related. It forms the conclusion of the VIIth Oration.   GIBBON.
See a farther account of it in the Preface.
† This rich man is Constantine, that eternal object of the hatred and malignity of Julian.   LA BLETERIE.
The beginning of this Fable is remarkably similar to that of Nathan's Parable, in 2 Sam. xii. 2. which Julian had read in the Septuagint. Πλυσιω ανδρι προβαλα ην πολλα, και αγιλαι βοων, says the Emperor. Τω πλυσιω ανδρι ην ποιμνια και βυκολια πολλα σφοδρα, says the Prophet.
‡ In the original, ιπποι μυριαι (" many mares.")
§ Constantius Chlorus reigned only over the Gauls, Spain, and Great-Britain. Constantine, with much good fortune, and perhaps too much address, made himself master of the whole empire.   LA BLETERIE.
‖ Constantine left three sons, between whom he divided the empire. Constantine, known in history by the name of the younger Constantine, had the Gauls, Spain, and Great-Britain. Constantius had the East. Constans, Italy, Illyricum,

among whom he divided his wealth *, before he died, but without inftructing them how to manage it, how to acquire more, if it fhould fail, or, when it was acquired, how to preferve it. So grofs was

Illyricum, and Africa. We are acquainted only with two daughters of Conftantine the Great; Conftantina and Helena. He married the former to Flavius Claudius Hannibalianus, his nephew, fon of his brother Dalmatius the Cenfor. This princefs afterwards married the Cæfar Gallus. Helena was married to Julian. It is not at firft eafy to conceive how he can fay, that " the father of the " family divided his eftate between his fons and *his daugh-* " *ters* ;" as, among the Romans, the daughters were excluded from the empire. But this paffage of Julian informs us of two things; 1. That if Conftantine gave his nephew Hannibalianus the title of King, with Armenia the Lefs, Pontus, and Cappadocia, it was on account of his marriage with Conftantina, on whom, befides, he conferred the title of Augufta, and a right to wear the diadem. 2. That if he raifed Dalmatius, the brother of Hannibalianus, to the dignity of Cæfar, and gave him Thrace, Macedonia, and Achaia, it was becaufe Dalmatius was to efpoufe Helena, who was then a child. Hannibalianus and Dalmatius were included in the maffacre which followed the death of Conftantine. One fault of that able politician, a fault much more real than that with which Julian here reproaches him, is that of having raifed his brothers and his nephews to fuch a height as to make them formidable to his children. If he could imagine that he fhould have authority enough over both to prevent the ufual effects of jealoufy and ambition during his life, fhould he have flattered himfelf that they would have fuch refpect to his memory as to remain within the limits which he had prefcribed them? The greateft princes ought always to think that they will not reign after their deaths.

LA BLETERIE.

* Whether, after the death of Faufta, the mother of Conftantius and his brothers, Conftantine contracted any other marriage does not appear from the memorials, ftill remaining, of thofe times; except that in general Julian here fays, that " he had many wives," ἐγένοντο δὲ αὐτῷ γυναῖκες πολλαὶ, though without naming them. SPANHEIM.

his

his ignorance, that he thought nothing neceſſary but riches; nor in that art had he much experience, having acquired it, not by any fixed principle, but rather by uſe and habit, like empirics, who by practice only cure diſeaſes, and conſequently muſt be ignorant of many. Thus thinking that the number of his ſons would ſufficiently ſecure the continuance of his family, he uſed no endeavour to make them virtuous *.

This was the firſt origin of their diſſenſions. For each of them deſiring, like his father, to have great riches, and ſingly to poſſeſs all, attacked his brother. The calamities occaſioned by their folly and ignorance extended alſo to their neareſt relations, who had had no better education. A general ſlaughter enſued, ſo as to realiſe by divine vengeance the moſt tragical cataſtrophe. They divided their patrimony by the ſword, and every thing was thrown into confuſion. The ſons deſtroyed the temples of their anceſtors, which before indeed had been deſpiſed by their father, and ſtripped of their offerings, dedicated by many, but chiefly by his forefathers. But when they deſtroyed the temples, they repaired the old and erected new ſepulchres †, as if they had foreſeen, that for their

* Julian, in his firſt panegyric on Conſtantius, ſays, that the children of Conſtantine had the moſt excellent education that could be given to princes. He then perhaps flattered. Now perhaps he ſlanders. LA BLETERIE.

† By "ſepulchres" he muſt mean churches. So they were called by the Pagans, becauſe they were built over the tombs of the martyrs. *Ibid.* See p. 102, note †.

ALLEGORICAL FABLE.

contempt of the Gods they would ere long want many sepulchres themselves.

Amidst these disorders, marriages also being contracted which were no marriages *, and the laws both of Gods and men being thus alike infringed, Jupiter was moved with compassion, and addressing himself to the Sun †, he said to him,

* Constantius first married the daughter of Julius Constantius, his uncle. Though history does not inform us who were the wives of Constantine the younger and Constans, it may be presumed that they also married their cousin-germans. Such marriages were not forbidden among the Romans till Theodosius, whose law was afterwards repealed by Justinian. However, even before the prohibition of Theodosius, they were unusual, because they were odious. It was thought that they bordered upon incest. This we learn from St. Augustine, *de civitate Dei*, *l.* xv. c. 16. *Raro per mores fiebat quod fieri per leges licebat... Factum etiam licitum propter vicinitatem horrebatur illiciti; et quod fiebat cum consobrinâ penè cum sorore fieri videbatur, quia et ipsi inter se propter tam propinquam consanguinitatem fratres vocantur, et pene germani sunt.* Allowing this, it will be easy to conceive how a passionate enemy, like Julian, may so severely reprobate the marriages of the children of Constantine. This key, I think, may serve for want of better historical light.' LA BLETERIE.

Julian, whose mind was biassed by superstition and resentment, stigmatises these unnatural alliances between his own cousins with the opprobrious name of γαμωι τι ου γαμων. The jurisprudence of the canons has since revived and enforced this prohibition, without being able to introduce it either into the civil or the common law of Europe.

GIBBON.

One of these " no marriages" was that of Julian himself with his cousin Helena. Another, that of Gallus and Constantina.

† After what has been said before, it is needless here to observe, that Julian means by the Sun that intelligence produced from all eternity by the supreme God, &c. in a word, the Logos of Plato. LA BLETERIE.

" Of

ALLEGORICAL FABLE.

" Of all the Gods my moſt ancient offſpring,
" being born before heaven and earth, doſt thou
" ſtill retain the memory of the inſults thou haſt
" received from that diſdainful and arrogant man,
" who, by forſaking thee *, entailed ſo many
" calamities on himſelf, his family, and his children?
" Though you have not perſonally wreaked your
" vengeance on him, nor have launched your ar-
" rows againſt his children, are you leſs the author
" of that deſtruction which has deſolated his
" family? But let us ſummon the Fates, and en-
" quire of them whether any aſſiſtance can be
" given it."

The Fates inſtantly attended; but the Sun, as if abſorbed in contemplation, continued to fix his eyes on Jupiter. The eldeſt of the Fates thus replied: ' Juſtice and Sanctity, O Father, forbid
' it. But it depends on yourſelf, ſince you have
' ordered us to be ſubſervient to them, to prevail
' on them alſo.' " True," anſwered Jupiter,
" they are my daughters, and therefore I may
" interrogate them.—Venerable Goddeſſes, what
" do you adviſe?" ' That, Father,' they replied,
' is as you direct; but be careful leſt that worſt

---

* The devotion of Conſtantine was peculiarly directed to the Genius of the Sun, the Apollo of Greek and Roman mythology; and he was pleaſed to be repreſented with the ſymbols of the God of light and poetry. GIBBON.
 Among the many coins of this Emperor, found at Reculver, in Kent (the Roman Regulbium), ſome have, on their reverſe, the figure of Apollo, with a ſtar, and *Soli invicto comiti*. This device would have ſerved equally well for Julian.

' of

' of all crimes, a zeal for impiety, should univer-
' sally prevail in the world.' " To that," said Jupiter, " I will certainly attend." The Fates then
approached, and spun as the Father directed. Afterwards Jupiter thus addressed the Sun: " You
" see this infant *, the nephew of that rich man,
" and the cousin of his heirs. Though destitute
" and despised, he is your off-spring. Swear,
" therefore, to me, by my sceptre and your own,
" that you will take especial care of him, that you
" will be his guide, and secure him from evil.
" You see he is enveloped, as it were, with smoke,
" and filth, and darkness, and that the flame which
" you have kindled in him is in danger of being
" stifled:

" And owns no help but from thy saving hands †.
" Take him therefore, and superintend his edu-
" cation. This I and the Fates allow." At
this the Sun much rejoiced, and was pleased with
the child, perceiving in him a small spark of
himself still remaining. From that time he educated the boy, withdrawing him

Far from alarms, and dust and blood ‡.
But Jupiter ordered the motherless and chaste
Minerva to have a share also in his education.

Thus instructed, when the youth had attained
that age,

* Julian himself.
† Iliad IX. 231. Pope, 304. Part of the speech of
Ulysses to Achilles, requesting him to assist the Greeks.
‡ Iliad XI. 164. Pope, 216. applied to Hector, when
protected by Jupiter and Fate.

When

ALLEGORICAL FABLE.

When springs the down, when youth has all its charms *,
Being apprised of the numerous calamities which had befallen his relations and cousins, he was so terrified, that he would have rushed headlong into Tartarus, had he not been prevented by the benevolent Sun and provident Minerva †, who threw him into a slumber, which banished that idea. Awaking from this, he returned to his solitude, and there, sitting on a stone, he considered with himself how he should escape such a variety of evils; for now every thing appeared adverse, and he was abandoned even by hope.

Mercury then, who had an affection for him, assuming the appearance of one of his young companions, thus kindly accosted him: "Follow "me, and I will shew you a smoother and easier "way, as soon as you have gone through this "winding and rugged path, which obliges, as "you see, all who enter it to turn back." The

---

* Iliad XXIV. 348.

† In the original, της Προνοιας Αθηνας. In his IVth Oration, Julian considers Pronœa as another name for Minerva. After the example of Plato, whose philosophy he adopted, Julian, like other Heathens, acknowledged God's Providence. Not to mention his master Jamblichus (*de Myster. l. 1. c. 9.*) " the Providence of God" is mentioned by Euripides, in his Orestes, ver. 1181. On some excellent coins of Commodus it appears under the symbol of a woman extending her right hand, and holding a spear in her left, or before an altar, with another figure of a man standing, and on each side a tree, with the inscription ΠΡΟΝΟΙΑ. And on the Roman coins is sometimes seen a temple, and sometimes a radiated figure of the sun, with PROVIDENTIA inscribed, &c.   SPANHEIM.

youth

youth then proceeded cautiously, with his sword, his shield, and spear, but with his head unarmed. Relying on his guide, he came to a road, though unfrequented, highly pleasant, and embroidered with fruit-trees and flowers innumerable, such as are pleasing to the Gods, and also with ivy, laurel, and myrtle.

When they arrived at the foot of a high mountain, " On the summit of that," said Mercury, " dwells the Father of the Gods; be careful " therefore, for great is your danger, to worship " him in the most religious manner. Ask of him " whatever you please. You will wish, my child, " for what is best." So saying, Mercury disappeared, though the youth was very desirous of being informed by him what petition he should prefer to the Father of the Gods. Thus deserted, he could only advise with himself, and he could not have been advised better. " Though I do not " yet see," said he, " the Father of the Gods, " let me solicit him for his best gifts. O Father " Jupiter, or by whatever other name thou pleasest " to be called, for that to me is indifferent, teach " me the way that leads to thee. For the region " of thy residence is incomparably beautiful, if I " may judge of its excellence by the pleasantness " of the path through which I have been con- " ducted hither." After having thus prayed, he fell fast asleep. During this slumber, or trance, Jupiter shewed him the Sun in person. Astonished at this sight, the youth exclaimed, " For this and
" all

ALLEGORICAL FABLE.

"all thy other favours, O Father of the Gods, I
"offer and dedicate myself to thee." Then embracing the knees of the Sun, he intreated his protection. But he, calling Minerva, bade her first observe what arms he had brought. Seeing only a sword, a shield, and a spear, "Where, my
"son," said she, "are your ægis and helmet?"
He answered, "I could scarce provide even these;
"neglected and despised, I had no friend in the
"family of my relations." "What then," replied the Sun, "will you say, when I tell you,
"that you must necessarily return to it?" Hearing this, the youth intreated him, with many tears, not to send him thither again, as, in that case, he should never see him more, but should certainly perish there, overwhelmed with misfortunes. "You
"are young," said the Sun, "and have not yet been
"initiated. Return therefore to earth, and when you
"are initiated *, dwell in safety; return and pu-
"rify

---

* By the hands of Maximus [See the first note on Epistle XV.] Julian was secretly initiated at Ephesus, in the twentieth year of his age. His residence at Athens confirmed this unnatural alliance of philosophy and superstition. He obtained the privilege of a solemn initiation into the mysteries of Eleusis, which, amidst the general decay of the Grecian worship, still retained some vestiges of their primæval sanctity; and such was the zeal of Julian, that he afterwards invited the Eleusinian pontiff to the court of Gaul, for the sole purpose of consummating, by mystic rites and sacrifices, the great work of his sanctification. As these ceremonies were performed in the depth of caverns, and in the silence of the night; and as the inviolable secret of the mysteries was preserved by the discretion of the initiated; I shall not presume to describe the horrid sounds, and fiery apparitions,

"rify yourself from all impiety. You must then invoke me, and Minerva, and the other Gods."

The youth, at these words, remained silent. The Sun then conducting him to a mountain, (whose summit shone with light, but whose lower parts were covered with thick darkness, through which, however, as through a mist, the rays of the Sun appeared dim and faint), thus addressed him: 'You see your cousin the heir [*]: Do you see also those herdsmen and shepherds?' He replied in the affirmative. 'How is he,' said the Sun, 'and how are his shepherds and herdsmen, employed?' "He," said the youth, "seems to me asleep; he lives in retirement, and devotes himself to pleasure. Few of his shepherds are well-disposed; most of them are wicked and cruel; for they either devour or sell his sheep, and thus doubly injure their master; they ruin his flocks, and, though they receive much and return him but little, they complain that they are defrauded of their wages; but it were better that they should be paid the whole, than the sheep be destroyed." 'But suppose,' said the Sun, 'I and Minerva, by the command of Jupiter, should appoint you guardian of all these flocks, in the room of this heir?' This the youth again

---

apparitions, which were presented to the senses, or the imagination, of the credulous aspirant, till the visions of comfort and knowledge broke upon him in a blaze of celestial light. GIBBON.

[*] Constantius.

opposed,

opposed, and earnestly intreated to remain there. The Sun replied, "Be not obstinately disobedient, "lest my hatred should be equal to the love that "I have borne you." The youth then answered, 'O most excellent Sun and Minerva, and thee 'too I attest, O Father Jupiter, dispose of me 'absolutely as you please.' After this, Mercury, again appearing, inspired him with additional courage. For now he thought he had found a guide in his return, and during the time that he was to pass on earth.

Minerva then thus accosted him: "Good son "of this excellent and divine father and of me, "attend! The best shepherds, you observe, do "not please this heir; but profligates and flatterers "have enslaved him. Consequently he is not "beloved by the good and virtuous, and by those "who seem his friends he is injured and dis- "honoured. Be careful therefore, when you re- "turn, never to prefer a flatterer to a friend. "Take another advice, my son. That man sleeps, "and of course is often deceived; but be you "sober and vigilant *. A flatterer often assumes "the confidence of a friend; just as if a smith, "covered with smoke and ashes, should, by a "painted face and a white garment, induce you to

---

* Συ δε νηφε, και γρηγορει.
The same words as those of the Apostle, Νηψατε, γρηγορησατε, 1 Pet. v. 8.
This is not the first passage in which we have seen our author availing himself of his Christian erudition.

" give him one of your daughters in marriage.
" Thirdly, let me exhort you to have a particular
" regard to yourself. Respect us in the first place;
" among men, those who resemble us most, and
" no one besides. You see how much this poor
" wretch has suffered from a false shame and a
" foolish timidity."

To this the Sun added, ' Those whom you select
' for your friends treat as friends, not as servants
' and domestics. Behave to them with freedom,
' candour, and generosity, not thinking of them
' one thing, and saying another. What was so
' destructive to this young heir as unfaithfulness
' to his friends? Love your subjects, as you are
' loved by us. Whatever relates to our worship
' prefer to all other virtues. For we are your
' benefactors, and friends, and preservers.'

Delighted at these words, the youth clearly shewed his desire to obey the Gods implicitly in all things. " Depart now," said the Sun, " with
" joyful hopes, for I, and Minerva, and Mer-
" cury will every where be with you, and also
" all the Gods who dwell on Olympus, or in the
" air, or on earth, and all the other deities; so
" you shall be pious to us, faithful to your friends,
" and humane to your subjects, teaching them to
" excell by your example, and never being en-
" slaved by their passions or your own. Retain
" the armour that you brought hither, and receive
" from me this torch, which will afford you such
" light on earth, that you will not need that of
" heaven.

" heaven. Accept also from good Minerva an
" ægis and a helmet, for she has many, as you
" see, which she bestows on whom she pleases.
" Mercury, besides, will give you a golden wand.
" Depart therefore, relying on this armour, and
" traverse earth and sea, inviolably obeying our
" laws. Let neither man, nor woman, your
" own countrymen, nor foreigners, persuade you
" to neglect our precepts. While you observe
" them, you will be loved and esteemed by us,
" and also respected by our good servants, and
" formidable both to wicked men and evil dæ-
" mons *. Know that you were invested with a
" mortal body in order to discharge these duties.
" For the sake of your ancestors, we wish to
" purify your family from every stain. Remember,
" therefore, that your soul is immortal, and sprung
" from us; and that, if you follow us, you will be
" a God, and with us will behold our Father."

Whether this be a fable, or a true narrative, I cannot tell †.

* It is well known that the Platonists admitted of good and evil Genii, and that they included both under the name of dæmons.   LA BLETERIE.

† Thus St. Paul, *Whether in the body, or out of the body, I cannot tell; God knoweth.* 2 Cor. xii. 3.

The Duties of a Priest.
Extracted from the Fragment of an Oration, or Epistle *.

A. D.
362 or 3.

*** IF any are detected misbehaving to their prince, they are immediately punished; but those who refuse to approach the Gods, are possessed by a tribe of evil dæmons, who, driving many

---

* This Fragment was interwoven with the Epistle to Themistius, as has been observed in the notes on that Epistle. We have therefore published it separately. It is part of an epistle which Julian wrote to some High Priest, teaching him the example which he ought to set to those of his own order both at home and abroad. And there are many things in this Fragment which he wishes his people to practise in imitation of the Christians.   PETAU.

Mr. Gibbon styles this " a long and curious Fragment " without beginning or end ;" and adds, " The Supreme " Pontiff derides the Mosaic history, and the Christian " discipline; prefers the Greek poets to the Jewish pro- " phets; and palliates, with the skill of a Jesuit, the *re-* " *lative* worship of images."

A more full account of it has been given in the Preface by the Abbé de la Bleterie, whose reasons for not translating the whole I deem conclusive. But, omitting the offensive parts, the extracts which I have selected shew the great use which Julian made of that *sound form of doctrine which was once delivered to* him by transplanting into his own religious code, but without acknowledgment, many of the moral

many of the atheists * to distraction, make them think death desirable †, that they may fly up into heaven, after having forcibly dislodged their souls. Some of them prefer deserts to towns; but, man being by nature a gentle and social animal, they also are abandoned to evil dæmons, who urge them to this misanthropy; and many of them have had recourse to chains and collars ‡. Thus, on all sides, they are impelled by an evil dæmon, to whom they have voluntarily surrendered themselves by forsaking the immortal and tutelar Gods. But enough of these. I now return to the subject from which I have digressed.

The practice of virtue, in obedience to the laws of their country, should certainly be enforced by the governors of states; but it is also your duty to exhort the people by no means to

moral precepts of the gospel, particularly that *new commandment, Love your enemies, do good to them that hate you,* &c. And, on the whole, if great part of the charge (as it may be called) which he here delivers to his Pagan priesthood, was observed by our Christian clergy, they would be more respectable, and more respected, than they are.

* The usual elogium of the Christians with this apostate.
SPANHEIM.

† Julian seems here to allude to the religious frenzy, the horror of life, and the desire of martyrdom, which possessed the enthusiastic Donatists.

‡ The solitary fanatics, whose iron chains, &c. the philosopher here ridicules, were the monks and hermits who had introduced into Cappadocia the voluntary hardships of the ascetic life. See Tillemont, *Mem. Ecclef. tom.* ix. p. 661, 662. GIBBON.

These solitary ascetics then abounded in Ægypt, Palestine, and Mesopotamia, as is evident from other remains of that age. SPANHEIM.

transgress

DUTIES OF A PRIEST.

transgress the sacred laws of the Gods. The office of a priest being necessarily more respectable than that of any other citizen, it may be proper for me now to consider that, and to teach you its obligations. Some perhaps may be better informed: I wish I could say all; but I hope it of those who are naturally temperate and virtuous. Such will own this discourse to be adapted to them.

In the first place, above all things cultivate philanthropy; as this is attended by many other blessings, and particularly by that, which is the greatest and most excellent of all, the favour of the Gods. For as those who kindly participate in the concerns of their masters, in their friendships, their studies, and amours, are more beloved than their fellow-servants; so it must be supposed that the Divine Being, who, by his nature, is a lover of mankind *, is delighted with those who love each other. Of philanthropy there are various kinds; one is the punishing offenders sparingly, and that for the good of the punished, as masters correct their scholars; another is the relieving the wants of the poor, as the Gods relieve ours. Observe the many blessings with which they supply us from the earth; food especially, of every kind, and that more in quantity than they have afforded to all other animals united. As we are born naked, they cloath us with the hair of beasts, and with such raiment also as is furnished

---

* Φιλάνθρωπον. Φιλανθρωπία, in like manner, is ascribed to God by St. Paul (Tit. iii. 4.), from whom Julian probably borrowed it.

DUTIES OF A PRIEST.

by the earth and trees. And not contented merely with rudeness and simplicity, with such coats, as, Moses says, they made of skins *; consider also how many gifts we enjoy of industrious Minerva. What other animal is indulged with wine? what other with oil? unless we impart to them what we refuse to men. What fishes feed on corn? or what beasts on marine productions? I do not mention gold, brass, and iron, with all which the Gods have enriched us; not to incur their resentment by overlooking the vagrant poor, especially when any of them are in morals irreproachable, but, having inherited nothing from their parents, are reduced to poverty by a nobleness of mind which despises wealth. On seeing these, the generality of mankind are apt to arraign the Gods. Indigence, however, is by no means chargeable to the Gods, but to the infatiable avarice of us who are rich, to which are owing the false ideas which men form of the Gods, and the calumnies with which they reproach them. Do we desire that God would rain down gold on the poor, as he did formerly on the Rhodians †? Were this to be granted, immediately sending out our servants, and every where placing vessels, we should drive away all

---

* Gen. iii. 21.—*the Lord God made coats of skins, and cloathed them.*

† Jupiter is said to have rained gold on the Rhodians at the time when Vulcan, cleaving his skull with a hatchet, delivered him of Minerva. See Pindar. Olymp. VII. and Homer, Il. II. 670.

With joy they saw the growing empire rise,
And showers of wealth descending from the skies.
                              POPE 813.

others,

others, that we alone might snatch the common blessings of the Gods. Some perhaps may wonder at our wishing for what cannot possibly happen, and would be utterly useless; since what is absolutely in our power we do not practise. Who was ever impoverished by what he gave to others? I, for my part, as often as I have been liberal to the poor, have in return been abundantly rewarded by the Gods; though I have never been a vile hoarder, nor have I ever repented of my generosity. I say nothing of the present time (as it would be absurd to compare private generosity with Imperial munificence), but, when I was a subject *, I remember that this often happened †. Thus when the estate of my grandmother ‡, which had been forcibly with-held, at length devolved to me entire; of the little which I then had I expended and bestowed on the poor. We ought therefore of our abundance to be communicative to all men, but especially to the virtuous; and to

---

* Consequently, while he yet frequented the churches of the Christians. SPANHEIM.

† This had of old been divinely said by another, the wisest of princes: *He that hath pity upon the poor,* (or, which is the same thing, *who giveth to the poor), lendeth unto the Lord, and that which he hath given, will he pay him again.* Prov. xix. 17. And in another place, *The liberal soul shall be made fat; and he that watereth, shall be watered also himself* xi. 25. Ibid.

‡ The name of Julian's maternal grand-mother is unknown. She espoused Anicius Julianus, who was a præfect, and from this marriage sprung Basilina (the mother of Julian), and the famous Count Julian. LA BLETERIE. See Epistle xlvi.

the

DUTIES OF A PRIEST.

the indigent, as far as will relieve their necessities. I will add, though it may seem paradoxical, that it is a duty to give cloathing and food to our enemies *; for we give it to their nature, and not to their conduct. And, therefore, I think that those who are imprisoned in dungeons, are also worthy of this attention, as such humanity by no means interferes with justice. For as many are imprisoned for trial, of whom some are to be condemned, and others acquitted, it would be much too severe to refuse compassion even to the guilty for the sake of the innocent, and rather to treat the innocent with cruelty and inhumanity on account of the guilty. The more I consider this, the more unjust I think it. We style Jupiter the Hospitable, yet we ourselves are more inhospitable than the Scythians. How, or with what conscience, can one, who would sacrifice to Jupiter the Hospitable, approach his shrine, when he forgets, that

By Jove the stranger and the poor are sent,
And what to those we give, to Jove is lent †?

---

* Can there be a doubt of the fountain from which Julian drew this living water, so different from the muddy streams of his favourite philosophers? *If thine enemy hunger, feed him; if he thirst, give him drink.* Rom. xii. 20. *Inasmuch as ye have done it unto one of the least of these my brethren, ye have done it unto me.* Matth. xxv. 40.

† Odyss. VI. 207. Broome 247. Part of the speech of Nausicaa to Ulysses on finding him shipwrecked on Phæacia. The same lines occur again in Odyss. xiv. 56. and are also quoted by Julian in Epistle xlix. They are there differently translated by Pope. Thus also Odyss. ix. 270.

────── the Gods revere;
The poor and stranger are their constant care. Pope 301.

And

And how can a worshipper of social Jupiter, if he sees any one in distress, and does not give him part of a drachm, think that he worships Jupiter as he ought? When I reflect on these things, I am quite astonished, seeing the surnames of the Gods, coeval with the world, considered as so many painted images, but in fact by no means treated by us as such. The Gods are styled by us Houshold Gods, and Jupiter the Domestic Deity; but we behave to our relations as if they were strangers. For man is related, with or without his consent, to every other man; whether, as is said by some, we all proceed from one man and one woman; or whether the Gods produced not one man and one woman only, but many at once, in great numbers, together with the world. For they who could create one man and one woman, were also able to create many, and in the same manner that they produced them, they might also produce these. Consider not only the variety of customs and of laws, but, which is more important, more excellent, and more prevalent, that tradition of the Gods which has been transmitted to us by the most ancient ministers in things sacred; namely, that, when Jupiter formed the world, some drops of sacred blood were spilled on the earth, from which sprung mankind. Thus we are all relations; since from one man and one woman, or from two persons, many men and women have sprung, as the Gods declare, and we must necessarily believe on the testimony of the facts themselves,

selves, as we all derive our origin from the Gods. That many men were produced at once is testified by facts, but will be more clearly shewn in another place. * * * * *.

It is proper also to observe, as has been said by those who have preceded us, that 'man is by nature a social animal. Shall we then, who deliver and establish these maxims, act unsocially towards our neighbours? Urged by such customs and inclinations, let every one of us discharge the duties of piety towards the Gods, of benevolence towards men, of chastity in regard to the body, and all the offices of religion. Let us endeavour always to retain in our minds some religious idea of the Gods, and viewing their temples and images with honour and veneration, let us revere them as much as if we saw the Gods themselves there present. For the images, and altars, the custody of the sacred fire, and all other things of that kind, were established by our ancestors as symbols of the presence of the Gods; not that we suppose them to be Gods, but that we may worship the Gods by them *. . . . . .

Besides the images of the Gods, their temples, their shrines, and their altars are to be reverenced. It is also reasonable that the priests should be honoured, as the ministers and servants of the

---

* This plea in defence of image-worship has been since adopted, as is well known, by the Romish Church. Other arguments equally futile and jesuitical follow. But the above may suffice.

Gods,

Gods, who dispense to us what relates to them, and contribute much towards procuring us their favours. For they celebrate sacrifices, and offer up prayers, for all. And therefore it is just to pay them not less but rather more honour than to the civil magistrates. But if any one should think that the civil magistrates are entitled to equal honour, as they discharge a kind of priestly function, by being guardians of the laws; yet no less respect is due to the others. The Greeks advised their king to reverence a priest *, though an enemy; and shall we not reverence those who are our friends, and who pray and sacrifice for us?

As my discourse has returned to the point from which it digressed, it is proper for me now to explain how a priest ought to act in order to be justly esteemed. As to what relates to ourselves, that need not here be discussed or examined.

As long as a priest retains his rank, he should be honoured and respected; when he is wicked, let him be degraded from the priesthood, and when he is unworthy, despised. But as long as he sacrifices, and makes libations, and attends on the Gods, we should behold him, as we do their most valuable possessions, with regard and veneration. For it is absurd to love the stones of which altars are formed, on account of their being consecrated to the Gods, and because they are of such a shape

---

* Hom. Il. I. 23. Speaking of Chryses. Αιδωσθαι θ' ιερηα, &c. The priest to reverence, &c.

and

and figure as are suitable to the holy office, for which they are intended; and not to think a man, who is dedicated to the Gods, worthy of honour. Some perhaps may think that the same honour is also due to one who acts unjustly, and is guilty of many transgressions in his holy office. Such a one, I say, should be censured, lest by his wickedness he should offend the Gods; but till he has been censured, let him not be despised. Nor is it reasonable, having this opportunity, to deny not such only, but those who deserve it, the honour that is their due. Like a magistrate, therefore, let every priest be respected, as this is the oracle of the Didymæan God *:

They whom depravity and folly lead
To scorn the priests of heaven's immortal powers,
And to the wise intentions of the Gods
Their own vain thoughts contemptuously oppose,
In safety live not half their days, condemn'd
To perish by th' eternal Gods, who deem
Their servants honour sacred as their own †.

And again, in another place, the God says,
For all my servants by destructive vice, &c.
and declares, that for that he will inflict punishments upon them. As there are many such sayings

---

* Didymæan Apollo. This title was given to Apollo, or the Sun, by reason of his own light, and that which he communicates to the Moon. Macrob. Sat. I. 17.
Others derive the name from a temple and oracle of Apollo at Didyma in Miletus. See Strabo, *Geog.* l. xiv. Pliny, and Lucian *de Astrologiâ*.
† Julian quotes this oracle again in his LXIId Epistle.

of

of the God, which may instruct us how much we ought to honour and venerate the priesthood, I will discuss them more fully on some other occasion. It may be sufficient at present, as I would say nothing inconsiderately, to quote this prophecy and mandate of the God in his own words. If any one therefore thinks me in these matters an instructor worthy of credit, let him revere and obey the God, and pay distinguished honour to the priests.

What a priest ought to be, I will now endeavour to explain; not on your account (for had I not been firmly persuaded, not only by the testimony of our chief *, but by that of the supreme Gods, that you would ably discharge this office, as far as your will and inclination are concerned, I should not have ventured to entrust to you a work of such importance) but that you may instruct others in your neighbourhood, both in town and country, by stronger arguments, and with superior authority, as not being merely your private sentiments, or your own practice only, but as being also my opinion, who, in what relates to the Gods, seem to be Supreme Pontiff †, and though by no means worthy

---

* Καθηγεμονος. Probably Maximus, the perverter of Julian to Paganism (see p. 113. note *) whom, writing to another priest (Epistle LXIII.) he calls by the same name, " Κοινος καθηγεμων, their common master;" and on whose advice, in these ecclesiastical arrangements, it appears that he chiefly relied.

† It is remarkable, that Julian here does not expressly style himself Sovereign Pontiff, but that " he seemed to be" so, δοκωλα ειναι, though Constantine and the succeeding Emperors

worthy of so high an office, yet study to be so, and for that purpose constantly supplicate the Gods. Be assured, that they have given us great hopes after death, and on them we may with confidence * rely, as they are incapable of deceiving, not only in such matters, but in any of the concerns of human life. If, by their excellent power, they can correct all the disturbances and monstrous abuses that happen in this life, how much more in the other (where the contending parts are disunited, the immortal soul being separated, and the body dead), will they be able to perform all the promises that they have made to mankind? Knowing therefore that the Gods have assigned to their priests great rewards, let us make those whose lives are conformable to their examples, which ought to speak to the vulgar, sponsors in every thing for their dignity. This we must begin with piety towards the Gods. Thus it becomes us to minister to them as supposing them present and seeing us (though we see not them), and, with a sight superior to every kind of splendor, pene-

---

perors (as has been observed by Spanheim, from ancient marbles, coins, &c. *Obs. ad Jul. Orat.* I. p. 278.) retained this dignity till the reign of Gratian.

Neither was Gallienus, as Spanheim asserts, nor Claudius, as others, the last on whose coins the titles of Pontifex Maximus, and the tribunitial power, are recorded.
CLARKE.

* This is not so much a Chaldæan, or an Hermetic, or even a Platonic, as a Christian confidence. SPANHEIM.

trating our most secret thoughts *. That this is not my sentiment, but that of God, expressed in several passages, it may be sufficient to shew by one instance, which will establish these two points, that the Gods see all things, and that they delight in the pious:

> Nothing escapes the wide-extended beam
> Of Phœbus; solid rocks it penetrates,
> And seas cœrulean; nor the starry host
> Eludes it, through the firmament, untir'd,
> Revolving, by necessity's wise law;
> Nor all the nations of the dead, beneath
> Immers'd by Tartarus in shades of night.
> But not high Heaven delights me more than
>   goodness.

Therefore as every soul, especially the human †, is more nearly connected with and allied to the Gods than stones or rocks, it is probable that the eyes of the Gods can penetrate them with much more ease and efficacy. Observe too the philanthropy of God, in saying, that he is " as much " delighted with the thoughts of religious men, " as with the purity of Olympus." Will he not therefore raise the souls of us all, who piously approach him, from darkness and from Tartarus?

---

* Thus the Psalmist, *Thou understandest my thought afar off. Thou art acquainted with all my ways*, &c. Pf. cxxxix. 2, 3.

† By this distinction, or preference, Julian seems to suppose that beasts also have souls, as he must allude to some beings inferior to the human.

For

DUTIES OF A PRIEST.

For he knows even those who are confined in Tartarus, that not being exempted from the divine power. But to the pious, instead of Tartarus, he promises Olympus *.

Above all, therefore, it is indispensibly necessary for the priests to be active in works of piety, that they may approach the Gods with religious awe †, and not say or hear any thing that is shameful. For priests ought not only to abstain from all impure and immodest practices, but also from all such words and sights. Far, therefore, from us be all licentious jests, and all scurrilous discourse ‡. That you may more clearly understand my meaning, let no priest read Archilochus ||, nor

---

* It is curious to hear a heathen philosopher thus inculcating the immortality, or future existence, of the soul, the resurrection, &c. But, as the woman of Samaria said to our Lord, *the well is deep*; and Julian, like her, *had nothing to draw with* but what he borrowed from Christianity. Where, for instance, did he learn, that "the pious are "promised Olympus?" Virgil, improving on Homer, speaks only of Elysian fields, or pleasant earthly mansions, *locos lætos, et amœna vireta*, &c. in which sages and heroes were placed after death. But that the just shall be *caught up into heaven*, or are promised Olympus, that where God himself is, *there they shall be also, was brought to light by the gospel*.

† Thus the Psalmist, *Serve the Lord with fear, and rejoice with trembling*. Psalm ii. 11.

‡ Thus St. Paul, *Neither filthiness, nor foolish talking, nor jesting, which are not convenient*, &c. Eph. v. 4.

|| Julian characterises the poetry of Archilochus in his VIIth oration. He was the first inventor of Iambics.

Archilochum proprio rabies armavit Iambo,
—— —— Archilochus by rage
Was with his own Iambic arm'd,

as Horace expresses it, in which he wrote so severely against Lycambes,

nor Hipponax *, nor any other writer of that class: let him also avoid every thing that has the same tendency in the old Comedy †. Much preferable and more suitable to us is the study of philosophy

Lycambes, who had promised him his daughter in marriage, but gave her to another, that he hanged himself. His poems are now lost.

* A witty poet of Ephesus, whose Iambics are said to have had the same tragical effect as those of Archilochus. They are also lost.

How little Julian observed this rule himself will be evident to any one from several of his works, in which he more than once alludes to the sayings both of Archilochus and the old comic poets, but particularly from the Cæsars and the Misopogon, which are not only seasoned with sarcasms and jokes, but also abound with scoffs more cutting and severe than any of the Iambics of Archilochus or Hipponax. So that what Cyril said, in his books against him, was not undeserved, that " he studiously covets the reputa-
" tion of great and various erudition." SPANHEIM.

† The old Comedy was so called on account of the alterations that happened afterwards, and which occasioned three sorts of comedy; the old, the middle, and the new. The old, in which there was nothing fictitious, either in the subject, or in the names of the actors: The middle, where the subjects were not fictitious; they were true histories, but the names were invented: And the new, in which every thing was feigned; the poets invented not only the subjects, but also the names. Eupolis, Cratinus, and Aristophanes, [all mentioned by Horace, l. 1. sat. 4. 1.] are the three greatest poets of the old comedy, and were contemporary, about 400 years before our Saviour. The liberty which they took of naming notorious offenders, such as Cleon, Hyperbolus, Cleophantes, &c. they often abused; Cratinus did not spare even the great Pericles, and Aristophanes respected not the wisdom of Socrates. Not contented with making men's actions the subjects of their pieces, they represented their faces to the life by means of masks, which were made to resemble them. DACIER.

How closely Foote, the modern Aristophanes, trod in the steps of these ancients is notorious.

alone,

DUTIES OF A PRIEST.

alone, of those sects especially which boast the Gods as the first promulgers of their doctrine, such as those of Pythagoras *, Plato, and Aristotle, and also those who follow Chrysippus † and Zeno ‡. Not that we should listen to all, or to the tenets of them all, but to those tenets only which are productive of piety: and as to the Gods, these teach us, first, that they are; secondly, that they regard things below §; and lastly, that they do not the least evil to men or others, or are envious, slanderous, or contentious, as has been related by our poets, but for which they are despised, while the Jewish prophets, for strongly asserting the same, are admired by those wretches who adhere to the Galileans ‖. To us those histories are most suitable which relate real facts; but let those fictions, which the ancients have composed in the form of histories, be avoided; such as love-tales,

---

* See p. 21.   † See p. 8.   ‡ See p. 39.
§ Thus St. Paul—*he that cometh to God must believe that he is, and that he is a rewarder of them that diligently seek him.*
Heb. xi. 6.
‖ The sentiments of Julian were expressed in a style of sarcastic wit, which inflicts a deep and deadly wound whenever it issues from the mouth of a sovereign. As he was sensible that the Christians gloried in the name of their Redeemer, he countenanced, and perhaps enjoined, the use of the less honourable appellation of *Galileans*.   GIBBON.
There might be a mixture of policy in it too, as knowing the efficacy of a nick-name to render a profession ridiculous.   LA BLETERIE.
This nick-name, however, did not originate with Julian. Epictetus gave the Christians the same appellation near 300 years before.   See his Discourses IV. § 2. &c.

DUTIES OF A PRIEST.

and every thing in that strain. As all ways * are not proper for a priest †, but require being pointed out to him, neither does every kind of reading suit him. For the mind is affected by books, and the passions, being soon raised, on a sudden burst forth into a dreadful flame. Against this, I think, we should watchfully guard long before.

Let no admittance be given to the doctrine of Epicurus ‡, nor to that of Pyrrho §. The Gods indeed

---

* This refers to the "Sacred Way," a street in Rome. so called, because the priests went that way on the ides of each month to sacrifice. Horace met his Impertinent in it. *Ibam forte viâ sacrâ*, &c. l. 1. Sat. 9.

† As to this institution there is a remarkable passage of Athenæus, at the end of his sixth book, where he treats of the remains of ancient frugality and parsimony, which were still retained in the offices of religion: "We walk in "some prescribed and appointed ways; we carry [in our "processions] and repeat in our prayers what we are en-"joined, and in our sacrifices we act with simplicity and "œconomy. For we wear nothing more than nature re-"quires, either next to our bodies, or in our outward "garments; our cloaths and our shoes are cheap, and the "vessels with which we minister are of earth or brass."
PETAU.

‡ Epicurus, the disciple of Xenocrates and Aristotle, supposed the world to be formed by chance, or a fortuitous concourse of atoms. He maintained also that pleasure was the end of man, of which he constituted sense the judge. He denied the natural relation of mankind to each other, taught irreligion and injustice, and his principles led to oppression, adultery, and murder, in the opinion of Epictetus and others

§ Pyrrho, the founder of the sect of the Pyrrhonists [or Sceptics] was born at Elis, and flourished about the time of Alexander. [He was contemporary also with Epicurus and Theophrastus.] He held, that there is no difference between just and unjust, good and evil; that all things are equally

DUTIES OF A PRIEST.

indeed have wisely abolished them, many of their writings being lost *; but it cannot be improper to mention them, for the sake of example, to shew what kind of books the priests ought principally to shun. And if books, much rather should thoughts, be avoided. For the guilt of the mind, and that of

equally indifferent, uncertain, and undistinguishable; that neither our senses nor understanding give us either a true or a false information: therefore, that we ought to give them no credit, but to remain without opinion, without motion, without inclination; and to say of every thing, that it no more is than it is not; that it is no more one thing than another; and that against one reason there is always an equal reason to be opposed. His life is said to have been conformable to his principles; for that he never avoided any thing; and his friends were obliged to follow him, to prevent his running under the wheels of a coach, or walking down a precipice. But these stories perhaps are nothing but mere invention, formed to expose the absurdities of his system. Once, when he saw his master Anaxarchus fallen into a ditch, he passed by him, without offering him any assistance. Anaxarchus was consistent enough with his principles not to suffer Pyrrho to be blamed for this tranquil behaviour; which he justified, as a laudable instance of indifference, and want of affection. A fine picture this of sceptical friendship!

For a more complete account of the system of Pyrrho, see Diogenes Laertius, in his life; and Lipsius *Manuduct. ad Stoic. Philosoph.* l. 11. dis. 3.   Mrs. CARTER.

* The exultation of Julian that these impious sects, and even their writings, are extinguished, may be consistent enough with the sacerdotal character; but it is unworthy of a philosopher to wish that any opinions, and arguments the most repugnant to his own, should be concealed from the knowledge of mankind.   GIBBON.

" With the sacerdotal character, of a Pagan or a Papist, " such exultation may be consistent;" but surely not with that of a Protestant, who is taught to " prove all things," and whose secession from the church of Rome was grounded on freedom of enquiry, and justified by reason.

DUTIES OF A PRIEST.

the tongue, are not, in my opinion, of an equal dye; but the mind should in the first place be guarded, as by it the tongue is taught to offend. The hymns therefore of the Gods should be learned, which are many and beautiful, composed both by ancients and moderns; and chiefly those which are sung in the temples. For most of them the Gods have by supplications been induced to deliver; though some, the effusions of divine inspiration, and of souls inaccessible to evil, have been made by men in honour of the Gods. These deserve to be studied; and the Gods should frequently be addressed, in private as well as in public; generally three times a day; or, at least, at the dawn, and in the evening. Nor is it proper for a priest to pass a whole day and night without a sacrifice; for as the dawn is the beginning of the day, so is the evening of the night; and therefore it is reasonable to offer the first-fruits, as it were, of both these intervals to the Gods when we rest from our priestly function. The rites that are performed in the temples are performed in obedience to the laws of our country, and neither more nor less is required than they prescribe. These are the property of the Gods. Therefore to render them the more propitious, we should imitate their nature: And indeed if we consisted of souls only, as the body would then be no obstruction to us, it might be proper to prescribe a particular mode of life to the priests. But since the

the priests do not merely consist of souls *, that which they are to study in the time of their ministration is not the whole of their employment. What then is allowable to one who is appointed to the priestly office at the seasons when he is not engaged in his sacred vocation? I am of opinion that a priest should in every respect be immaculate, both by night and day; that he should purify himself every night with those lustrations that our ordinances require; and that he should confine himself within the precincts of the temple as many days as the laws enjoin. To us at Rome thirty days † are commanded; other places differ. All those days he should reside, I think, and philosophise in the temple; and not go either home, or to the forum; nor see even a magistrate, except in the temple; but take upon himself the superintendence of divine worship, and inspect and regulate the whole. Those days being completed, when another has succeeded to his office, and he returns to the ordinary business of life, let him freely resort

---

* Something here is wanting; I have supplied it by conjecture.

† It is remarkable that the least residence enjoined by their local statutes to the prebendaries in most of our cathedrals consists of exactly the same number of days, viz. thirty. But their " strict residence," as it is called, being in general indispensible, of twenty-one days *in continuum*, is much less strict than that of these Pagan priests, as it is satisfied by their appearing in their stalls once every day, and sleeping in their houses every night. Thirty days residence being enjoined (as above) at Rome to every priest, the number allotted to each temple must have been twelve at least.

DUTIES OF A PRIEST.

to the houses of his friends, and, when he is invited, to the entertainments, not indeed of all, but of persons whose characters are respectable. At such times also there is no indecorum in his going, but rarely, to the forum; or in visiting the duke * and præfect * of the province, and to the utmost of his power relieving the indigent.

Let me add, that I think it becoming for the priests to wear in the temple, during their ministration, a most magnificent habit, but out of it a common plain dress. For it is absurd to pervert what is given us in honour of the Gods to the purposes of pride and vanity. And therefore in the forum we should renounce our costly vestments, and totally relinquish all ostentation. The Gods, admiring the modesty of Amphiaraus, though they had doomed that army to destruction, in which, apprised of this decree, he served, and therefore his fate was inevitable, removed him from this life to another, and gave him a divine inheritance. For when all the chiefs who besieged Thebes inscribed devices on their shields † before they were forged, and thus erected trophies, as it were, on the calamities of the Cadmeans ‡, this converser with the Gods went on that expedition with armour unin-

---

* The military and civil commanders, the general and the governor. The former was styled ηγεμων, or *dux*.

† The ostentatious devices, or armorial bearings of these chiefs, may be seen in Æschylus.

‡ The Thebans, so called from Cadmus, the supposed founder of their city.

scribed *, so that even his enemies attested his clemency and moderation. Priests therefore, I think, should [imitate his example †], in order to insure the favour of the Gods. For we offend them not a little by exposing to the populace the sacred vestments, and improperly divulging them to the public view as a wonderful sight. From whence it happens, as we are approached by many who are impure, that the symbols of the Gods are defiled. But for us to wear the habit, and not to lead the lives, of priests, is in itself a summary

---

* Thus Æschylus, in his Seven Chiefs against Thebes,
────────── with awful port the prophet
Advanc'd his massy shield, the shining orb
Bearing no impress; for his generous soul
Wishes to be, not to appear, the best §;
And from the culture of his modest worth
Bears the rich fruit of great and glorious deeds. POTTER.

As this modest and amiable augur was fighting bravely, the earth opened beneath him, and he descended alive to the infernal regions, with all his arms, and in his chariot. Statius has exerted the utmost force of his genius in describing this righteous hero. *Ibid.*

Amphiaraus wearing his shield entirely plain is accounted for in the same manner by Euripides, who has imitated the above, in his Phœnician Virgins:

────────── no unseemly pride
In his armorial bearings was express'd,
But on his modest buckler there appear'd
A vacant field. WODHULL.

Homer styles him, Odyss. xv. 245.
The people's saviour, and divinely wise, i.e.
Belov'd by Jove and him who gilds the skies POPE, 274.
"By Jove," says Eustathius, "because he was a king, and by Apollo, because he was a prophet."

† Some such words are wanting here in the original.

§ *Esse quam videri.*

of

of every transgression, and the greatest contempt of the Gods. On that therefore I will be more particular.

I address you on this subject, as I deem you a model. At obscene theatrical entertainments let not a priest by any means be present; nor admit them in his own house; as nothing can be more unbecoming. And if such exhibitions could be totally banished from the stage, and if all houses could be kept pure from Bacchus *, I would use my utmost endeavours to effect such a reform. But as I think this scarce possible, and, if it were, that it might not be expedient, I have abandoned that vain pursuit. I think it, however, highly proper for priests to absent themselves from theatres, and to leave their lasciviousness to the people. Let no priest therefore enter the theatre, nor form a friendly connection with any actor, or charioteer †, and

---

* That his own "cup" was "temperate" we have not only his own word (Epist. XLVI.) but that of his contemporaries. What he practised he had therefore a right to preach. St. Paul, in like manner, teaches his bishops and deacons to be *not given to wine, to be lovers of hospitality, lovers of good men, just, holy, temperate*, &c And, though omitted here, Julian directs his priests also to be *no strikers*, in a particular Epistle (the LXIID) on that subject.

† Those who drove the chariots in the Circensian or public games, whose company, like that of our *black legs*, was shunned by all who had a regard for their own reputation. Nero therefore could not more effectually degrade his own character than by assuming that. Had he been a British prince, he would have rid his own horses at Newmarket, or driven a stage-coach on the road. Actors were viewed by Julian, and the lovers of decorum, in the same disgrace-

DUTIES OF A PRIEST.

and let no dancer or mimic approach his door. I allow the priests to go only, if they please, to the sacred games; provided they are those at which women are forbidden not only to enter the lists *, but to be present. As to the hunting-matches which are exhibited in some cities within the theatres †, need I say, that from them not merely the priests, but even their sons, should be excluded?

disgraceful light. Though Æsopus in extravagance might rival Cleopatra, neither he nor Roscius was deemed, like our Garrick, a companion for priests and senators.

* Juvenal (Sat. I.) mentions the women in his time as ambitious of shewing their courage in encountering wild beasts, though with the forfeiture of their modesty.

   Cum ——————— Mævia Tuscum
    Figat aprum, &c.
When —— the mannish whore
Shakes her broad spear against the Tuscan boar.
DRYDEN.

Martial compliments the emperor Domitian on the same account; and the women are exposed by Juvenal (Sat. VI.) for engaging even as gladiators.   KENNET.

† The *Venatio direptionis* seems to have been an institution of the later Emperors. The middle part of the *Circus* being set all over with trees, removed thither by main force, and fastened to huge planks, which were laid on the ground; these, being covered with earth and turf, represented a natural forest, into which the beasts being let from the *caveæ*, or dens under ground, the people at a sign given by the Emperor fell to hunting them, and carried away what they killed to regale upon at home. The beasts usually given were boars, deer, oxen, and sheep.   Ibid.

The amphitheatral beasts sometimes broke loose from their dens, and made great havock in the city, as is mentioned by Pliny, Ammianus, and others.

For similar hunting-matches in the Greek amphitheatres bears and panthers were provided, as Julian mentions in his xxxvth Epistle, for the Argives.

I should

DUTIES OF A PRIEST.

I should perhaps have previously mentioned from whence, and how, the priests should be chosen. But there is no impropriety in making this the close of my discourse. Let them consist of persons of the best characters in every city. In the first place, they should be ardent lovers of the Gods; and, secondly, of mankind also *; of the poor as well as the rich. As to that, let no distinction be made between the noble and the mean. For he whom his modesty sequesters is by no means to be rejected on account of the obscurity of his merit. Therefore, though a man be poor, or a Plebeian, if he have these two endowments, love towards the Gods, and love towards men *, let him be elected into the priesthood. His love towards the Gods will appear by his instructing his family in religious duties; and his love towards men by his distributing from a little liberally † to the necessitous, by giving with a willing mind, and endeavouring to do as much good as possible. But this part requires the utmost attention, as some preventive remedy must be provided.

* What are these but the two Christian commandments, the love of God and of our neighbour, on which, says our Saviour, *hang all the law and the prophets?*

† Thus Tobit, iv. 8. *If thou hast abundance, give alms accordingly: if thou have but a little, be not afraid to give according to that little.*

DUTIES OF A PRIEST.

Obferving, I fuppofe, that our priefts neglect the poor *, the impious Galileans have adopted this philanthropy, and on the femblance of this duty have founded a moft enormous crime; like thofe who allure children with cakes, which having given them twice or thrice, they inveigle them from their parents, and, conveying them on fhipboard, fell them in diftant countries; and thus for a tranfient fweet the remainder of their lives is imbittered †. In the fame manner, they, be-

* The author muft have known, from the facred books which he read as lecturer in the church of Nicomedia, that this was an unfair reprefentation, and that the Chriftians had a prior and much more cogent obligation in their divine law, whofe characteriftic is philanthropy and univerfal benevolence. But he is not afhamed firft to plunder and then to revile it.

† He infinuates, that the Chriftians, under the pretence of charity, inveigled children from their religion and parents, conveyed them on fhip-board, and devoted thofe victims to a life of poverty or fervitude, in a remote country. Had this charge been proved, it was his duty not to complain but to punifh.   GIBBON.

Though I have tranfcribed this note, I cannot affent to the conftruction which the ingenious writer has put upon the fentiments of Julian in the firft part of it. The "inveigling of children," (above-mentioned) I apprehend to be only (as I have tranflated it) "by way of fimile;" nor is it faid or implied that Chriftians only were the inveiglers. The fimile, as ufual, begins with Ωσπιρ ("As") and the application is made by Τον αυτον και αυτος τοπτον ("They, in "like manner") fo that the charge againft the Chriftians is confined to their charity and miniftration to the poor (*Forgive* them *this wrong!*) for which indeed (as above remarked) Julian affigns an unworthy and difingenuous motive, qualified by a "fuppofe" (οιμαι) which he could not really "fuppofe" to be true. But ready as he was to calumniate the faithful, let us not impute to him charges which he never brought.

ginning

DUTIES OF A PRIEST.

ginning with what they call a love-feast, and a hospital *, and the ministry of tables † (for, as the work, so also is the word, frequent among them), pervert the faithful to impiety ‡. * * * * * *

* "Hospital" (υποδοχη) I have here restored to its original sense, as derived from *hospitium*, a sense which, from the disuse of such charitable foundations for age and want, independently of accidents and diseases, seems almost lost amongst us, the term being now generally confined to receptacles for casualty and sickness. But the hospitals established by our ancestors, in the true primitive spirit of the gospel, at and near Canterbury, at Guildford, Croydon, &c. which are still in being, were appropriated, in the former sense, to the lodging and relief of the old and necessitous.

† Διακονιας τραπεζων. The same expression is used by St. Luke, in Acts vi. 2.

From hence it appears, as has been related by Tertullian and others, that, on account chiefly of the poor, those common tables, common banquets, κοιναι τραπεζαι, κοιναι ευωχιαι, as the ancient teachers of the Christians afterwards called them, [misprinted ευχωχιαι. See Athenæus, *l.* VIII. *c.* 16.] were furnished by the rich. And also, as is mentioned by Theophanes, that *xenodochia*, or receptacles, were built for receiving any foreign poor, whether Gentiles or Christians; and in the same place he informs us of the certain quantity of corn which was distributed in the province of Galatia for the relief of strangers and the poor.

SPANHEIM.

‡ The Fragment here ends abruptly. Other charges, equally absurd, might perhaps follow; though, as this is styled the "close" of it (τυς λογυς λεξαι), it could not be much longer.

THE

THE CÆSARS*.

JULIAN. IT is the season of the Saturnalia †; the God, therefore allows us to be merry; but as I have no talent for the ludicrous, I am inclined, my friend, to blend wisdom with mirth.

FRIEND.

Dec. 361.

---

* Julian composed this satire after he was Emperor. I would say, that the friend with whom he converses was either Sallust the Second, or Sallust præfect of Gaul, if the satire of the Cæsars were the same as the work, entitled, The Saturnalia, as he seems to say himself (*Orat.* IV.) that he had addressed that to Sallust. But a passage in the Saturnalia, quoted by Suidas, and which is not in the Cæsars, proves that they were different works. [That passage is as follows: "But we believe Empedotimus ‡ "and Pythagoras, and what, derived from them, has been "delivered by Heraclides § of Pontus, and was lately "communicated to us by that excellent hierophant "Jamblichus."] It is needless to add that the word *Cæsar* here means *Emperor.* Even after that name had been appropriated to a new dignity, the Augusti still retained it, though those who were only Cæsars never bore the name of Emperors or Augusti.   LA BLETERIE.

Julian composed this satire in the winter that he spent at Constantinople.   SUIDAS.

† He wrote on Natural History.
‡ Julian mentions him also in the Fragment, by the name of "the great Empedotimus," and classes him with Socrates and Dion, as being unjustly put to death.
§ A native of Heraclea in Pontus, a hearer of Plato and Aristotle. He left several works, enumerated by Diogenes Laertius, but all now lost. A little treatise "on Commonwealths" is however ascribed to him.

VOL. I.   L   The

FRIEND. Can any one, Cæsar, be so absurd as to joke seriously? I always thought that this was intended only for relaxation, and to alleviate care.

JUL.

The book of Henry Stephens, preserved in the London library, mentions, in the Catalogue of his books, Συμποσιον, ἡ Κρονια, ("The Banquet, or Saturnalia,") and does not name the Cæsars. PETAU.

The philosophical fable, which Julian composed under the name of the Cæsars, is one of the most agreeable and instructive productions of ancient wit. Spanheim, in his preface, has most learnedly discussed the etymology, origin, resemblance, and disagreement of the Greek *Satyrs*, a dramatic piece, which was acted after the tragedy, and the Latin *Satires* (from *Satura*), a miscellaneous composition, either in prose or verse. But the Cæsars of Julian are of such an original cast, that the critic is perplexed to which class he should ascribe them. The value of this agreeable composition is enhanced by the rank of the author. A prince who delineates with freedom the vices and virtues of his predecessors, subscribes, in every line, the censure, or approbation, of his own conduct. GIBBON.

Thus agreeable, and thus instructive, it seems extraordinary that this should be the first attempt (at least I know of no other) to translate the Cæsars into English.

† The festivals of Saturn were instituted in the consulship of Sempronius Atratinus, and Minucius; or, according to others, in that of Titus Lartius. Others make them commence in the time of Janus, king of the Aborigines, who received Saturn in Italy, survived him, and placed him among the Gods. The better to represent that peace and abundance which were enjoyed in the reign of that God, these festivals passed in entertainments and rejoicings. The Romans quitted the *toga*, and appeared in public in an undress. They sent presents to each other as on new-year's day. Games of chance, forbidden at other times, were then allowed, the senate adjourned, the business of the bar ceased, and the schools were shut. The children proclaimed the festival by running through the streets, and crying *Io Saturnalia*. In ancient times it was held on the 17th of December, according to the year of

Numa,

THE CÆSARS.

Jul. You are in the right; but that is by no means my difpofition; as I have never been addicted to fcoffs, fatire, or ridicule. In order, however, to comply with the ordinance of the God, fhall I, by way of amufement, repeat to you a fable, which you will not perhaps be difpleafed to hear?

Friend. You will oblige me. For I am fo far from defpifing fables, that I value thofe which have a moral tendency, being of the fame opinion with you, and your, or rather our, Plato, who has difcuffed many ferious fubjects in fictions.

Jul. True.

Friend. But what, and whofe, fhall it be?

Jul. Not an ancient one, like thofe of Æfop, but a fiction from Mercury. This I will repeat to you as I received it from that God, and whether it contain truth, or falfhood blended with truth, I will leave you to judge when you have heard it.

Friend. Enough, and more than enough, of preface. One would think you were going to deliver an oration rather than a fable. Now then proceed to the difcourfe itfelf.

Numa, and continued only one day. Julius Cæfar, when he reformed the calendar, added two days to that month, which were inferted before the Saturnalia, and given to that feftival. Auguftus afterwards added to it a fourth day, and the Emperor Caius a fifth, named *Juvenalia*. In thefe five days was included that which was appropriated to the worfhip of Rhea, called *Opalia*. There was afterwards celebrated for two days the feftival in honour of Pluto, called *Sigillaria* (or feaft of ftatues) from fome fmall images that were offered to that God. All thefe feftivals were appendages to the Saturnalia, which thus lafted feven whole days, from the 15th to the 21ft of December. Sanadon.

THE CÆSARS.

Jul. Attend;

Romulus, sacrificing at the Saturnalia, invited all the Gods, and Cæsars also, to a banquet. Couches were prepared for the reception of the Gods on the summit of heaven, on Olympus, the firm mansion of th' Immortals *.

Thither, it is said, like Hercules, Quirinus ascended. For thus, in compliance with the rumour of his divinity, we must ſtyle Romulus. Below the moon, in the higheſt region of the air, a repaſt was given to the Cæſars. Thither they were wafted, and there they were buoyed up, by the lightneſs of the bodies with which they were inveſted, and the revolution of the moon. Four couches †, of exquiſite workmanſhip, were ſpread for the ſuperior Deities. That of Saturn was formed of poliſhed ebony, which reflected ſuch a divine luſtre as was inſupportable. For on viewing this ebony the eye was as much dazzled by the exceſs of light, as it is by gazing ſtedfaſtly on the ſun. That of Jupiter was more ſplendid than ſilver, and too white to be gold, but whether this ſhould be called *electrum* ‡, or what other name ſhould

---

* Odyſſ. vi. 42.

† The Roman mode of reclining, at their meals, on beds or couches, is too well known to need explanation. Every couch held three.

‡ Pure gold was in uſe to the days of Alexander Severus, who permitted a fifth part of ſilver to be mixed with four parts of gold. This they called *electrum*; and, in conſequence of his regulations, medals were conſecrated to him as the reſtorer of the coin: a compliment due with equal juſtice

should be given it, Mercury, though he had enquired of the metallists, could not precisely inform me.

On each side of them sat on golden thrones the mother and the daughter, Juno near Jupiter, Rhea near Saturn. On the beauty of the Gods Mercury did not descant; as that, he said, transcended my faculties, and was impossible for him to express. For no terms level to my comprehension, however eloquent, could sufficiently extol or do justice to the inimitable beauty of the Gods.

Thrones, or couches, were prepared for all the other Deities, according to their seniority. As to this, there was no disagreement; for, as Homer, instructed, no doubt, by the Muses themselves, observes, " each God has his own throne assigned " him, where he is firmly and immoveably fixed *." When therefore they rise at the entrance of their Father, they never confound or change their seats, or infringe on those of others. Every one knows his proper station.

Thus all the Gods being seated in a circle, Silenus † fondly placed himself near young and beautiful

---

justice to the providence of the present most august Sovereign of Great Britain; who, in this and many other respects, may be compared to that most excellent and virtuous Emperor. CLARKE.

Julian (as will be observed in the sequel) has not done justice to this prince.

* I do not recollect this passage in Homer, nor has the Index of Seberus enabled me to find it.

† The mixed character of Silenus is finely painted in the sixth eclogue of Virgil. GIBBON.
Servius

beautiful Bacchus (who was close to his father Jupiter), as his foster-father and governor, diverting the God, who is a lover of mirth and laughter, with his facetious and sarcastic sayings.

As soon as the table was spread for the Cæsars, the first who appeared was JULIUS CÆSAR. Such was his passion for glory, that he seemed willing to contend for dominion with Jupiter himself. Silenus, observing him, said, " Behold, Jupiter, one " who has ambition enough to endeavour to de- " throne you : He is, you see, strong and hand- " some, and, if he resembles me in nothing else, " his head, at least, is certainly the fellow of " mine *."

Amidst these jokes of Silenus, to which the Gods paid little attention, OCTAVIANUS entered. He assumed, like a camelion, various colours, at first appearing pale, then black, dark, and cloudy †, and,

---

Servius remarks that Virgil took the hint of his Silenus from Theopompus. According to our ideas of the Heathen Gods, the part assigned to him by Julian seems rather more suitable to Momus.

* It should be remembered that Silenus was represented very short, flat-nosed, with large eyes, and a fat paunch. Cæsar, on the contrary, was tall, well-made, and of a genteel shape. His aquiline nose, his piercing eyes, and his noble air seemed to announce the master of the world. But he was bald, like Silenus, which so much concerned him, that of all the distinctions that were lavished upon him by the Roman senate and people, none, it is said, gave him more pleasure than that of always wearing a crown of laurel.   LE BLETERIE.

† This marks the various characters which the policy of Augustus knew how to assume, as occasion required ; the supple-

THE CÆSARS.

and, at laſt, exhibiting the charms of Venus and the Graces. In the luſtre of his eyes he ſeemed willing to rival the ſun *; nor could any one encounter his looks. " Strange!" cried Silenus; " what a changeable creature is this! what mis-" chief will he do us!" ' Ceaſe trifling,' ſaid Apollo, ' after I have conſigned him to Zeno, I will ex-' hibit him to you pure as gold. Hark ye,' added he to that philoſopher; ' Zeno, undertake the care ' of my pupil †.' He, in obedience, ſuggeſting to

---

ſuppleneſs with which he cringed at firſt to the republican party, his cruelty in the proſcription, &c. his conduct compounded both of good and evil till he had deſtroyed the Triumvirs his collegues; and, laſtly, the gentleneſs and equity of his government when he was abſolute maſter. On his death-bed he aſked his friends, whether he had performed his part well in the world; *ecquid iis videretur mimum vitæ commode tranſegiſſe?* He might have been anſwered, that the actor was inimitable, and that the piece would have been applauded without exception, if its beginning had been leſs tragical. *Ibid.*

* Theſe particulars are found in Suetonius: " His " eyes were bright and lively, and he affected to have it " thought there was a certain divine vigour in them, and " was wonderfully pleaſed, if any one, when he looked " earneſtly upon him, turned down his eyes to the ground, " as at the luſtre of the ſun." *Suet. Aug. c.* 79. *Ibid.*

This image employed by Julian, in his ingenious fiction, is juſt and elegant; but when he conſiders this change of character as real, and aſcribes it to the power of philoſophy, he does too much honour to the power of philoſophy and to Octavius. GIBBON.

† It is pretended that the converſation of the philoſophers, in particular that of Athenodorus the Stoic, contributed greatly to correct the faults of Auguſtus. Athenodorus ſhall be mentioned in the cloſe of theſe remarks. Let it be obſerved, by the way, that Julian places the philoſophers in heaven, with the exception, no doubt, of Epicurus and Pyrrho, whoſe tenets he deteſted. LA BLETERIE

him a very few precepts, as if he had muttered the incantations of Zamolxis, soon rendered him wise and virtuous.

The third who approached was TIBERIUS, with a grave but fierce aspect, appearing at once both wise and martial. As he turned to sit down, his back displayed several scars, some cauteries and sores, severe stripes and bruises, scabs and tumours, imprinted by lust and intemperance. Silenus then saying,

" Far diff'rent now thou seemest than before *",
in a much more serious tone, ' Why so grave, my
' dear?' said Bacchus. " That old satyr," replied
" he, has terrified me, and made me inadvertently
" quote a line of Homer." ' Take care that he
' does not also pull your ears,' said Bacchus; ' for
' thus, it is said, he treated a certain grammarian †.'
" He

---

* Ἀλλοῖος μοι, ξεῖνε, φαίνης νιον ἢ το παροιθεν.
This is what Telemachus says, in the xvith book of the Odyssey, to his father Ulysses, whom he did not yet know, and in whose outward appearance Minerva had just wrought a metamorphosis. LA BLETERIE.

" Before," in English, is as equivocal as παροιθεν, in Greek. This the French translator, as he observes, could not retain, *auparavant* not signifying the same as *par devant.*

† This fact is unknown. But we know that Tiberius had at his table some men of learning (they were at that time distinguished by the name of grammarians), whom he delighted to embarrass by frivolous and absurd questions. He asked them, for instance, who was the mother of Hecuba; what name Achilles bore at the court of Lycomedes; what the Sirens sung, &c. Those who had the misfortune to displease this tyrant did not always escape so well as he whom Julian mentions. As the questions of

Tiberius

"He had better," returned Silenus, "bemoan himself in his solitary island (meaning Capreæ) and tear the face of some miserable fisherman *."

While they were thus joking, a dreadful monster [CALIGULA] appeared. The Gods averting their eyes, Nemesis delivered him to the avenging Furies, who immediately threw him into Tartarus, without allowing Silenus to accost him. But on the approach of CLAUDIUS, Silenus began to sing the beginning of the part of Demosthenes in the Knights of Aristophanes †, cajoling

---

Tiberius often related to what he had read, the grammarian Seleucus took care to learn what books the Emperor was reading. Tiberius being apprised of it, not contented with banishing him from the palace, forced him to destroy himself. *Suet. Tiber.* 70 and 56. LA BLETERIE.

* A few days after Tiberius had retired into the island of Capreæ, a fisherman came over the rocks, and presented him with a barbel of an extraordinary size. Tiberius, who thought himself in this retreat inaccessible, being terrified at the boldness of this fisherman, ordered his face to be scratched with his fish. And the poor man rejoicing that he had not also presented him with a monstrous crab that he had caught, Tiberius commanded his face to be torn with the crab. *Suet. Tib.* 60. *Ibid.*

† In the first scene of that comedy, whose object is to depreciate in the eyes of the people one Cleon, who had gained their entire confidence, Demosthenes and Nicias, two Athenian generals, complain bitterly of the tyranny which this new-comer exercises in the house, meaning the state, over the other slaves, that is, those who had a share in the government. " Alas! alas!" says Demosthenes, " how much reason we have to complain! May the just " Gods confound that wicked Paphlagonian, both him and " his projects! That slave, lately purchased, since he has " been introduced into the family, incessantly beats the
" servants."

Claudius. Then turning to Quirinus, "You
"are unjuſt," ſaid he, "to invite your deſcendant
"without his freed-men, Narciſſus and Pallas.
"But, beſides them, you ſhould alſo ſend for his
"wife Meſſalina, for without them, he appears
"like guards in a tragedy, mute and inanimate."

While Silenus was ſpeaking, Nero entered,
playing on his harp, and crowned with laurel. Silenus then turned to Apollo, and ſaid, "This man
"makes you his model." 'I ſhall ſoon uncrown
'him,' replied Apollo: 'he did not imitate me in
'every thing, and when he did, he was a bad imi-
'tator.' Cocytus therefore inſtantly ſwept him
away, diveſted of his crown.

"ſervants." Among the Greeks, the term *Paphlagonian*
was an affront; it meant a Barbarian, a blockhead, a
ſtammerer. In every ſenſe it ſuited the Emperor Claudius,
who was born in the Gauls; who, with ſome learning and
genius, never reaſoned when he was in fear, and he was in
fear during his whole life, even on the throne; and his
words were ſo badly articulated, that he could ſcarce be
underſtood. But the Paphlagonian of Ariſtophanes ill-
treated the ſlaves; while the Paphlagonian of Silenus was
governed and ill-treated by the ſlaves. Claudius was always the ſervant of his freed-men. He only complained
of it, and that even in the ſenate. He ſaid there one day,
ſpeaking of a certain freed-woman of his mother, "She
"has always conſidered me as her maſter. I ſay it to her
"commendation, becauſe there are at this time ſome in
"my own family who do not think me their maſter." *Suet.
Claud.* 39. The mixture of truth and irony, in the verſes
of Ariſtophanes applied to Claudius, throws, I think, more
humour into the pleaſantry of Silenus. M. Spanheim has
but half underſtood it.   La Bleterie.

THE CÆSARS.

After him, seeing many come crowding together, VINDEX *, OTHO, GALBA, VITELLIUS, Silenus exclaimed; " Where, ye Gods, have you found " such a multitude of monarchs? We are suffocated " with smoke; for beasts of this kind spare not " even the temples of the Gods †." Jupiter then looked at his brother Serapis ‡, and said, pointing to VESPASIAN, ' Send this miser, as soon as possible, ' out of Ægypt, to extinguish these flames. Bid ' his eldest son [TITUS] solace himself with a prosti-

---

* C. Julius Vindex, governor of Celtic Gaul, descended from the ancient kings of Aquitaine, was the first who revolted from Nero. Virginius Rufus, governor of Upper Germany, marched against him; but the two generals had a conference, in which they agreed against the tyrant; this, however, did not prevent the two armies from engaging, in spite of Virginius and Vindex, who could not restrain them. The latter was defeated, and killed himself in despair. Julian thinks that he designed to make himself Emperor. Yet he had written to Galba to offer him his forces and allegiance, if the latter would accept the empire. LA BLETERIE.

† Silenus has here chiefly in view the burning of the famous temple of Jupiter Capitolinus, which was perpetrated under Vitellius, and by those of his party. This passage, which throws light on what Vespasian says afterwards, and to which the Latin translators, not even F. Petau, have attended, I have corrected from an excellent Greek MS. of the works of Julian. SPANHEIM.

‡ Julian (*Orat.* IV.) says, that " Serapis is the same " as Pluto," to whom he assigns some functions very different from those which are ascribed to him by the poets. Here Jupiter addresses himself to Serapis, because Vespasian was first acknowledged by the legions that were in Ægypt, and proclaimed in Alexandria, July 1, 69. The years of his reign are reckoned from this day. Besides, it is pretended that this prince had received several striking marks of the protection of Serapis. *Tacit. Ann.* IV. 81. LA BLETERIE.

VOL. I.   L 6   ' tute,

THE CÆSARS.

'tute *, but chain his younger son [DOMITIAN †],
'near the Sicilian tyger ‡.'

Then

* Μίξα της Αφροδίτης της πανδήμου, *cum Venere publicâ.* The manners of Titus, before he was Emperor, were far from irreproachable. See *Suet. Tit.* 7. His passion for Berenice was very scandalous. The tragedy of Racine has long accustomed the French to consider her as a virtuous princess, worthy to ascend the throne of the Cæsars. Great poets sometimes determine reputations unjustly. Virgil and Racine have made two celebrated queens what they were not. The prudence of Berenice was always very equivocal at least. She became a widow very young; and her zeal for the Jewish religion, which she professed, did not prevent her being accused of entertaining more than friendship for her brother Herod Agrippa. In order to put a stop to a report so injurious to her honour, she married Polemon, king of Cilicia, after having obliged him to embrace Judaism; but she did not live long with him, and left him, it is said, through libertinism. This account, taken from Josephus, makes me suspect that she is principally alluded to by Silenus, under the name of *Venus publica*. If the colours seem too strong, let it be remembered, that those of satire in general, and of this in particular, are not always exact. Is Julian, for instance, excusable in saying nothing of the good qualities of Titus, and in characterising him only by one vice, which ought scarce to be admitted into his portrait, even by way of shade, as he was divested of it when he was Emperor? " This report," says Suetonius, " turned to his advantage, and was after-
" wards changed into the highest praises; when there was
" found in him no one vice, but, on the contrary, the most
" consummate virtues. . . . . He immediately dismissed
" Berenice from the city, with the utmost reluctance
" on both sides." All that can be said in excuse of Julian is, that the reign of Titus was so short, that one cannot venture to affirm, that his manners were really changed. This was probably the idea of the poet Ausonius, when he styled him " happy in not having reigned
" long:" *Felix brevitate regendi.*   LA BLETERIE.

The reverse of this, *Infelix brevitate regendi*, M. de la Bleterie applies to Jovian, as a motto to his History of that prince.

The

Then came an old man [NERVA §], of a beautiful aspect (for even old age is sometimes beautiful), in his manners most gentle, and in his administration mild. With him Silenus was so delighted, that he remained silent. 'What!' said Mercury, 'have you nothing to say of this man?' "Yes, "by Jupiter," he replied; "for I charge you all "with partiality, in suffering that blood-thirsty "monster to reign fifteen years, but this man "scarce a whole year." 'Do not complain,' answered Jupiter; 'many good princes shall succeed him.'

TRAJAN immediately entered, bearing on his shoulders the Getic ‖ and Parthian trophies. Silenus, observing him, said, in a low voice, but loud enough to be heard, "Our lord Jupiter must "now be careful, or he will not be able to keep "Ganymede to himself." After him advanced a

✝ The cruelties of Domitian are well known.
‡ Phalaris.
§ Nerva, when he was raised to the empire, was sixty-three years old, at least. LA BLETERIE.
‖ Though the name of Getes was given more peculiarly to the nations beyond the Danube, who bordered on the mouths of that river, the Greeks gave the same name also to the Dacians, that is, the Transylvanians, the Wallachians, and the Moldavians. Trajan subdued them. In his reign the power of the Romans was at the greatest height it had ever attained. In the North, he reduced Dacia to a province. In the East, he made himself master of Armenia, Mesopotamia, and Assyria. The Parthians, to whom he had given a king, were in some sort become subject to the Romans. *Ibid.*

venerable

venerable sage [HADRIAN], with a long beard * ;
an adept in music, gazing frequently on the heavens,
and

* Hadrian was the first of the Emperors who wore a
beard. "He let his grow," says Spartianus, " in order to
" conceal some natural deformity;" *ut vulnera, quæ in facie
naturalia erant, tegeret.* In reading the history of Hadrian,
and even the little which Julian says of him in this satire,
I am struck with some marks of resemblance between these
two Emperors. They had both as much genius as it was
possible to have, and of the same kind. They were greedy
of glory, jocose, and sarcastic, fond to extravagance of
the Greeks and the Grecian literature, both friends of
the arts and sciences, both authors, both full of zeal for
idolatry, superstitious, persecutors, astrologers, desirous of
knowing every thing, perpetually inquisitive, so as to be
accused of magic, fickle, obstinate, singular, and vain of
being so. They both made very wise laws, and performed
many acts of mercy. Hadrian sometimes seemed cruel,
and it is said that Julian was humane only through vanity.
Julian had not the infamous vices of Hadrian, and was not
even suspected of them; but he had almost all his faults
and absurdities. LA BLETERIE.

More striking to me are some marks of resemblance
which may be traced between this Imperial sophist and the
royal philosopher of Sans-souci. Both are authors of no
small repute in various branches of literature. The Memoirs of himself and his family, which Julian has inserted
in his Epistle to the Athenians, may be compared with
those of the House of Brandenburgh, and the History of
his Gallic campaigns, now lost, but mentioned by Libanius,
with the Commentaries, yet unpublished, of the Prussian
monarch. That Julian was a poet as well as Frederick, appears
from a collection of his verses mentioned also by Libanius
(*Orat. parent.* p. 161.) though two small pieces (which I
have quoted and translated in the notes on the Misopogon),
are all that now remain. Both solaced their leisure with
the charms of music. The epistles of both have an air of
familiar elegance. If the Cæsar lamented the loss of his
friend Sallust, recalled by his jealous cousin, the prince
deplored the fate of his favourite Kat, condemned to
death by his cruel father. Both were married, early in
life,

and curiously investigating the abstrusest subjects *. "What," said Silenus, think you of this Sophist? "Is he looking for Antinous †? If so, one of you may tell him that the youth is not here,

life, by their predecessors, to princesses not of their own choice, yet neither of them was ever charged with any illicit amour. "The chastity of Julian," says Mr. Gibbon, " is confirmed by the impartial testimony of " Ammianus, and by the partial silence of the Christians." " Fortune," said the Prussian hero, after his defeat at Kolin, " is a female, and I am no gallant." The Roman carried the simplicity of his dress to an indecent extravagance; his beard and its inhabitants, his inky nails, &c. are recorded by himself. The German, by the scantiness of his wardrobe, his boots, and his snuff, as Dr. Moore informs us, is almost as singular in these more polished times. Early attached to Grecian literature, Julian neglected and despised the language and writers of Italy. Equally enamoured of the French language, Frederick has always professed a kind of aversion for those of Germany. If the Emperor invited Maximus, Priscus, and other Platonists from Greece, the King sent for Voltaire, Maupertuis, and other academicians from France. In war too, as well as in literature, these heroes have acted a distinguished but not always a successful part. In two particulars, however, they materially differ: Julian was a superstitious Pagan: Of Paganism or superstition Frederick has never been suspected; yet the former believed the immortality of the soul, which, it appears from his Epistle to Marshal Keith, &c. the latter does not.

* It is said, that Julian here meant to describe himself. He informs us (*Orat.* iv.) that " from his infancy, he " stopped to contemplate the stars with so much pleasure, " that he was even then deemed an astrologer (ἀστρομάντις) " though he did not yet know what astrology was." Is the title of *curiositatis omnis explorator*, which Hadrian so justly deserved, and that of " Sophist," less applicable to the censor of Hadrian? LA BLETERIE.

† The deification of Antinous, his medals, statues, temples, city, oracles, and constellation, are well known, and still dishonour the memory of Hadrian. GIBBON.

" and

" and thus check his madness and folly." To
these succeeded a man of moderation, not in ve-
nereal * but political pursuits [ANTONINUS PIUS.]
Silenus, on seeing him, exclaimed, "Strange!
" how important is he in trifles! This old man
" seems to me one of those who would harangue
" about a pin's point †.

At the entrance of two brothers, MARCUS AU-
RELIUS and LUCIUS VERUS, Silenus contracted his
brow, as he could by no means jeer or deride them ‡.

MARCUS,

---

* Our satyr here obliquely charges Antoninus Pius with
lasciviousness; an imputation which was not true, it being
certain that that Emperor was temperate and chaste. But
he seems to have been accused, though not justly, of avarice, for adopting, when he was Emperor, the simple diet
and parsimony of a private subject.   PETAV.

Titus Antoninus, surnamed *Pius*, that is, " the good,"
was one of the greatest and best princes that the Romans
had. Pausanias justly says, that " he deserved not only
" the name of Pius, but also that of Father of Mankind,
" which was formerly given to Cyrus." Antoninus had
in fact the frailties with which Silenus reproaches him; but
he early corrected them.   LA BLETERIE.

† Εις των διαπριοντων την κυμινον. " One that cuts cumin;"
which seems analogous to our English phrase of " skinning
" a flint." This we apply, however, only to misers; but,
as M. de la Bleterie observes, " that of the Greeks refers
" not only to avarice, but a littleness of mind. Anto-
" ninus was generous, but not at the expence of any other
" person; *largus sui, alieni abstinens*." Our " splitting a
" hair " may perhaps come nearer to it.

‡ They were brothers only by adoption. Silenus had
too much to say of Lucius Verus. Indeed he was a good-
natured prince, a sincere friend, and incapable of disguise.
He always considered himself as the lieutenant rather than
the collegue of his brother. But he indulged himself,
without moderation, in all kinds of debaucheries, and was

a slave

THE CÆSARS.

MARCUS, in particular, though he strictly scrutinised his conduct with regard to his son and his wife *; as to her, in his immoderate grief for her death, though she little deserved it; as to him, in hazarding the ruin of the empire by preferring him to a discreet son-in-law †, who would have made a better prince, and studied the advantage of his son more than he did himself. Notwithstanding these failings, Silenus could not but admire his exalted virtue. Thinking his son ‡ [COMMODUS] unworthy of any stroke of wit, he silently dismissed him. And he, not being able to support himself, or associate with the heroes, fell down to the earth.

---

a slave to the ministers of his pleasures. Excepting that he was not cruel, that he did not drive chariots in the circus, nor act on the stage, he much resembled Nero.
LA BLETERIE.

* The greatest and perhaps the only fault of Marcus Aurelius was his excessive good-nature, which made him blind or too indulgent as to his brother, Lucius Verus, his wife, the too famous Faustina, and his son, Commodus. We shall mention him more than once in the sequel. *Ibid.*

† Claudius Pompeianus, originally of Antioch, and son only of a Roman knight, but a man of extraordinary merit. Marcus Aurelius caused him twice to be nominated consul, and gave him in marriage his daughter Lucilla, the relict of Lucius Verus. *Ibid.*

‡ One of the most wicked princes that ever reigned. "The enemy of the Gods and of his country, the parricide, the executioner of the senate, the gladiator, more cruel than Domitian, more infamous than Nero," is part of the funeral elogium which the senate made on Commodus. This assembly, which thought it had always a right to sit in judgment on the Emperors, would have ordered his body to be thrown into the Tiber, had not Pertinax prevented it. *Ibid.*

PERTINAX then approached, still lamenting the mortal wound that he received at a banquet *. This excited the compassion of Nemesis, who said, " The authors of this deed shall not long exult; " but, PERTINAX, you were culpable † in being " privy to the conspiracy that destroyed the son " of MARCUS." He was succeeded by SEVERUS ‡, a prince inexorable in punishing. ' Of him,' said Silenus, ' I have nothing to say; for I am terrified ' by his stern and implacable looks.' His sons would have accompanied him, but Minos prevented them, and kept them at a distance. With a prudent distinction, however, he dismissed the youngest

---

* The senate and people flattered themselves with having again found Marcus Aurelius in Pertinax; but he only reigned eighty-seven days. The Prætorian guards, who could not bear an Emperor so different from Commodus, massacred him in the palace. LA BLETERIE.

† The reproof given him by Silenus [rather Nemesis] for being concerned in the conspiracy of Letus and Marcia seems not well founded; but Julian perhaps follows some historian unknown to us. The death of Pertinax was revenged by Didius Julianus, who put Letus and Marcia to death; and by Severus, who cashiered the Prætorians. Julian is right in not naming among the Emperors Didius Julianus, worthy of eternal oblivion, for buying the empire which the Prætorian guards had put up to auction.
Ibid.

‡ Severus was perhaps the most warlike of all the Emperors. Like Hannibal an African, he had all his virtues; but he had also all the vices which the Romans ascribe to the Carthaginian general. What Sylla said of himself may be said of Severus; " no one was a better friend or a worse enemy." *Ibid.*

[GETA],

THE CÆSARS.

[GETA], and ordered the eldeſt [CARACALLA] to be puniſhed for his crimes *. That crafty murderer MACRINUS †, and the youth of Emeſa ‡ [ELAGABALUS], were driven from the ſacred incloſure. But ALEXANDER THE SYRIAN §, being placed in the hinder ranks, bewailed

---

* The antipathy of Caracalla and Geta is well known. The latter ſeemed to have ſome good qualities. The former ſtabbed his brother in the arms of Julia, their common mother, who herſelf received a wound in the hand. He was as wicked, and almoſt as ſtupid, as Caligula. He was a profeſſed enemy to men of learning. LA BLETERIE.

† Macrinus, Prætorian præfect, knowing that Caracalla intended to kill him, cauſed that prince to be aſſaſſinated, on the road from Edeſſa to Carræ. The army, who did not think him guilty of that murder, choſe him Emperor; and their choice was confirmed by the Senate. But fourteen months after, Varius Avitus Baſſianus, afterwards known by the name of Elagabalus, having aſſumed the title of Auguſtus, marched againſt him, and attacked him on the borders of Syria and Phœnicia. Macrinus ſhamefully fled, while the event of the battle was yet undetermined. Endeavouring to eſcape into Europe, he was overtaken by his purſuers, and put to death. *Ibid.*

‡ Elagabalus was of Emeſa in Syria, the ſon of Varius Marcellus, a Roman ſenator, by Soëmia, the daughter of Mæſa, ſiſter to the Empreſs Julia. He may in ſome manner be conſidered as the nephew of Caracalla. He pretended even to be his ſon. All the infamous, extravagant, and cruel practices that can be committed by a young man without genius, taſte, or the leaſt ſpark of virtue or ſentiment, who, to indulge his caprice, endeavours to exhauſt the power and wealth of a Roman Emperor; this is an abſtract of the reign of that prince, or, to ſpeak more properly, that monſter. *Ibid.*

§ Alexander Severus is conſidered by many, even at preſent, as a moderate prince, *magis extra vitia quàm cum virtutibus*, of a narrow genius, timid, the ſlave of an imperious mother, &c. He owes this reputation to the hiſtory

wailed his misfortune. Silenus added, " O thou
" fool and madman! highly exalted as thou wert,
" thou didst not govern for thyself, but gavest

of Herodian, an author by no means exact, but agreeable and interesting, whom two translations, one in Latin, the other in French, as good at least as the original, have put within the reach of every one. Herodian discovers an extravagant prejudice against the Emperor Alexander, for which we might perhaps be able to account, if the historian were known to us otherwise than by his work. It were to be wished that a pen as brilliant as his would endeavour to re-establish the memory of a prince in all respects the most amiable and accomplished that is mentioned in ancient history. He wanted neither courage nor firmness. If he had a great deference for his mother Mamméa, it was as much owing to his discernment as to his gratitude and tenderness for her. The œconomy with which they are reproached was a virtue more necessary than ever in the state to which the senseless prodigality of Elagabalus had reduced the finances. Alexander died at twenty-nine years of age, and consequently was younger than Trajan, T. Antoninus, and Marcus Aurelius were when they ascended the throne; and yet he deserves at least to be compared with them. Julian has followed the Memoirs of Herodian; and, besides, it should not be forgotten, that Mamméa was probably a Christian; that Alexander, instead of persecuting the Christians, worshipped Jesus Christ, whose statue he honoured, in his oratory, with those of Apollonius Tyanæus, Abraham, and Orpheus; that he had a design of building a temple to Jesus Christ, and of causing him to be received among the deities adored by the Romans. This was more than sufficient to make Alexander despised by Julian. Among the strokes of satire which are couched under the name of *Syrian*, which he gives to the son of Mamméa, and which, however, he did not deserve, except by his birth, I have no doubt that Julian includes the character of a worshipper of Jesus Christ. We know that Judea, where the Christian religion had its rise, was an appendage of Syria, and that the disciples of Jesus Christ were first styled Christians at Antioch.

La Bleterie.

" thy

ID
"thy wealth to thy mother, and could'ſt not be
"perſuaded that it was much better to beſtow it
"on thy friends than to hoard it *." 'All, how-
  'ever,'

* MAXIMIN, of the Gothic nation, the firſt of the Barbarians of the North, whom I find inveſted with the Roman dignities, made a ſenator by Alexander, and commanding ſome troops, conſpired againſt his benefactor, cauſed him to be aſſaſſinated near Mentz, and uſurped the ſupreme power. This Maximin was a kind of giant, being eight feet high, and with ſtrength proportioned to his ſtature; he was a great warrior, but ſo cruel and blood-thirſty, that he was named Cyclops and Phalaris. He obliged the whole empire to revolt againſt him, and, with his ſon, was at length ſlain by the ſoldiers, who thus revenged the death of Alexander.

It is ſurpriſing that Julian ſays not a ſingle word of any of the Emperors who reigned from Alexander to Valerian; namely, PUPIENUS and BALBINUS, GORDIAN the younger, the two PHILIPS, TRAJAN-DECIUS, and Æmilian. If he had omitted only the two firſt Gordians, and ſome others, Æmilian, for inſtance, it might be ſuppoſed that he conſidered them only as the phantoms of Emperors. Yet ſtill they deſerved to be named as much as Galba, Otho, and Vitellius, and more ſo than Vindex. Will it be ſaid, that ſome of them were unworthy to reign? Yet others were worthy; and, beſides, Julian has juſt mentioned Elagabalus. Will it be ſaid, that all thoſe princes had a tragical end? But he preſently introduces Valerian. It may alſo be obſerved, that Julian appears to have eſteemed the younger Gordian by offering ſacrifices and libations on his tomb, while he was marching againſt the Perſians.

In the IVth century, at lateſt, it was ſaid, that the Emperor Philip the father had been a Chriſtian, and that he had ſubmitted to public penance; a tradition the more ſtriking, as the Chriſtians had little intereſt in claiming the murderer of Gordian. The Chriſtianity of Philip, real or pretended, and the manner ſo unchriſtian in which he arrived at the throne, might have ſupplied the Silenus of Julian with ſome ſingular ſtrokes. Trajan-Decius would have been reckoned among the good princes, if he had

'ever,' said Nemesis, 'who were accessary to his
'death, I will deliver to the tormentors.' And
thus the youth was dismissed.

GALLIENUS then entered, with his father [VA-
LERIAN], the latter dragging the chain of his captivity, the other effeminate both in his dress and
behaviour. Silenus thus ridiculed the father:

"―― By those snowy plumes distinguish'd,
"Before the ranks who marches in the van *."

And

not been a persecutor of the Christians; and doubtless it
is not on that account that Julian erases him from the list
of Emperors. Certain it is that no satisfactory reason can
be assigned for all these omissions. It seems therefore very
probable to me that the text is here mutilated. It is not
the only chasm that I think I perceive in the satire of the
Cæsars. LA BLETERIE.

* Wodhull's translation.
These two verses are taken from the Phœnician Virgins
of Euripides. By α λευκολοφας, " with the white plume,"
I imagine that Silenus alludes to the age and white hairs
of Valerian. No one is unacquainted with his captivity,
any more than the barbarity with which he was treated by
Sapor I. Upon a false report of the death of Valerian, the
Romans placed him among the Gods. Thus this unfortunate prince had altars in Rome, while in Persia he was
trodden under foot. He was perhaps flead alive. Certain
it is, that the Persians tanned his skin, dyed it red, and
covered it with straw, in order to preserve it in a temple.
Valerian had some excellent qualities; and his fate would
perhaps have had more claim to pity, if he had not deserved it by shedding the blood of the Christians. The
most dreadful circumstance of his misfortune was, the
having on the throne a son who did not send even to
demand his release. " He would have been revenged,"
says M. de Tillemont, " if he had not had a son." When
Gallienus was informed of the imprisonment of his father,
he answered by an apophthegm; " I knew that my father
" was liable to the misfortunes of human nature." How
much

And to the son he said,

" Him gold adorns, all dainty as a bride *."

Jupiter ordered them both to depart from the banquet †.

They were succeeded by CLAUDIUS ‡, on whom all the Gods fixed their eyes, admiring his magnanimity,

much are princes to be pitied! The flatterers of Gallienus discovered philosophy, and even heroism, in the indifference of this unnatural son. LA BLETERIE.

* This is an imitation of a line of Aristophanes, in his comedy of The Birds. Gallienus was a cowardly, slothful, effeminate prince, a good orator, a good poet, but a very bad emperor. While he was engaged in his debaucheries, and amusing himself in some misplaced studies, in some effusion of wit, in making some pretty verses, or uttering some good jokes on the loss of provinces, Italy itself was ravaged by the Barbarians. Without reckoning Zenobia and Odenathus, eighteen usurpers assumed the purple. Gallienus, to prevent such revolts, excluded the senators from all military employments; a fatal policy, which, in the sequel, contributed to raise to the throne mere cyphers, men who had nothing Roman but the name. In short, the reign of Gallienus is the æra of the fall of the empire, which never perfectly recovered the violent shocks which it then received. *Ibid.*

† Gallienus deserved to be excluded. But Julian seems to represent the Gods as ungrateful. Ought they thus to treat the fate of the unfortunate Valerian, who was so zealous for their worship? Misfortune, after all, is not a crime. But it should be remembered that Valerian was taken by his own fault, and that, according to the Pagan ideas, being a prisoner, he ought to have shortened his disgrace, and not have survived his liberty. When Perseus, king of Macedonia, applied to Paulus Æmilius not to lead him in triumph, the Roman considered him as a coward, and answered, " That depended, and still depends, on himself." *Ibid.*

‡ Claudius II. had every civil virtue and military talent. His reign lasted only two years; but he signalised it by a great

nanimity, and granted the empire to his descendants, thinking it just that the posterity of such a
lover of his country should enjoy the sovereignty
as long as possible *.

After him entered AURELIUS †, as if to escape
those who were accusing him before Minos. For
many

---

great victory gained over the Germans, and by the defeat of
320,000 Goths. It is said, that he devoted himself for the
safety of his country. This devotement (if we understand by it a solemn devotement, like that which the Decii
made of their persons in the time of the republic) is a fiction, contrary to the relation of the best historians, who
say, that Claudius died of a pestilential fever at Sirmium.
Julian, however, manifestly alludes to it. He believed, or
was willing to believe, an incident so honourable to the
memory of Claudius, whom he considered as the founder
of his family. Constantius-Chlorus, the grandfather of
Julian, was the son of Claudia, the daughter of Crispus,
one of the brothers of Claudius II. The surname of Constantine came from the family of Glaudius, as he had a
sister named Constantina. Julian passes over Quintillus,
the brother and successor of Claudius, because he reigned
only twenty days at most.   LA BLETERIE.

In his first oration in praise of Constantius, Julian celebrates also " the eminent virtues" of their common ancestor
the Emperor Claudius; " the battles which he fought with
" the Barbarians beyond the Danube, his condescending
" manners, and that modesty of dress which was still ob-
" servable on his statues."

* In Julian this was not adulation, but superstition and
vanity.   GIBBON.

† Aurelian, the conqueror of the Barbarians, of Zenobia,
and of Tetricus, completed the recovery of what Gallienus
had lost. If he did the state too many services to be placed
in the rank of bad princes, he was too severe and too cruel
to be reckoned among the good. He was born in Pannonia, or Dacia, of a very obscure family. The mother
of Aurelian, priestess of the Sun in her village, inspired
her son, no doubt, with the zeal which he always professed

THE CÆSARS.

many charges of murder, which he could not palliate or excuse, were brought against him. But my Lord the Sun *, who had patronised him on other occasions, assisted him also on this, by informing the Gods, that the Delphic oracle

" That he who evil does, should evil suffer,

" Is righteous judgment,"

had been fulfilled.

The next was PROBUS, who in less than seven years re-built seventy cities, and also enacted many wise laws. Having suffered unjustly, he was honoured by the Gods, and his death was revenged by the punishment of his murderers. Silenus, nevertheless, endeavoured, in like manner, to ridicule him; and many of the Gods urging him to be silent, " Let those who shall follow," said

---

fessed for that God. He chose him for his tutelar deity, as Julian did afterwards.

TACITUS, a prince truly respectable, and worthy of the senate who chose him, ought to have been placed at the feast of the Cæsars. Nevertheless, he is not even named. Is the omission owing to Julian, or the transcribers? As Tacitus reigned only six months, I will not venture to determine. As to his brother, Florian, who reigned only three, or perhaps two, and who, besides, took possession of the empire, as of an inheritance, without being chosen by the senate, or even proposed by the army, he deserved to be omitted. LA BLETERIE.

* Aurelian adored that Deity as the parent of his life and fortunes. His mother had been an inferior priestess in a chapel of the Sun: a peculiar devotion to the God of light was a sentiment which the fortunate peasant imbibed in his infancy, and every step of his elevation, every victory of his reign, fortified superstition by gratitude. GIBBON.

he, " grow wiser by his example. Dost thou
not know, O PROBUS, that physicians make bitter
" potions palatable, by infusing them in mead?
" But thou, who wert always so severe and cruel
" that none could equal thee *, hast suffered, how-
" ever unjustly, in like manner. For no one can
" govern brutes, much less men, but by sometimes
" gratifying and indulging them; as physicians
" humour their patients in trifles, that they may
" insure their compliance in things essential."
'What! dear father,' said Bacchus; ' do you now
' play the philosopher upon us?' " Why not?"
replied Silenus. " Were not you too, my son,
" instructed by me in philosophy? Know you not
" that Socrates also held, like me, the first rank
" in philosophy among his contemporaries, if you
" credit the oracle of Delphi? Allow me therefore
" to speak not always jocosely, but sometimes
" seriously."

While they were thus talking, CARUS with his
sons [CARINUS and NUMERIAN] would have

---

* This censure of Silenus is extravagant. Probus can only be reproached for having enforced military discipline with a strictness of which the Roman armies were no longer capable. In time of peace he employed them in useful labours. One day happening to say inadvertently, that " there should soon be no more need of soldiers," this expression cost him his life. The same army, however, who had murdered him, erected a monument to him, with this inscription: *Hic Probus Imperator et vere Probus situs est, victor omnium gentium barbararum, etiam tyrannorum.*

LA BLETERIE.

entered,

entered, had not Nemesis repulsed them *. Diocletian †, accompanied by the two Maxi-

* History represents Carus as a prince above mediocrity: *virum medium, inter bonos, magis quàm inter malos, collocandum.* But he had the misfortune to succeed Probus, and to have Carinus for his son. On the other hand, he defeated the Persians, and took Seleucia and Ctesiphon, when a flash of lightning terminated his conquests and his life. It must not, however, be said that the sentence of Julian is too severe, as Carus dared to assume, or suffered flattery to give him, the title of "Lord and God." Besides, Julian thought perhaps that Carus was guilty of the death of his predecessor Probus; but the fact is at least doubtful. His second son, Numerian, was not unworthy of a place at the banquet. History speaks of him advantageously. As to what is said of Carinus, the justice of Nemesis cannot but be applauded. LA BLETERIE.

† Diocletian reigned for twenty years with great prosperity and address; but he disgraced the latter part of his reign by the most barbarous of all persecutions. He was a soldier of fortune, and having learned nothing but the art of war, he was a profound politician, and had a subtle genius that penetrated every thing, but was itself impenetrable. He always attended to what was solid. His projects, though grand and vast, were never chimerical, unless it were that of extinguishing the Christian name; yet of that he was not the author. He had the art of doing good himself, and of employing others to do evil. Being master of his passions, he could disguise all his vices, except pride, which made him introduce into the court of the emperors the ceremonial of the court of Persia. He should be considered as the founder of a new empire, which had not, it may be said, any thing in common with that which was founded by Augustus, but the name. The effective partition of the provinces subject to the Romans annihilated the ancient plan, and gave the finishing stroke to the senate, which till then had always had an influence in public affairs, and whose authority was much restored after the death of Aurelian. The aversion of Diocletian to the city of Rome prepared the great event of the foundation of Constantinople. *Ibid.*

MIANS, and my grandfather CONSTANTIUS *, then approached, magnificently dreſſed. Theſe, though they held each other by the hand, did not walk on a line with DIOCLETIAN. Three others † alſo
ſur-

*. Conſtantius-Chlorus.

† Diocletian firſt divided the empire with Maximian, afterwards ſurnamed Herculius, his old friend, a great general, very liberal, and not deficient in genius; but unpoliſhed and cruel, without education, and without manners. They gave in conjunction the title of Cæſar to Conſtantius-Chlorus and Maximian-Galerius, and divided the Roman empire, which was governed by two Emperors and two Cæſars, into four parts.

Conſtantius-Chlorus was the only one of the four who was of high birth. With all the talents of his collegues, he had none of their faults. His ſole ambition was to make his people happy. No prince ever loved money ſo little, or ſo much loved by his ſubjects. Through fear of oppreſſing them, he denied himſelf neceſſaries. Such is the picture that is drawn of him even by the authors who have written ſince his family has been extinct.

As for Maximian-Galerius, ſurnamed *Armentarius*, or "the Herdſman," he was rather a Barbarian than a Roman. He had great talents for war, and all imaginable vices, which he nevertheleſs concealed a little; ſo much was he afraid of Diocletian. He had almoſt an equal hatred to the Chriſtian religion and to learning, and forced Diocletian to become a perſecutor. Theſe four princes governed with a perfect union, whoſe tie was the reſpect which Maximian-Herculius, and the two Cæſars, had for Diocletian, whom they regarded as their father, and almoſt as their God. Diocletian, on his ſide, did not exalt himſelf above them; and, in particular, he took care to ſtifle bad reports. What Julian here ſays of the modeſty of that prince and his collegues admits, however, of ſome exception. Diocletian ſometimes treated Galerius with great haughtineſs; and Galerius, tired of trembling before him, made him tremble in his turn, and forced him to abdicate the empire. Diocletian and Herculius quitted the purple on the ſame day; the firſt at Nicomedia, and the
other

surrounded him, in the manner of a chorus; but when, like harbingers, they would have preceded him, he forbade them, not thinking himself entitled to any distinction. Transferring only to them a burthen which he had borne on his own shoulders, he walked with much greater ease. Admiring their union, the Gods assigned them a seat superior to many. But MAXIMIAN * behaving with imprudence and haughtiness, Silenus, though he did not think him worthy of ridicule, would not admit him into the society of the Emperors. And, besides, he was not only addicted to all kinds of lasciviousness, but by his impertinent officiousness and perfidy often interrupted the harmonious concert. Nemesis therefore soon banished him, and whither he went I know not, as I forgot to ask Mercury.

---

other at Milan. The abdication of Diocletian has been considered as the greatest effort of human virtue; nevertheless, it was not so voluntary as is generally supposed. But he made it honestly, and without return; wiser than Herculius, who, after resuming the purple, and occasioning many disturbances, was obliged to destroy himself.

LA BLETERIE.

* I know not why Julian excludes only one of the two Maximians. As a proof that neither of them deserved to be admitted, we do not immediately discover which he means. However, as this Maximian alone disturbed the concert formed by the union of Diocletian and his collegues, Julian must necessarily speak of Maximian-Galerius. He died at Sardis, of a dreadful disorder, considering his death as a punishment of the cruelties which he had exercised against the Christians. Ibid.

To

To this most melodious tetrachord a harsh, disagreeable, and discordant sound succeeded *. Two of the candidates Nemesis would not suffer to approach even the door of the assembly. LICINIUS came thus far, but having been guilty of many crimes, he was repulsed by Minos. CONSTANTINE entered, and sat some time; and near him sat his

* Diocletian had flattered himself that the partition of the empire between two Emperors and two Cæsars would subsist in future; but one of the chagrins which he felt in his retirement was the ambition and misunderstanding of his successors, each of whom thought only of making himself master of the whole empire. Those whom Julian has here in view are Maxentius, Maximin-Daïa, Licinius, and Constantine.

Maxentius, the son, or supposed son, of Maximian-Herculius, was a prince ill-made, without genius, cowardly, slothful, cruel, debauched. When he harangued his soldiers, it was to exhort them to make good cheer, to spend money, to enjoy life; *fruimini*. He obliged Sophronia, daughter of the governor of Rome, to renew the tragical history of Lucretia. It is well known that he perished in the Tiber, in his endeavour to destroy Constantine.

Maximin-Daïa, as despicable as Maxentius, and a still more cruel persecutor than his uncle Maximian-Galerius, being vanquished by Licinius, escaped to the city of Tarsus, and took poison at the end of a great entertainment. This poison, failing of its entire effect, occasioned him a horrible and long malady. I do not find in all antiquity a death more shocking than his.

Though Licinius had courage and success in war, he was still more wicked than Maximin. He considered literature as the pest of a state. Constantine vanquished him, obliged him to quit the purple, and, soon after, deprived him of life. Of Constantine and his sons more in the sequel.   LA BLETERIE.

THE CÆSARS.

fons. As for MAGNENTIUS *, he was refused admittance, because he had never done any thing laudable, though many of his actions might appear brilliant. But the Gods, perceiving that they did not flow from a good principle, dismissed him much afflicted.

* Magnentius, who derived his origin from the Franks and the Saxons, served with reputation in the Roman troops, when he assumed the purple at Autun, and caused the Emperor Conſtans to be put to death. He was vanquished by Conſtantius in the battle of Murſa in 352, and in the following year, through fear of falling into the hands of the conqueror, he killed himſelf in the Gauls, after having killed all his family. He had profeſſed Chriſtianity, though he was perhaps a Pagan in his heart. Courage is aſcribed to him, or that which often produces the ſame effect, the art of concealing his timidity, with a taſte for books, learning, a lively and animated eloquence, and reſpect and zeal for the laws, when they were no obſtacle to his ambitious projects. No writer charges him with debauchery, and this ſilence expreſſes much. Such vices, however, are given him as are always given to unſucceſsful uſurpers. Julian, in particular, elſewhere paints Magnentius in the moſt hideous colours; but it is in his panegyrics of Conſtantius. The opinion which he forms here ſeems much more credible, and ſufficiently agrees with that of Zoſimus. "Magnentius," ſays that hiſtorian (*l.* ii.) "was bold in "proſperity, and timid in adverſity. He knew ſo well "how to diſguiſe his natural perverſeneſs, that thoſe "who did not know him took him for a man of ſim- "plicity and of an excellent character. I think myſelf "obliged to make this remark," continues Zoſimus, "becauſe ſome have thought that he governed the ſtate "well. Let them be no longer deceived in him. Magnentius "did nothing from good motives, from a principle of "virtue." Let us obſerve, by the way, that the true or falſe idea which Julian gives of Magnentius is exactly the ſame which we ought to have of Julian.

LA BLETERIE.

In this manner was the banquet prepared. At the table of the Gods nothing was wanting, for all things are theirs. But that of the heroes Mercury thought imperfect, and Jupiter was of the same opinion. Quirinus had long requested to introduce another of his descendants. But Hercules said, "I will not suffer it, Quirinus. For
" why have you not invited my ALEXANDER also
" to the feast? If therefore, Jupiter, you intend
" to enroll any of the heroes among us, send,
" I intreat you, for ALEXANDER. When we
" are canvassing the merits of men, why should
" the bravest be omitted?" What the son of Alcmena proposed was approved by Jupiter. ALEXANDER therefore entered the assembly of heroes; but neither CÆSAR, nor any one else, rose up to him; so that he was obliged to take the seat which the eldest son of SEVERUS had left vacant*, he, for his fratricide, having been expelled.

---

* What is the reason that Alexander takes the seat intended for Caracalla, when there are so many others vacant? This is one of those little circumstances that give narrations a greater air of truth. Besides, this recalls some facts. Caracalla was inflamed with a foolish passion for Alexander. Not contented with filling the cities, the temples, Rome, and the capitol with the statues of that prince, with having a phalanx whose officers bore the names of the generals of Alexander, and dressing in the Macedonian manner, he endeavoured to identify himself with his hero in some fantastic pictures, where the face was composed of half that of Alexander and half that of his own. He persecuted the Peripatetic philosophers, because Aristotle was suspected of being concerned in the death of that conqueror. LA BLETERIE.

Silenus

Silenus then scoffing at Quirinus, said, 'Take care,
' or this one Greek will excell all your Romans.'
" By Jove," replied Quirinus, " I think that many
" of them are, in every respect, his equals. My
" posterity indeed have so much admired him, that
" of foreign generals they style and think him
" only great; not that they deem him superior to
" their countrymen, or are void of national preju-
" dice. But that we shall soon determine when we
" have brought their merits to the test!" Saying
this, Quirinus blushed [*]; and seemed evidently
anxious for his descendants.

After this, Jupiter asked the Gods, whether all
should enter the lists, or whether they should adopt
the practice observed in wrestling, where whoever
conquers him who has gained the most victories is
deemed the only victor, even of those who have
been vanquished by his antagonist, though they
have not been his competitors? This was generally
approved, as a just determination. Mercury then
proclaimed that CÆSAR should advance first, OCTA-
VIANUS next, and TRAJAN third, those being the
greatest warriors. Silence being commanded, Saturn, turning to Jupiter, expressed his surprise at
seeing martial Emperors summoned to this contest,

---

[*] We must not forget that Julian is a Greek to the
bottom of his soul. His only comfort in being a Roman
was his having been born at Byzantium, and his considering
Rome as a colony of Greeks. LA BLETERIE.

but no philosophers *. "These," he said, "are
" equally dear to me. Call therefore, and intro-
" duce MARCUS [AURELIUS]." He being summoned, advanced with a serious aspect †, occasioned by the labours of his mind. His eyes were
hollow, his brow was contracted ‡, and his whole
form displayed unstudied beauty; for his hair was
uncombed, his beard was long, his dress simple
and œconomical, and by scanty nourishment § his
body

* It is right for Saturn, a pacific God, and the father
of the golden age, to be interested for philosophical princes,
and for Marcus Aurelius in particular, the greatest philosopher of them all; who, in spite of the various scourges
with which the empire was afflicted in his time, promoted
the happiness of the Romans. It is said of this Emperor,
that Providence gave him to mankind in mercy, to temper
the severity of the chastisements which it had inflicted upon
them in justice. LA BLETERIE.

† It is pretended, that, even in his childhood, neither
joy nor sorrow ever made him change countenance: but his
gravity had nothing in it sad or austere. *Sine tristitiâ gravis*.
Ibid.

‡ He is thus represented on his medals, especially those
which were struck in the latter years of his life. *Ibid.*

§ At the age of twelve years, Marcus Aurelius took the
habit of a philosopher, and soon after he was desirous of
practising all the austerities of the Stoic philosophy, even
to the lying on the ground under his cloak. His mother
used her utmost endeavours to persuade him to lie on a
wooden bedsted covered with a single skin. A life so
hardy made no abatement in the sweetness of his temper,
but it impaired his health. Nevertheless, his habitual in-
firmities never prevented him from fulfilling all his duties,
and from finding time besides for study. His soul appeared
to have gained what his body had lost.

Julian piqued himself on being an imitator of Marcus
Aurelius, slept hardly, and lived on vegetables. Some of
the

body was transparent and splendid, like the purest and clearest light. When he was admitted within the sacred inclosure, Bacchus said, " King Saturn " and Father Jupiter, can any thing imperfect be " allowed among the Gods?" No answer being returned, " Let us send then," proceeded he, " for some lover of pleasure." 'But,' replied Jupiter, ' it is not lawful for any one to be admitted ' here who does not worship us *.' " Let judgment " therefore," said Bacchus, " be pronounced on " him in the vestibule. We will call, with your " leave, a prince, not indeed unwarlike †, but
" softened

the Epistles of Julian give us reason to think that he was frequently ill. But it is more easy to wear the beard of Marcus Aurelius, to copy his austerities, and to ruin one's health, like him, than to acquire his solidity of genius, his love of virtue for virtue's sake, his contempt of glory, and, if I may venture so to express myself, that sobriety of wisdom, which was the foundation of his character.

LA BLETERIE.

* Ου ϑεμιϊον εισω φοιϊαν ανδρι μη τα ημιϊερα ζηλωϊι. M. de la Bleterie translates this, " Whoever does not take us for " his model cannot set foot here;" but I understand it, " Whoever is not a worshipper of us," &c. in allusion to Constantine, who was a Christian. It is observable, however, that Constantine and his sons are before mentioned as entering the assembly and sitting some time.

† If Constantine had been a slave to his pleasures, so far as to deserve, though he had declared for Christianity, the protection of Bacchus, he would not have been so distinguished in war and in peace; he would not have reigned so gloriously for more than thirty years, that is, much longer than any Emperor had reigned since Augustus. This general reflection may be sufficient to shew the injustice of Julian. History represents Constantine to us as a prince always engaged in some useful project, giving frequent audiences,

"softened by pleasure and enjoyment. Let Con-
"stantine come as far as the vestibule."

This diences, drawing up his laws and dispatches himself, borrowing from his sleep time to read the holy scriptures, and to compose some religious discourses, which he pronounced in public, endeavouring to obtain the assistance of Heaven by prayer, fasting, and abstinence from lawful pleasures.

If we deduct from these elogiums whatever may be taken from panegyrics, if we set aside the good that is said of him by Christian writers, and even the praises that are given him by such of the Pagans as may be suspected of flattery, having written in his reign, or in that of his sons, I mean Libanius, and the historian Praxagoras; in a word, if Constantine be judged by the testimony of Eutropius, who dedicates his work to Valens, and by what is said of him by that Victor who wrote in the reign of the sons of Theodosius I. the result will be, that Constantine was a prince of an elevated genius, active, vigilant, laborious, and, even independently of what he did for the Christian religion, and notwithstanding the blemishes that are found in his life, that he deserved the title of Great. The testimony of those authors is the more important, as they spare neither his faults nor failings.

Zosimus, a partial writer, and the declared enemy of the Christian Emperors, is the only one, besides Julian, who accuses him of being devoted to pleasures. Yet Zosimus throws this reproach only on the latter years of his reign. In fact Constantine could have given no pretext for that accusation till after the foundation of New Rome. Tired of wars, and even of victories, he thought that he had acquired a right to taste the fruit of his labours. Without remaining in inactivity, or living in voluptuousness (for, to the end of his life, he employed himself in affairs of state, and in those of the church), he gave some brilliant entertainments. His court was magnificent; he procured himself some amusements that had nothing criminal in the eyes of the world, and which perhaps he thought were allowed him because he had not yet been baptised.

It

THE CÆSARS.

This being allowed (the mode of their contention having been previously settled) Mercury advised, that every one should severally speak for himself, and that the Gods should then give their votes. But of this Apollo disapproved, insisting, that truth only, and not eloquence, or the charms of oratory, ought to be discussed and examined by the Gods. Jupiter, wishing to oblige all, and, at the same time, desirous to prolong the assembly, replied, " There can be no inconvenience in di-
" recting each of them to speak by a certain
" measure of water *, and afterwards we may
" interrogate them and scrutinise their thoughts."
Silenus jocosely added, ' Take care, Neptune, or
' Trajan and Alexander †, mistaking the water
' for

It is supposed that the imagination and malignity of Julian working on this canvas might make Constantine a slave to pleasure. Let us never forget that Julian detested his uncle as the destroyer of Paganism; and that he was by taste, by principle, by vanity, an enemy to all pleasures. How much must the magnificence of Constantine have wounded a man who gave into the opposite extreme, who carried philosophy to such an excess, as to despise decorum, and who, by the manners which he ascribes to himself in the Misopogon, seems to have been desirous that his picture should be the companion of that of Diogenes!

La Bleterie.

* When the Greeks and Romans would give orators a certain fixed time, they employed hour-glasses of water, to which they gave the name of *clepsydra*, which the modern Latinists apply very improperly to our sands. *Ibid.*.

† It is well known that Alexander was very fond of wine, and that in drunkenness he was capable of the greatest

' for nectar, will swallow it all, and so leave none
' for the rest.' Neptune answered, "They were
"much more fond of your draughts, Silenus,
"than of mine. It behoves you therefore to be
"rather afraid of your own vines than of my
"springs." Silenus was chagrined, and made no
reply, but afterwards attended solely to the dis-
putants. Mercury then proclaimed,

* ' The arbiter of prizes due
  ' To signal merit now begins.
  ' Delay no longer, Time exhorts,
  ' But lend your ears to what the voice
  ' Of herald Mercury proclaims.
    ' Ye kings, to whose superior sway
    ' Of old submissive nations bow'd,
    ' Who launch'd in fight the hostile spear,

greatest excesses. His last debauch cost him his life. As for Trajan, he was obliged to forbid the execution of any orders which he might give at coming from a great entertainment. One of the methods of which Hadrian availed himself to gain his friendship was to carouse with him at table. LA BLETERIE.

* See Lucian, at the end of his Demonjacs. PETAU.
The three first lines only (in the original) are quoted from that work.

This proclamation, in the taste of those which were made in Greece at the opening of the games, consists of forms used on those occasions, and of ends of verses taken from the Greek poets that we have, and those whom we have not. This kind of cento has in the original, or rather had, a merit which we may imagine, but which it is impossible to transfuse into another language.
LA BLETERIE.
M. de la Bleterie has only given the sense. The English is almost literal.

' Advance,

'Advance, contend, with prudent minds
'Oppose your rivals, and await
'The just, th' impartial will of Heaven!
'Wisdom these think the end of life,
'Those, vengeance on their foes to wreak,
'And serve their friends: of life, of toil,
'Pleasure some make the single view,
'Feasts, nuptials, all that feeds their eyes:
'From dainty ornaments of dress,
'Or rings, with precious gems adorn'd,
'Others superior bliss derive.
'Jove will the victory decree.'

Mercury having made this proclamation, the combatants drew lots: and the lot happened to concur with the love of pre-eminence habitual to Cæsar. This augmented his pride and arrogance; so that Alexander would have declined the contest, had he not been encouraged and persuaded by Hercules. Alexander obtained the next turn of speaking after Cæsar. When all the rest had had their proper turns assigned them, Cæsar thus began:

"It was my good fortune, O Jupiter and ye
"Gods, to be born, after many heroes, in that
"illustrious city, which has extended her do-
"minion farther than any other; so that they all
"may be satisfied, if they obtain the second place.
"For what other city, deducing its origin from
"three thousand men, has, in less than six hun-
"dred years, carried its conquests to the utmost
"extremities

THE CÆSARS.

"extremities of the earth? What other nation has produced so many distinguished warriors and legislators, or such devout worshippers of the Gods? Born in a city so renowned, I surpassed, by my actions, not only my contemporaries, but all the heroes that ever lived. Of my own countrymen I know not one that will deny me the superiority. But as this Grecian is so presumptuous, which of his actions will he pretend to put in competition with mine? His Persian trophies perhaps, as if he knew not how many I won from Pompey. And who was the most experienced general, Pompey or Darius? Which of them commanded the bravest troops? Instead of the refuse of mankind, Pompey had in his army more warlike nations than were ever subject to Darius; of Europeans, those who had often routed the hostile Asiatics, and of them the most valiant; Italians, Illyrians, and Gauls. Having mentioned the Gauls, can the Getic exploits of ALEXANDER be compared with my conquest of Gaul? He passed the Danube once; I twice passed the Rhine; and of my German victories no one can dispute the glory. I fought with Ariovistus *.

"I was the first Roman who dared to cross the German ocean †. Though this was a wonder-

* The antithesis is this: "Alexander met with no opposition in his Getic expedition, and therefore he marched with impunity. But I was resisted by Ariovistus."
PETAU.

† In the original, τῆς ἔξω θαλασσης, "the outward sea." The inner was the Mediterranean.

"ful

"ful atchievement, however it may be admired,
"more glorious was my intrepidity in being the
"first who leaped on shore *. Of the Helvetic
"and Iberian nations I say nothing; nor have I
"mentioned my actions in Gaul, where I took
"above three hundred towns †, and defeated two
"millions of men. Great as these actions were,
"that which followed was greater and more il-
"lustrious. Being obliged to wage war with my
"fellow-citizens, I vanquished the unconquered
"and invincible Romans. If we should be judged
"by the number of our battles, I fought thrice
"as many as are ascribed to ALEXANDER by his
"greatest panegyrists; if by the number of towns
"taken, not in Asia only, but also in Europe, I
"reduced more. ALEXANDER saw and traversed
"Ægypt; I, while I feasted there, subdued it.
"Will you also compare the clemency of each of
"us, when victorious? I pardoned my enemies,

* He alludes here to the descent which Cæsar made on Britain. But the memory of Julian deceives him. He attributes to Cæsar what Cæsar himself says (*l.* v. *de bello Gallico*) of the eagle-bearer of the tenth legion. "He
" who bore the eagle of the tenth legion, after beseeching
" the Gods, that the event might be prosperous to the
" legion, said, 'Leap ashore, soldiers, unless you would
' betray the eagle to the enemy.' " Saying this, with a
" loud voice, he threw himself out of the ship, and ad-
" vanced with the eagle towards the enemy, &c." It was Alexander, who, after passing the Hellespont, first leaped ashore completely armed. Such a proceeding is more suitable to the impetuous valour of Alexander than to the phlegmatic and sedate courage of Cæsar. LA BLETERIE.
† See Plutarch.

" and

" and received from them such a return as Nemesis
has revenged. He never spared his enemies, nor
even his friends. In particular, as you dispute
the pre-eminence, and will not immediately yield
to me, like the rest, you compel me to mention
your cruel behaviour to the Thebans *. On
the contrary, how great was my humanity to
the Helvetii! The cities of the former were
burnt by you; the cities of the latter, burnt by
their own inhabitants, were rebuilt by me †.
Which, in short, was most illustrious; your
defeating ten thousand Greeks, or my repulsing
the attacks of a hundred and fifty thousand Romans? Much more could I add, both of ALEX-
ANDER and myself; but as I never had leisure
to study the art of oratory ‡, you must excuse
me, and, forming a just and impartial judgement both from what I have said, and what I
have omitted, will, I doubt not, give me the
superiority."

* When Alexander took Thebes by storm, the inhabitants were slain and destroyed for several hours without
regard to sex or age; and the city was afterwards razed,
the house of Pindar only excepted.

† The Helvetii having abandoned their country, and
burnt their towns, as they were preparing to enter Gaul,
were defeated by Cæsar, sent back to their country, and
ordered to re-build their houses.

‡ In the original, το λεγειν εξεμελιτησα, or εξεμιλησα. Perhaps he does not mean to say, that Cæsar had no excellence in speaking; for he was reckoned among the
orators of his time; witness Cicero, in his Brutus; but
that he was not used to speak without premeditation.

CANTOCLARUS.

CÆSAR

THE CÆSARS.

Cæsar thus concluded, but seeming desirous of saying still more; Alexander, who before had with difficulty restrained himself, could refrain no longer, but, with much anxiety and emotion, thus began:

"How long, O Jupiter and ye Gods, shall I
" silently bear the insolence of this boaster *! He
" sets no bounds, you see, to his praise of himself,
" or to his abuse of me. Much better would it
" have become him to have abstained equally from
" both, as both are alike intolerable, but chiefly
" that of depreciating my conduct, which he made
" the example of his own. Such is his assurance,
" that he has dared to ridicule his own model.
" You should have recollected, Cæsar, the tears
" which you shed on hearing of the memorials
" that were raised in honour of my deeds †. But
" you afterwards owed your elevation to Pompey,
" who, though he was really insignificant ‡, was
" idolised by his countrymen. As to his African

---

* This is not unlike the beginning of Cicero's Oration against Catiline, *Quousque tandem abutêre, Catilina, patientiâ nostrâ?*

† At Gades, observing in the temple of Hercules a statue of Alexander the Great, he sighed, and, as if ashamed of his own supineness in having done nothing memorable at an age when Alexander had conquered the world, he importunately urged to be recalled to Rome, that he might be ready on the spot to embrace any occasion that might offer for more important undertakings. *Sueton. Jul. Cæsar. c. 7.* See also Plutarch.

‡ It is plain that Julian had read the Epistles of Cicero to Atticus.   La Bleterie.

" triumph,

"triumph *, no great exploit, his fame was owing
"to the weakness and inactivity of the consuls †.
"The servile war ‡ was not waged with men, but
"with the most abandoned slaves, and it was con-
"ducted by Crassus and Lucius §, though Pompey
"had the name and the reputation. Armenia and
"the neighbouring provinces were conquered by
"Lucullus; yet for these also Pompey triumphed.
"He was then flattered by his fellow-citizens,
"and named the Great. But than whom of his
"predecessors was he greater? Which of his
"actions is comparable to those of Marius, or of
"the two Scipios? or of Camillus, who was almost
"as much the founder of Rome as this Quirinus,
"having rebuilt his city when it was almost falling?
"For they did not arrogate to themselves the
"works of others, as is usual in buildings founded
"and finished at the public expence, where the
"magistrate, who has only plaistered the walls,
"on completing the edifice, inscribes the foun-
"dation-stone. But these heroes, as public ar-
"tificers and architects, have justly immortalised
"their own names. It is no wonder therefore,
"that you vanquished Pompey, scratching his

---

* Pompey, at the age of twenty-nine, when he was only a knight, was sent into Africa to encounter the party of Marius.   La Bleterie.

† M. Tullius Decula and Cn. Cornelius Dolabella.

‡ The war of Spartacus.

§ Lucius Gellius. See Plutarch's Life of Crassus, and Appian, *Bell. Civil.* I.

"head,

" head *, and more resembling a fox than a lion.
" When he was deserted by Fortune, who had
" long favoured him, you easily conquered him
" single. But that your success was owing to no
" superior abilities is evident; for being in want
" of provisions (which, you know, is no small fault
" of a general †), you fought, and were defeated ‡.
" And if Pompey, by his imprudence, or folly, or
" because he could not govern his army, when he
" should have protracted the war, gave battle §,
" and did not pursue his victory, his failure was
" the consequence of his own misconduct, not of
" your military skill. The Persians, on the con-
" trary, though in every respect well prepared and
" amply provided, submitted to my dominion.
" And as it becomes a good man and a wise

* In the original, δακτυλω κνωμενω, which the French translator has paraphrased, " who, for fear of disarranging " his hair, did not venture to touch his head but with his " finger's end." Yet Ammianus (xvii. 11.) mentioning two ludicrous faults that the envious imputed to Pompey, says that this was one, *quod genuino quodam more caput uno digito scalpebat*; " that he scratched his head, in a par- " ticular manner, with one of his fingers."

† Julian himself committed the same fault in his Persian expedition.

‡ At the battle of Dyrrhacium.

§ This interpretation agrees better with the sense, and with history, than the proper signification of the Greek words, (which is, " when he should have declined to give " battle."] For certain it is, from Appian, Plutarch, and other writers, that Pompey did not act like a prudent ge- neral in offering battle to Cæsar at Pharsalia, when Cæsar was in such a situation, that he must easily have been re- duced by his want of necessaries.   CANTOCLARUS.

" prince

" prince to act not only with moderation, but with
" juftice, I took arms to revenge the Greeks on
" the Perfians, and to free Greece from civil war.
" Nor was it ever my intention to ravage Greece,
" but thofe only, who would have prevented my
" march againft Perfia, I chaftifed. You, after
" fubduing the Gauls and Germans, turned your
" arms againft your own country. What can be
" worfe, what more infamous?

" You have mentioned, with a fneer, ' my de-
' feating ten thoufand Greeks.' " That you your-
" felves fprung from the Greeks, and that the
" Greeks inhabited the greateft part of Italy, I
" well know; but on this I will not infift. With
" a fmall nation of them, the Ætolians, your
" neighbours, you thought it of great confequence
" to make an alliance; but after they had fought
" for you, why did you reduce them, and that
" not eafily, to fubjection? If then, in the old age,
" as it has been called, of Greece, you could
" fcarce reduce, not the whole, but one fmall
" nation, which was fcarce known when Greece
" was in her vigour, what would have been the
" event, if you had been obliged to contend with
" the Greeks when flourifhing and united? How
" much you were alarmed by the invafion of
" Pyrrhus you need not be reminded. As you
" think the conqueft of Perfia fuch a trifle, and
" depreciate an enterprife fo glorious, tell me
" why, after a war of above two thoufand years,
" you have never fubdued a fmall province be-
" yond

" yond the Tigris *, subject to the Parthians?
" Shall I inform you? The darts of the Persians
" prevented you. Antony, who served under
", your command, can give you an account of
" them †. But in less than ten years I conquered
" both Persia and India. After this, do you dare
" to contend with me, who, trained to war from
" my childhood, performed such deeds, that the
" remembrance of them, though they have not
" been sufficiently celebrated by historians, will
" live for ever, like those of the invincible Her-
" cules, of whom I was the follower and imitator?
" I rivalled, in short, my ancestor Achilles, and,
" admiring Hercules, I trod in his steps as nearly
" as a mortal can follow a God. Thus much, O
" ye Gods, it was necessary for me to say in my
" own defence against an opponent, whom per-
" haps it might have been better to have silently
" despised. If I was guilty of any cruelties, the

* Meaning Babylonia, where the Romans never made any solid conquest. It was the northern part of Mesopotamia. LA BLETERIE.

† Antony, having entered Media, thought himself happy to escape with the remains of his army, after losing twenty thousand men, and all his baggage. Julian might have quoted many other Roman generals and Emperors [Crassus in particular], who were worse treated even than Antony, in their expeditions against the Parthians, or Persians. But he did not foresee that he himself would soon add to the number of those unfortunate heroes. *Ibid.*

It is impossible to read the interesting narrative of Plutarch (tom. v. p. 102—116.) without perceiving that Mark Antony and Julian were pursued by the same enemies, and involved in the same distress. GIBBON.

" innocent

"innocent were not the objects, but such as had "frequently and notoriously offended, and had "made no proper use of their opportunities. "And my offences even against them were fol- "lowed by Repentance*, a very wise Goddess, "and the preserver of those who have erred. As "for my chastising the ambitious, who always "hated and had often injured me, in that I "thought myself excusable."

This military harangue being concluded, the attendant of Neptune gave the hour-glass to OCTAVIANUS, measuring to him a very small quantity of water, and at the same time, reminding him of his insolence to that Deity †. On which having reflected with his usual sagacity, omitting to say any thing of others, he thus began:

"Instead of depreciating the actions of others, "O Jupiter and ye Gods, I will confine my whole "speech to what concerns myself. In my youth

---

* Μεταμέλεια. This Goddess, thus deified by Julian, seems rather taken from the Christian scriptures, than the Heathen mythology. The French translator styles her *Métanée*, from Μετάνοια, and "a celebrated retreat for pe- "nitents, known in Ecclesiastical history by the name of "*la Métanée.*"

† In the war which Octavius waged against Sextus Pompey, many reproach him as well for some of his expressions, as for his conduct, having said, when his fleet was lost in a storm, that "he would gain the victory even "in spite of Neptune." And accordingly, when the Circensian games were next performed, he excluded the image of that God from the solemnity. *Suet. Aug. c.* XVI.

Julian himself, in like manner, swore afterwards, in a passion, that he would never sacrifice again to Mars. See *Ammianus*, XXIV. 6.

"I had

THE CÆSARS.

"I had the government of my native city, like
"this illustrious ALEXANDER. The German wars,
"like my father CÆSAR, I happily concluded.
"Involved in civil dissensions, I subdued Ægypt
"at Actium in a sea-fight. I defeated Brutus and
"Cassius at Philippi, and I made the son of Pom-
"pey contribute to my glory. Such, however,
"was my attachment to philosophy, that, instead
"of being disgusted at the freedom assumed by
"Athenodorus *, I was pleased with it, and re-
"vered him as a preceptor, or rather as a parent.
"Areus † also was my friend and confident. And,
"upon the whole, I was never guilty of the least

---

* A very bold action is related of this philosopher: Augustus, whose behaviour was never very guarded, sometimes made some private assignations which might have
been fatal to him. One day, when a Roman lady was to
go to the palace incognito, Athenodorus got into a close
chair, and ordered himself to be carried to the apartment
of the Emperor. Then, stepping out, with a sword in
his hand, " See," said he, " to what you expose yourself !
" Are you not afraid that some republican, or an enraged
" husband, should take such an opportunity of putting
" you to death ?" Augustus thanked the philosopher for
his lesson, and promised to reform. He took greater precautions, no doubt, for the future, but his reformation
went no farther. Livia, it is well known, to maintain her
ascendant over him, was obliged to connive at his infidelities.
                                     LA BLETERIE.

† Julian in his Epistles mentions more than once the
philosopher Areus, and the esteem which Augustus had
for him. Certainly if by philosophy are meant the philosophers, he cannot but be well satisfied with Augustus.
Such equivocal expressions are too common.   *Ibid.*

Areus is mentioned in the Epistle to Themistius, (see p.
25. and note *) and in Epistle LI.

VOL. I.   O   " offence

"offence against philosophy. As Rome, I saw, had
"been frequently reduced to the last extremity by
"intestine divisions, I so re-established her affairs,
"as to render them, by your assistance, O ye
"Gods, firm and adamantine. Without indulg-
"ing an insatiable ambition, I studiously endeav-
"oured to enlarge her dominions; but I concurred
"with nature in fixing the rivers Danube and
"Euphrates as their boundaries. After having sub-
"dued the Scythians and Thracians, I did not
"employ the long reign with which you indulged
"me in meditating war after war, but devoted my
"leisure to the correction of the evils which war
"had occasioned, and to legislation; in which, I
"apprehend, I did not consult the public wel-
"fare less than my predecessors; nay, if I must
"boldly speak the truth, I consulted it more than
"any who have governed such an empire. For
"some who have commanded armies, when they
"might at length have rested in peace, have made
"one war the pretence for another, as the litigious
"contrive law-suits. Others, when forced into a
"war, have been immersed in pleasure *, and have
"preferred the most infamous pursuits, not only
"to their glory, but even to their lives. Well
"weighing all these things, I do not think myself
"entitled to the lowest place. But it becomes
"me to acquiesce in whatever you, O ye Gods,
"may please to determine."

* Alluding to Antony.

TRAJAN was appointed to harangue next. Though he had a talent for speaking *, such was his indolence, that he usually employed Sura to compose his orations. Bawling, rather than speaking, he displayed to the Gods his Getic and Parthian trophies. He then lamented his old age, as if that had prevented him from extending his Parthian conquests. 'You fool,' said Silenus, 'you
'reigned twenty years, and this ALEXANDER only
'twelve. Why, then, do you not condemn your
'own indolence, instead of throwing the blame on
'want of time?' Provoked at this taunt, for he was not deficient in eloquence, though it was often blunted by intemperance, TRAJAN added,

" O Jupiter, and ye Gods, when I assumed the
" reins of government, I found the empire in a
" torpid and divided state, occasioned partly by

---

* Trajan, it is said, had written the history of his wars with the Dacians. There is a short Greek epigram by him in the Anthologia. He was not learned; but he esteemed and favoured men of letters. When he triumphed over the Dacians, he had in his car the sophist Dion, Chrysostom, and, during the procession, he frequently turned to speak to him. L. Licinius Sura was the confident of Trajan, who loaded him with riches, and raised him thrice to the consulship. The enemies of Sura accused him of a design against the life of the Emperor. Trajan, by way of answer, went to sup with Sura, had his eyes examined by the surgeon, and was shaved by the barber, of Sura, and supped with great gaiety. On the next day he said to the accusers, " Confess that, if Sura wanted to dis-
" patch me, he yesterday missed a fine opportunity." After the death of Sura, Trajan borrowed the pen of Hadrian.
LA BLETERIE.

" the tyranny which had long prevailed at home,
" and partly by the infults of the Getes abroad *.
" I did not hefitate, however, fingly to attack the
" nations beyond the Danube. That of the Getes
" I fubdued and extirpated; of all the moft war-
" like, not only by their bodily ftrength, but by
" the courage with which they are infpired by the
" doctrine of their renowned Zamolxis †. For the
" firm

---

* By the Getes may be underftood the Dacians. Decebalus, king of the Dacians, had obliged Domitian to purchafe a peace, of which he endeavoured to cover the difgrace by a magnificent triumph. " The poets of the " time," fays M. de Tillemont, " equalled his pretended " victory to thofe of Alexander and Cæfar." For that they were paid, or expected to be paid; but the Romans did not give them credit. Trajan, who was not difpofed to be tributary to the Barbarians, availing himfelf of the firft infraction which Decebalus made, or feemed to make, of the treaty, marched againft the Dacians. They defended themfelves with much courage, and even conduct. But at length Decebalus, being reduced to the laft extremities, deftroyed himfelf, and Dacia was made a province.   LA BLETERIE.

† Zamolxis was the lawgiver of the Getes. [See p. 152.] Some Greeks pretend that he had been the flave of Pythagoras; but Herodotus thinks Zamolxis much more ancient. The opinion of the Getes as to the immortality of the foul had an affinity to the metempfychofis : They faid that the dead went to find Zamolxis, and every five years they fent an exprefs to reprefent to him the exigencies of the nation. See Herod. *l*. IV. 49.

It muft not be fuppofed, that, before Zamolxis, thofe people believed that the foul perifhed with the body. Zamolxis only publifhed his own private ideas concerning the ftate of feparate fouls. No nation is or ever was perfuaded that all ends with death. No nation has received from its lawgivers the belief of another life; the lawgivers have
                      every

"firm perfuafion that they fhall not perifh, but
"only change their place of abode, makes them
"always prepared as for a journey. This enter-
"prife I completed in lefs than five years. Of
"all the Emperors who preceded me * not one
"was fo mild to his fubjects, nor can that be
"contefted with me even with this Cæsar, be-
"fore unrivalled in clemency, nor by any other.
"The Parthians, till they infulted me, I thought it
"unjuft to attack; but after they had infulted me,
"neither my age, nor the laws which allowed me
"to quit the fervice †, prevented my invading

every where found it. Some have not mentioned this doctrine, becaufe it was fufficiently eftablifhed. Others have mentioned it, not in order to prove it, which was by no means neceffary, but to particularife it, and to dif-play its confequences. The perfuafion of the immor-tality of the foul, as well as that of the exiftence of God, is the tenet of mankind, and the faith of nature. The contrary error is either the frenzy of a philofopher who chooses to be fingular, or the interefted wifh of a li-bertine.   La Bleterie.

* In the original, Παντων των προ εμε γεγονοτων αυτοκρατορων ωφθην τοις υπηκοοις πραοτατος, "Of all the Emperors who pre-"ceded me I was the mildeft to my fubjects." This paf-fage, by which Trajan confounds himfelf with his prede-ceffors, is fimilar to that of Milton (noticed by Addifon in the Spectator, N° 285.) in which Adam and Eve are ranked among their pofterity.

Adam, the goodlieft man of men fince born
His fons, the faireft of her daughters Eve.

† Regularly, every Roman, after twenty years fervice, was exempted from bearing arms. Trajan had ferved from his earlieft youth. He was fifty-five years old, at leaft, perhaps fifty-feven, when he made war with Cofroes, king of Parthia.   La Bleterie.

O 3   "them.

" them. Thus circumstanced, am not I, who was
" eminently mild to my subjects and formidable
" to my enemies, and who revered your divine
" daughter, Philosophy, justly entitled to superior
" honours, and even to the first rank?"

TRAJAN having concluded, it was allowed that he excelled all in clemency, a virtue particularly pleasing to the Gods.

MARCUS AURELIUS then beginning to speak, Silenus said, in a low voice, to Bacchus, ' Let us
' hear which of his wonderful paradoxes and
' aphorisms this Stoic will produce.' But he, fixing his eyes on Jupiter and the other Gods, thus addressed them:

" I have no occasion, O Jupiter and ye Gods,
" to harangue or dispute. If you were ignorant
" of my actions, it would be proper for me to ac-
" quaint you with them; but as you are privy to
" them, and nothing is concealed from you, you
" will honour me as I deserve."

Thus MARCUS, as in every thing else, seemed worthy of admiration for his extraordinary prudence in knowing when to speak, and when to be silent *.

---

* This is an imitation of a verse of Æschylus, quoted by Aulus Gellius. In this particular, the pretended copy of Marcus Aurelius did not resemble his original. Julian spoke much and often. *Linguæ fusioris et admodùm rarò silentii,* says Ammianus.   LA BLETERIE.

THE CÆSARS.

CONSTANTINE * was then summoned to speak. He entered the lists with confidence; but when he reflected on the actions of his competitors, his own seemed trivial and inconsiderable. He defeated, it is true, two tyrants †; one of them unwarlike and pusil-

---

* Every impartial reader must perceive and condemn the partiality of Julian against his uncle and the Christian religion. On this occasion the interpreters are compelled, by a more sacred interest, to renounce their allegiance, and desert the cause of their author. GIBBON.

The reflections, or sarcasms, on the other candidates are confined to Silenus, or their antagonists. On this occasion Julian is betrayed by his prejudice into a breach of the unity of character before observed, by taking, or rather making Mercury, his informant, take a decided part against Constantine.

† Julian uses his utmost endeavours to depreciate the exploits of his uncle. Constantine was a great general; and perhaps his most substantial fault is his having been too warlike. If he had good fortune, he deserved it; and the Pagans themselves acknowledged that his talents were equal to his good fortune. *Innumeræ in eo animi corporisque virtutes claruerunt*, says Eutropius. *Militaris gloriæ appetentissimus, fortunâ in bellis prosperâ fuit; verùm ita ut non superaret industriam.* I know that Maxentius was a kind of Sardanapalus, who, remaining at Rome, while his collegue made war, said, that he alone was Emperor, and that the others were his lieutenants; that he considered the going from his palace to the gardens of Sallust as a long journey, &c. But he had 200,000 troops, a great deal of money, and good officers. "To dethrone him, Constantine," says a contemporary author, " with an army less numerous " than that of Alexander when he marched against Darius," that is, with no more than 40,000 men, " must have forced " the pass of Succi, and have gained the battles of Turin, " Brescia, Verona, and Rome, of which the three first, " at least, must have been very obstinate and bloody."

With regard to Licinius, he was not above fifty years old when he was defeated at the battle of Cibal, and about

sixty

pusillanimous, the other unfortunate and advanced in years, and both of them odious to Gods and men. As for his exploits against the Barbarians, they were ridiculous. For he, in a manner, paid them tribute, to indulge his love of pleasure. He stood therefore at a distance from the Gods, near the entrance of the moon, of whom he was enamoured *, and, gazing only on her, was regardless of the victory.

How-

---

sixty when he lost the battles of Adrianople and Chrysopolis, which rendered Constantine master of the empire. Licinius, with all his vices, was brave and skilful in the conduct of war. He made his troops observe the ancient discipline with extreme severity. Whatever Julian may say of him, his age had not at all abated his courage, any more than the vigour of his constitution. He was always prosperous when he had not Constantine to encounter. Add, that the reproach with which some writers have branded Constantine of breaking his word with Licinius, by putting him to death after having promised him life, seems removed by the silence of Julian. As to the victories which he gained over the Barbarians, that is, over the Franks, the Germans, the Sarmatians, and the Goths, Julian is the only one who despises those " exploits." It is well known that Constantine, far from " paying tribute" to the Barbarians, freed the Romans from that which they paid to the Goths under the honourable name of pension. But as he took into the service of the empire 40,000 men of that nation, the pay which he gave them is probably that which Julian calls " tribute." La Bleterie.

* Why does Julian make Constantine " enamoured of " the moon?" This is an ænigma which I have endeavoured to solve. Am I so fortunate as to have at last succeeded? The reader shall determine. Antiquaries agree, that, from the earliest times, the crescent was the distinction, or, as we should now express it, the arms of Byzantium, as it still continues to be of Constantinople. Thus,

when

"However, as it was necessary for him to speak,
"In these particulars," said he, " I am superior
" to my opponents; to the Macedonian, in having
" fought against the Romans, Germans, and Scy-
" thians, instead of Asiatic Barbarians; to Cæsar
" and Octavianus, in not having vanquished,
" like them, good and virtuous citizens, but the
" most cruel and wicked tyrants. To Trajan
" also, for my strenuous exertions against tyrants,
" I deserve no less to be preferred. To recover
" the province * which he conquered seems to me
" equally

when Julian reproaches his uncle with being enamoured of the moon, and attending solely to her, instead of thinking of the victory, the author, without detriment to the other ideas to which this reproach may give rise, principally means, that Constantine, wholly devoted to the care of founding and embellishing his new city, had neglected the affairs of state, and suffered his laurels to wither. This is exactly what Zosimus, the copyer of Eunapius and the echo of Julian, imputes to him, by saying, that " Con-
" stantine, after the foundation of Constantinople, had no
" success in war; διηλιϛε πολιμον ηδενα καλορθωρκως, and that
" he suffered the Barbarians to insult him in his new ca-
" pital." La Bleterie.

The above ingenious solution of a difficulty, before insuperable, will, I doubt not, be approved by every reader, and adopted by all future commentators on the Cæsars.

* Meaning Dacia, which Trajan had reduced to a province. Aurelian having abandoned it, it was usurped by the Goths. There can be no doubt of Constantine having carried his arms beyond the Danube. The two Victors enumerate, among his great actions, his having made a bridge over that river. But it is certain, that he did not conquer the country of the Dacians. I am convinced that Julian, in order to render him ridiculous, represents him as affecting the importance of a conqueror on account

of

"equally meritorious: perhaps to regain is more laudable than to gain. As to this MARCUS, he, by saying nothing for himself, yields us all the precedency."

'But, CONSTANTINE,' said Silenus, 'why do you not mention, among your great works, the gardens of Adonis *?' "What mean you," replied CONSTANTINE, "by the gardens of Adonis †?"

. of some advantages which he had gained over the Goths settled in Dacia; and perhaps for some forts which he had erected on the left of the Danube. With the same view, Julian makes him draw, from the silence of Marcus Aurelius, the most absurd, and, I may venture to say, the most foolish conclusion that can be imagined.

LA BLETERIE.

* Thus Suidas: "The gardens of Adonis consisted of lettuce and fennel, which were sown in pots. It is used as a proverb of things immature, or, when in season, slight, and not rooted, not lasting, but adhering only to the surface." See Athen. l. iv. c. 8. and Arrian's Epictetus. CANTOCLARUS.

Thus Shakspeare says,
Thy promises are like Adonis' gardens,
That one day bloom'd, and fruitful were the next.
1 Hen. IV. Act. I. Sc. II.
And Mr. Bramstone, in his Man of Taste. (Dodsley's Poems, Vol. I.) says,
Pots o'er the door I'll place, like cits balconies,
Which Bentley calls the gardens of Adonis;
and refers to Bentley's Milton, b. IX. ver. 439.

————— those gardens feign'd
Or of reviv'd Adonis.

He might have referred to much more ancient writers than Milton or his commentator, whom one would not have expected to have been ridiculed for this expression by a scholar.

† Could Constantine, though a Christian, be ignorant of the rites of a religion which he had long practised? If I mistake not, he is here meant to be accused on the most common subjects. LA BLETERIE.

'Pots,'

'Pots,' answered Silenus, ' filled with earth, in which
' women sow herbs in honour of that lover * of
' Venus. They flourish for a short time, but soon
' fade.' At this Constantine blushed, knowing
it to be intended as a sarcasm on his own actions.

Silence being proclaimed, it was expected that the Gods would immediately have determined the pre-eminence by their votes. But they thought it proper first to examine the intentions of the candidates, and not merely to collect them from their actions, in which Fortune had the greatest share; and that Goddess, being present, loudly reproached them all, Octavianus alone excepted, who, she said, had always been grateful to her. Of this the Gods apprised Mercury, and commanded him to begin with asking Alexander " what he " thought the highest excellence, and what " was his principal view in all the great actions " and labours of his life?" He replied, ' Universal ' conquest.' " And in this," said Mercury, " did " you think you succeeded?" ' Certainly,' answered Alexander. Silenus added, with a sneering laugh, " You forget that you were often con- " quered by my daughters," meaning vines; and ridiculing Alexander for his intemperance. Alexander, well versed in the Peripatetic aphorisms, replied, ' Things inanimate cannot conquer. ' There can be no contention with them, but only ' with men or animals.' At this, Silenus ironically

* Ἀνὴρ (" husband") in the original.

expressing

expressing his admiration, exclaimed, "Alas! alas! "how great are the subterfuges of logicians! But "in what class will you rank yourself, among "things inanimate, or among the animate and "living?" ALEXANDER, with some displeasure, replied, ' Be less severe; such was my mag- ' nimity, that I was convinced that I should be, ' nay that I was, a God.' " You allow then," said Silenus, " that you were often conquered by " yourself, when anger, grief, or some other passion " debased and debilitated your mind." ' But,' answered ALEXANDER, ' for any one to conquer ' himself, and to be conquered by himself, are sy- ' nonymous. I am talking of my victories over ' others.' " Fie upon your logic!" returned Si- lenus; " how it detects my sophistry! But when " you were wounded in India *, and Peucestes lay " near you, and you, almost breathless, were car- " ried out of the city, were you conquered by him " who wounded you, or did you conquer him?" ' I not only conquered him,' replied ALEXANDER, ' but I also destroyed the city.' " Not you, indeed, " you Immortal," said Silenus; " you lay like Homer's

---

* Alexander, when he was besieging the capital of the Oxydracæ, according to Quintus Curtius, but, as others say, of the Mallians, was so rash as to leap alone into the city, where he was dangerously wounded with an arrow by an Indian, who, believing him dead, then ad- vanced to strip him. Alexander, however, recovering, killed him with his dagger, and was soon after rescued by his soldiers, and carried off to his tent almost dead.

LA BLETERIE.

" Hector,

"Hector*, languid, and almost expiring; others
"fought and conquered." 'True, answered
ALEXANDER, 'but under my command.' "How
"could they obey you," said Silenus, "who were
"carried out almost dead?"

He then sung these verses of Euripides †:
"Unjust the custom of the Greeks; the troops
"The battle gain, their leaders gain the glory."

'Say no more, my dear father,' said Bacchus,
'left he should treat you as he treated Clitus.'
At this ALEXANDER blushed, wept, and was
silent.

This discourse ended, Mercury thus interrogated
CÆSAR: "What, CÆSAR, was the principal view
"of your life?" 'To excell my contemporaries,'
he replied, 'and neither to be, nor to be thought,
'second to any." "This," said Mercury, "is
"not quite clear. In what did you particularly
"wish to excell, in wisdom or eloquence, in mili-
"tary skill, or political abilities?" 'In every
'thing,' answered CÆSAR. 'I was desirous of be-
'ing the first of men; but, as that was impossible,
'I endeavoured to be the most powerful of my
'fellow-citizens.' "And had you much power
"among them?" said Silenus. 'Certainly,' re-

---

* When he was wounded by Ajax. Il. XIV. 432. and XV. 246.

† In his Andromache. Clitus is said to have repeated these verses at a banquet of Alexander, in order to depreciate his exploits, by which he provoked Alexander to kill him, as Quintus Curtius informs us, in his eighth book, and Plutarch, in his Life of Alexander.   BARNES.

plied Cæsar, for I became their governor." "That," returned Silenus, "you might be; but you could never gain their love, though, for that purpose, you diffembled much humanity, acting a part like a player, and meanly flattering all men." 'What!' faid Cæsar; 'was I not loved by the people who perfecuted Brutus and Caffius?' "That," replied Silenus, "was not becaufe they had murdered you; for on that account the people made them confuls*; but for the fake of your money, as foon as they had heard your will, and found that no fmall reward was given to thofe who fhould be their enemies."

This difcourfe alfo being concluded, Mercury thus accofted Octavianus: 'Will you alfo tell us what was your principal view?' He replied, "To reign well." "What means that?" faid

---

* This is contrary to hiftory. Brutus and Caffius were not nominated to the confulfhip by the people. The former was to have filled that place four years after, but that was an arrangement made by Cæfar. Though, inftead of ὕπατος, "confuls," we fhould read ἀνθύπατος, "pro-confuls," Julian would ftill be miftaken. It was not the people, but the fenate, that invefted Brutus and Caffius with pro-confular power in the provinces of which thofe two republicans had taken poffeffion. La Bleterie.

M. de la Bleterie has altered this paffage, in his tranflation, to "they thought them worthy of the confulfhip for having killed you." I cannot allow myfelf fuch a liberty, remembering the rule of Rofcommon,

Your author always will the beft advife,
Fall when he falls ———

A tranflator may correct his author in the notes, but in the text he fhould let him fpeak his own language.

Silenus,

Silenus. "Explain, AUGUSTUS, as this is pretended even by the wicked. Even Dionyſius * thought that he reigned well; and ſo did the ſtill more abandoned Agathocles *." 'You know then,' replied OCTAVIANUS, ' ye Gods, that when I 'parted with my grandſon †, I prayed you to 'give him the courage of CÆSAR, the conduct of 'Pompey, and my good fortune.' "Many ſtatues of Gods," ſaid Silenus, " moſt curiouſly carved, of Gods of great merit, have been ſent us by this ſtatuary." 'Why,' anſwered OCTAVIANUS, 'do you give me that ridiculous appellation?' "As Nymphs are carved," he replied, " have not you formed Gods, one of whom, and the principal, is this CÆSAR?" OCTAVIANUS bluſhed ‡, and ſaid no more.

Mercury then, addreſſing himſelf to TRAJAN, asked, ' what end his actions had in view?' " The fame," he replied, " as thoſe of ALEXANDER, but with more moderation." 'So you were conquered,' ſaid Silenus, ' by more ignoble paſ-ſions. He was frequently ſubdued by anger, you by the vileſt and moſt diſgraceful plea-

---

* Tyrants of Syracuſe well known.

† Auguſtus wiſhed this to C. Cæſar, the eldeſt ſon of Agrippa and Julia, when he ſent him to wage war in the eaſt. LA BLETERIE.

‡ Auguſtus had reaſon to bluſh at thoſe extravagant apotheoſes; and Julian was in the right to ridicule them. But ſhould he not have reflected that many of the Gods whom he worſhipped were no more than images a little older? *Magis è longinquo reverentia.* *Ibid.*

' ſures.

'sures [*], "Plague on you!" said Bacchus. "Your
"sarcasms prevent their speaking for themselves.
"A truce with your jokes, and consider now what
"you can find reprehensible in MARCUS; for he
"seems to me, in the sense of Simonides [†], per-
"fect and faultless [‡]." Then Mercury, turning
towards MARCUS, said, 'And what, O sage, did
'you think the greatest happiness?' With a low
voice, and with great diffidence, he replied, "To
"imitate the Gods." This answer was immediately deemed highly noble and praise-worthy.
Nor would Mercury question him any farther,
convinced that MARCUS would always answer with
equal propriety. In this opinion all the other
Gods concurred. Silenus only exclaimed, 'By
'Bacchus, I will not spare this sophist [§]. Why
'did you formerly eat bread and drink wine, and
'not nectar and ambrosia, like us?' "Not in
"order to imitate the Gods," replied he, "but
"to nourish my body, from a persuasion, whether
"true or false, that your bodies also require

[*] Yet Pliny the younger makes an admirable elogium on the chastity of Trajan. Rely on panegyrists. LA BLETERIE.

[†] A native of Ceos, one of the Cyclades, distinguished by his elegiac verses. His answer to Hiero's question, "What is God?" is well known.

[‡] In the original, τιτράγωνος, "four-cornered," or "square." This expression occurs in one of the fragments of this poet still preserved.

[§] No one less deserves the name of sophist than Marcus Aurelius. "A great proof of the regard of the Gods for "me," says he, ... "is that having a very great love "for philosophy, I have never fallen into the hands of any "sophist; that I have not amused myself with reading "their books, or unravelling their vain subtleties, &c."
Meditations of Marcus Antoninus. LA BLETERIE.

being

" being nourished by the fumes of sacrifices *. I
" did not, however, think that you were to be imi-
" tated in this, but in your minds." Silenus, as
much stunned at this as if he had been struck by a
skilful boxer, replied, ' This is somewhat plau-
' sible †; but tell me now, in what did you for-
' merly think, that the imitation of the Gods con-
' sisted?' Marcus answered, " In having as few
" wants, and doing as much good, as possible."
' What! had you no wants?' said Silenus. " As
" to myself," replied Marcus, " I had none; but
" my body perhaps had a few." Marcus seeming in this also to have answered wisely, Silenus at
last insisted on what he thought improper and
unjust in the conduct of Marcus towards his
wife and son, his enrolling her among the God-
desses, and entrusting the empire to him. ' In
' this also,' said Marcus, ' I imitated the Gods.
' For I practised that maxim of Homer,

* Julian adopts this gross conception by ascribing it to his favourite Marcus Antoninus. The Stoics and Platonists hesitated between the analogy of bodies and the purity of spirits; yet the gravest philosophers inclined to the whimsical fancy of Aristophanes and Julian, that an un- believing age might starve the immortal Gods. Gibbon.

† The Gods of Julian are not jealous Gods. On the con- trary, they are of a good composition, according to the ar- rogant philosophy of the Stoics, who were so chimerical as to imagine, that man has no need of any inward support, and that he may become like to God without any other strength than that of nature. " In which man," said they, " has " the advantage of Jupiter himself. Jupiter is good by " nature, but the wise man is good by his own choice."
La Bleterie.

Vol. I.   P   ' The

'The wife whom choice and passion both approve,
'Sure every wife and worthy man will love *.
'And as to my son, I am justified in my behaviour
'by that of Jupiter himself. "I should long ago,"
'said he to Mars, "have transfixed thee with a
"thunder-bolt, if I had not loved thee, because thou
"art my son †." 'Besides, I never imagined that
'COMMODUS would have proved so profligate. And
'though his youth, assailed on all sides by strong
'temptations, was hurried away by the worst, I
'entrusted the government to one not yet cor-
'rupted. Afterwards, indeed, he became wicked.
'My tenderness therefore to my wife was copied
'from the example of the divine Achilles ‡, and
'that

* Pope, 450. This is said by Achilles, on the subject of Briseis, whom he considers as his wife, and whom Agamemnon had taken from him. Il. IX. 343. LA BLETERIE.

Julian, after Homer, styles Briseis "the wife" (γαμῶης) of Achilles, as he had before styled Adonis "the husband" (ἀνηρ) of Venus. One would think he had read Thelyphthora.

† This is the substance of what Jupiter says to Mars. Il. V. 896, &c.

‡ It is impossible fully to justify the weakness of Marcus Aurelius in regard to his wife. Julian, however, might have made him offer a more plausible excuse than a maxim true in general, but liable to some exceptions; and which, for having come from the mouth of the divine Achilles, an authority very weak in point of conduct, was not the more applicable to the case of Marcus Aurelius. He might have alleged, not in his justification, but as an excuse, that, never suspecting evil, and judging of others by himself, he had thought that his wife was what she ought to have been. Whatever some historians may say, Marcus Aurelius was ignorant of the irregularities of Faustina, as he thanks the Gods "for having given him a wife so good-
"natured

' that to my fon * was in imitation of the fupreme
' Jupiter; and, befides, in both thefe I was guilty
'of

" natured and obliging, full of tendernefs for her husband,
" and of a wonderful fimplicity of manners." *Meditations
of Marcus Antoninus*, l. i. XVII.

" This ought not to feem very furprifing," fays Madam
Dacier, " if we confider, on one fide, the fimplicity of
" Antoninus," (fo fhe always calls Marcus Aurelius) " and,
" on the other, the genius of Fauftina, who had no lefs
" art than beauty, and who had captivated the emperor
" by all the external demonftrations of a tendernefs, which
" appeared great in proportion to its falfhood. Half as
" much would have been fufficient to deceive a man much
" more diftruftful and fufpicious than Antoninus. If, after
" this, any are obftinately aftonifhed at his ignorance,"
continues Madam Dacier, " I have no objection, perfuaded,
" that thofe who are fo aftonifhed are in the fame fituation;
" for the world abounds with fuch examples, and there is
" nothing of which women are more capable than fuch
" diffimulation."

Madam Dacier adds, that, " if, in the fatire of the
" Cæfars, this prince, inftead of excufing himfelf on ac-
" count of his ignorance, alleges the maxim of Achilles,
" and the example of other emperors, who have paid the
" fame honours to their wives, though they were no more
" worthy than Fauftina, the reafon probably was, that
" Julian meant to include in this fatire the wives of Ha-
" drian, Vefpafian, and Auguftus." That may be. But
I rather think that Julian imagined he had anfwered every
thing when he had quoted fome verfe of Homer.
                                            LA BLETERIE.

The deification of Fauftina is the only defect which
Julian's criticifm is able to difcover in the all-accomplifhed
Marcus Aurelius.   GIBBON.

Another " defect," obferved by Julian in Marcus Aurelius, was the entrufting the empire to his fon. See p. 209.

* We will not fay, with the Emperor Severus, that
Marcus Aurelius ought to have put his fon Commodus to
death. But the faults, which paternal tendernefs made that
philofophical Emperor commit, are utterly inexcufable in fo
                                                    great

'of no innovation. It is the general custom for
'sons to succeed to the inheritance of their fathers,
'and this is also the wish of all. Nor was I
'the first who decreed divine honours to a wife,
'there being many precedents. To have intro-
'duced it might perhaps have been unreasonable;
'but to prevent the nearest relations from fol-
'lowing a custom established by others, would be
'unjust. But I forget myself, and have been too
'prolix in my apology to you, O Jupiter and ye

great a man. I know that he at first took all possible
methods to give his son an excellent education. But some
corrupters insinuated themselves into the favour of that
prince. It is said, that, when Marcus Aurelius removed
them, Commodus was so chagrined as to be ill, and that
his father had the weakness to restore them to him.
Be that as it may, one of these three things must be
allowed; either Marcus Aurelius was apprised of the bad
inclinations of his son; or he considered him as a young
man wavering between good and evil; or, lastly, he thought
him solidly virtuous. In the first case, the empire not being
hereditary, Marcus Aurelius should have caused the senate
to name him another successor, and not have falsified the
fair speeches which he himself had made: " May my
" children perish, if they less deserve to be loved than
" those of Cassius, and if their lives are not useful to the
" republic!" In the second case, was the love of his
country displayed by exposing it to the risk of having a vicious
Emperor? On the third supposition, how can this prince
be exculpated for having depended too much on the virtues
which he thought he saw in a child? He made the senate
confer on him, at the age of fifteen or sixteen at most, both
the consulship, and the tribunitial power, and even the title
of Augustus; and by that in a manner divested himself of
paternal authority. Antoninus had not done so much in
favour of Marcus Aurelius himself, though he was so early
attached to virtue. LA BLETERIE.

'Gods,

'Gods, who know all things. Pardon me this
'indifcretion.'

When MARCUS had finifhed his fpeech, Mercury interrogated CONSTANTINE, and afked him, "What good end he had in view?" 'Having amaffed great riches *,' he replied, 'to disburfe them liberally in the gratification of my own defires, and thofe of my friends.' At this, Silenus burft into a fit of loud laughter, and faid, "You now wifh to pafs for a banker †; but how can you

---

* It is difficult to conceive that Conftantine did not opprefs his fubjects. I mean, that he did not lay fome new burthen upon them, and even that he granted fome diminution of the old ones, according to M. de Tillemont. However, if we confider the ftate in which the empire muft be, after fo many civil wars, after having fuffered the reigns of that crowd of Emperors and Cæfars, or rather tyrants, each of whom expended as much as a fingle fovereign, we fhall allow that, in fuch circumftances, the defign of founding a new capital, and of making Conftantinople at once equal to Rome, the work of fo many ages, was not that of a prince fufficiently intent on the welfare of his fubjects. But to fay that, in amaffing wealth, his object was to fatisfy the paffions of others, is unjuftly to render him refponfible for the abufes which were made of his liberality by fome of his friends, whom perhaps he had not chofen with fufficient difcernment. To pretend that his view was to fatisfy his own paffions is a calumny, unlefs it means his paffion for New Rome : that paffion, however, did not fo exhauft his treafures as to leave him nothing to diftribute in immenfe charities, in building and endowing churches, and in magnificently rewarding men of letters and artifts.
LA BLETERIE.

† To underftand this farcaftic pleafantry of Silenus, we muft fuppofe that the bankers at that time lived and dreffed very penurioufly. " As by your own confeffion," fays Silenus,

" you forget your living like a cook, or a hair-
" dreſſer? This your hair and looks formerly

Silenus, " you employed yourſelf in receiving and counting
" money, like a banker, you ought to have lived and
" dreſſed like one. You ought not to have indulged your-
" ſelf in good cheer, in inventing new ragoûts, in paying
" ſo much attention to your hair." The table of Conſtantine was ſerved with magnificence. By his medals it is
thought that he was perhaps too curious in dreſs. Euſebius mentions ſome white hair that was among the pre-
ſents which were ſent him by Barbarian kings *. He wore
gold-flowered ſtuffs, and a diadem adorned with jewels and
pearls. What a ſcandal to Julian, who baniſhed from his
palace all the cooks, who lived on vegetables, who neglected his hair and his perſon, on whom the diadem ſat
ſo heavy that he retained it only through policy! He muſt
have been enraged at him who had made the uſe of it
common, and by that means laid his ſucceſſors under the
neceſſity of wearing it.   LA BLETERIE.

The dreſs and manners, which, towards the decline of
life, he choſe to affect, ſerved only to degrade him in the
eyes of mankind. The Aſiatic pomp, which had been
adopted by the pride of Dioclctian, aſſumed an air of
ſoftneſs and effeminancy in the perſon of Conſtantine. He
is repreſented with falſe hair of various colours, laboriouſly
arranged by the ſkilful artiſts of the times, a diadem of a
new and more expenſive faſhion, a profuſion of gems and
pearls, of collars and bracelets, and a variegated flowing
robe of ſilk, moſt curiouſly embroidered with flowers of
gold. In ſuch apparel, ſcarcely to be excuſed in the youth
and folly of Elagabalus, we are at a loſs to diſcover the
wiſdom of an aged monarch, and the ſimplicity of a Roman
veteran. Julian, in the Cæſars, attempts to ridicule his
uncle. His ſuſpicious teſtimony is confirmed, however,
by the learned Spanheim, with the authority of medals.
Euſebius alleges, that " Conſtantine dreſſed for the public,
" not for himſelf." Were this admitted, the vaineſt coxcomb could never want an excuſe.   GIBBON.

* See Euſebius's Life of Conſtantine IV.

"proved, but now yôur words demonstrate."
Thus severely sarcastic was Silenus.

Silence being proclaimed, the Gods gave their votes privately. Most were in favour of MARCUS [*], but Jupiter, after discoursing apart with his father, ordered Mercury to make the following proclamation: 'All you who have engaged in this con- 'test, know, that, by our laws and decrees, the 'victor is allowed to rejoice, but not to insult the 'vanquished. Depart then wherever you please, 'under the patronage of the Gods, and, for the '.future, residing here, let every one choose some 'guardian and protector.'

ALEXANDER immediately hastened to Hercules, and OCTAVIANUS to Apollo; but MARCUS attached himself closely both to Jupiter and Saturn. CÆSAR wandered about, and ran here and there, 'till Mars and Venus, moved with compassion, called him to them. TRAJAN joined ALEXANDER, as if he would seat himself in the same place. But CONSTANTINE not finding among the Gods the model of his actions, and perceiving the Goddess of Pleasure, repaired to her. She received him very courteously, embraced him, and then dressing him in a woman's variegated gown, and

---

[*] Julian was secretly inclined to prefer a Greek to a Roman. But when he seriously compared a hero with a philosopher, he was sensible that mankind had much greater obligations to Socrates than to Alexander. GIBBON. See his Epistle to Themistius, p. 24.

nicely curling his hair, led him away to Luxury *.
With her he found one of his sons †, who loudly
proclaimed,

* Ασωτια. Julian here personifies Luxury, or (as M. de
la Bleterie translates it) Debauchery, and places her among
the Gods, in the same manner as he had before deified
Pleasure (Τρυφη), and Repentance (Μιταμιλεια.)

† This son, whom Constantine finds with Debauchery, is
not one of the three who had followed him to the banquet,
and whom, Julian says a little lower, their father " led
" out of the assembly of the Gods." He here means
Crispus, the eldest of all, a pupil of the celebrated Lac-
tantius, and known by his tragical death still more than
by his victories. But why does Julian place near Debauchery that prince whom history mentions as an unfortunate hero? Is it because he thought him guilty of the
crime of which his step-mother accused him? No; that
would tend to the exculpation of Constantine. It is rather
owing to Julian's continuing to treat a manner of living
less singular than his own as effeminacy and debauchery.
Crispus was charged by the Empress Fausta with the same
crime of which Phædra had formerly accused Hippolytus,
and of intending to dethrone his father. Constantine, too
credulous, put his son to death, and soon after, having
discovered the innocence of Crispus, he punished the false
accuser with a rigour that was considered as a new crime.

These two deaths, and that of his nephew, young
Licinius, are indeed enormous crimes, which might have
been expiated by the baptism which Constantine received
before he died. But we may judge of the effect which
they produced on such superficial and corrupt minds as
imputed to religion the faults of its professors, both by the
blasphemies of Julian and of modern infidels. Without
pretending to penetrate into the judgments of God, we
may consider, with M. de Tillemont, as the chastisement of
these cruel actions of Constantine, both the faults which
the Arians made him commit, and the extinction of his
family, which seemed likely to continue for many ages; yet,
numerous as it was, perished in less than forty years, by
such a variety of bloody and untimely deaths, as excites
horror. *Now therefore the sword shall not depart from*
thine

THE CÆSARS.

proclaimed, " Let all, whether they be libertines, " or murderers, or whatever be their crimes *, " boldly

thine house . . . because thou hast given great occasion to the enemies of the Lord to blaspheme.   LA BLETERIE.
Such haughty contempt for the opinion of mankind, whilst it imprints an indelible disgrace on the memory of Constantine, must remind us of the very different behaviour of one of the greatest monarchs of the present age. The Czar Peter, in the full possession of despotic power, submitted to the judgment of Russia, of Europe, and of posterity, the reasons which had compelled him to subscribe the condemnation of a criminal, or, at least, a degenerate son.   •   GIBBON.

* One would think, at first, that Julian alludes to the story which the Pagans of the fifth century circulated on the subject of the conversion of Constantine. They said, that that prince, struck with remorse for having put his son and his wife to death, having asked Sopater, chief of the Platonic school, and the Pagan pontiffs, whether the religion of the Gentiles had any expiation to efface such crimes, answered him, that it had not; that, in consequence, Constantine had a conference with a certain Ægyptian, who had come from Spain to Rome, and was well known to the women of the palace; that this Ægyptian and some bishops assured him that the Christian religion would give him what the Pagans refused him; and that there was no kind of wickedness which could not be washed in the blood of Jesus Christ; and that, upon their answer, he embraced Christianity, and declared himself its protector.

This relation proves that the Pagans did not consider Constantine as a man without conscience; and that, more equitable than our free-thinkers, they ascribed his change, not to policy, but to conviction. If the story were true, there would be no more pretence to insult us for the faults of Constantine, as he must have committed them in the darkness of idolatry. But truth obliges me to say, that the fact cannot be supported. For, 1. as Sozomen remarks, the philosopher Sopater, being well versed in the religion of the Gentiles, could not be ignorant that it had some pretended expiations for such cases as that of Constantine.

"boldly advance, for by sprinkling them with
"water, I will immediately make them pure. And
"if

2. It is not credible that the pontiffs of the idols should have been so silly as to lay him under an absolute necessity of providing himself elsewhere. If they had not had expiations, they would have invented them, to quiet the conscience of an Emperor whom they saw on the eve of deserting them, and throwing himself into the arms of the Christians. 3. Crispus, Fausta, and young Licinius died in 326; and in the year 312 Constantine acknowledged the Christian religion as the only true one.

Julian was too well acquainted with the history of his family, and the æra of the conversion of Constantine, to have had in view a fable, which he considered as a fable, supposing that in his time it had been yet invented. I imagine therefore that this apostate introduces Crispus vaunting the efficacy of baptism and repentance, in order to insinuate, by that profane irony, that the prospect of the resources offered to sinners by the Christian religion had emboldened Constantine to shed the blood of his relations. It was a common calumny with the Pagans to say, that Christianity favoured the corruption of men by promising pardon to the greatest crimes; as if the gospel promises any thing to incorrigible sinners, or assures them that they shall have time and the will to reform.

This calumny is the more atrocious in the mouth of Julian, as, having been of the clergy, he must be better acquainted with the spirit of the church, with the wise precautions and long probations that she employs to be assured of the conversion both of catechumens and of penitents. A religion, which did not offer to the most miserable man a method of recovering the favour of God, would be an ineffectual religion, and little worthy of the goodness of God who would have all men saved. It would indeed favour corruption by plunging or leaving the guilty in despair. A religion, which should pretend to efface crimes by mere ceremonies, without reforming the criminal, would be no more than a farce, a despicable palliative, likely to exasperate the disease, but not to cure it. Christianity observes the just mean. Adapted to the wants of mankind,

and

"if they should relapse, they need only smite
"their breasts and beat their heads, and they will
"again be purified."

To and worthy of the sanctity of its author, it presents men, to whatever abyss of degradation and misery vice may have reduced them, with a line which conducts them strait to God, provided, and not else, that they become new men in and by Jesus Christ. In all times, some, separating the promise from the condition, have assumed, by a deplorable abuse, a kind of title to sin more boldly. But God forbid, that, on the word of an accuser, who guesses and cannot prove, we should think that Constantine was of that number, and that the expectation of baptism should have influenced him to actions for which he is justly reproached! After all, it is not the fault of physic, if, from the uncertain hope of the assistance that it offers, some are so extravagant as to aggravate their diseases.

Besides the slanderous imputation just mentioned, I perceive in the words of Crispus a satirical stroke which is not undeserved. By the confession of Eusebius (which is saying every thing) Constantine did not enough distinguish from true Christians those who embraced Christianity only to make their fortunes. " By their hypocrisy and artifice," says Eusebius, " they insinuated themselves into the favour " of the Emperor, and much injured his reputation." Julian therefore here means to reproach Constantine for having over-looked every thing, and pardoned every thing, provided his religion was professed. But why did not the censor perceive, that he himself is more justly entitled to the like censure? Neither the uncle nor the nephew had sufficient delicacy as to their proselytes. Yet they must have been well acquainted with a memorable story of Constantius Chlorus. That prince, at the time when his collegues were persecuting Christianity with fire and sword, assembled such officers of his palace, and governors of his provinces, as were Christians, and gave them the alternative, either of retaining their places, by sacrificing to the Gods, or of losing them by adhering to their religion. When they had all made their options, he said to the prevaricators,

To this Goddess Constantine gladly devoted himself, and with her conducted his sons out of the assembly of the Gods. But the Deities who punish atheism * and bloodshed avenged on him and them the murder of their relations †, till Jupiter, in favour of Claudius ‡ and Constantius, gave them some respite.

varicators, " You have base and venal minds. I cashier " you, and banish you for ever from my palace. He who " betrays his conscience is capable of betraying me. As " for you," said he to the others, " I give you my esteem " and confidence. A man is faithful to his prince and " the community when he is faithful to his God." He retained them in his service, and entrusted them with the guard of his person, and the principal affairs of state; considering them as his surest friends and real treasures. I shall conclude this long note, or rather dissertation, with observing that M. de Tillemont questions whether Crispus had received baptism. The speech which Julian assigns to him leaves no room to doubt it. But it was not before perceived that it is Crispus who speaks in this passage.

La Bleterie.

Dr. Bentley, under the borrowed name of Phileleutherus Lipsiensis, styles this " a ridiculous and stale banter, used " by Celsus and others, before Julian, upon the Christian " doctrines of baptism, and repentance, and remission of " sins," and has refuted it at large in his Remarks on a late discourse of Free-thinking, § xlii.

* Julian treats the Christians as atheists, because they reject the plurality of Gods, and acknowledge one only.

La Bleterie.

† After the death of Constantine, the soldiers laid violent hands on his three brothers, and five of his nephews. Constantius was considered as guilty of this massacre, and Julian probably means to charge with it Constantine the younger also, and Constans. Be that as it may, the two latter made war on each other, and Constantine the younger was killed near Aquileia by the troops of Constans. That Constantius put Gallus to death is well known. *Ibid.*

‡ Claudius II. mentioned p. 167.

" As

"As for you," said Mercury, addressing himself to me, "I have introduced you to the knowledge of your father the Sun *; obey then his dictates, making him your guide and secure refuge, while you live; and when you leave the world, adopt him, with good hopes, for your tutelar God."

* Julian, as soon as he rose, always addressed a prayer to Mercury. He thought himself under the protection of that God. We have said in the preface, and shall again observe in another place, that by the Sun he understands the Demiurgus, or Logos.　　　LA BLETERIE.

THE CÆSARS.

The following Lift of the Roman Emperors, from JULIUS CÆSAR to JULIAN, will give a fuccinct view of all that are mentioned, and all that are omitted, in the foregoing Satire.

	Before Xt.				A. D.
1	JULIUS CÆSAR, died	44	26	* Maximin, died	238
		A. D.		and	
2	AUGUSTUS	14		Maximus	238
3	Tiberius	37	27	Pupienus	238
4	* Caligula	41		and	
5	Claudius I.	54		Balbinus	238
6	* Nero	68	28	Gordian	243
	[Vindex]	68	29	Philip	249
7	Galba	68	30	Decius	251
8	Otho	69	31	Gallus	252
9	Vitellius	69	32	† Valerian	260
10	Vefpafian	79	33	† Gallienus	268
11	Titus	81	34	Claudius II.	270
12	* Domitian	96	35	Aurelian	275
13	Nerva	98	36	Tacitus	276
14	TRAJAN	117	37	Probus	282
15	Hadrian	137	38	† Carus	284
16	Antoninus Pius	161		† Carinus	285
17	MARCUS AURELIUS	180		and	
	and			† Numerian	284
	Lucius Verus	169	39	Diocletian ⎫	
18	† Commodus	193		and ⎬ refigned	305
19	Pertinax	193		Maximian ⎭	
20	*Julian* I.	193	40	Conftantius-Chlorus	d.306
21	Severus	211		and	
22	* Caracalla	217		† Galerius	311
	and		41	† CONSTANTINE THE	
	Geta	212		GREAT	337
23	† Macrinus	218		and	
	and			† Licinius	323
	Diadumenus	218	42	† Conftantine II.	340
24	† Eliagabalus	222		† Conftantius	361
25	Alexander Severus	235		and	
				† Conftans	350
			43	JULIAN II.	363

N. B. Thofe marked † were excluded the affembly; thofe * were thrown into Tartarus; and thofe in Italicks are not mentioned. Vindex, though mentioned, was not Emperor. And Tiberius, Commodus, and Elagabalus, though they efcaped Tartarus, deferved it.

The

The MISOPOGON, or the ANTIOCHIAN *.

ANACREON † compofed many ludicrous poems ‡, the Fates having endowed him with a fportive vein. But neither Alcæus §, nor
Archi-

A. D. 363.

---

* Being jeered by the Antiochians, and feveral afperfions having been thrown on his beard in particular, Julian took his revenge in this fatire, in which, by a figurative reprehenfion of himfelf, he drew his keen pen againſt the manners and luxury of the people of Antioch. This work, and its fubject, are mentioned by Ammianus, *l.* xxii. Zofimus, *l.* iii. Gregory Nazianzen, *Orat.* ii. on Julian, and Socrates, *l.* iii. *c.* 17.   PETAU.

It feems as if Julian meant in fome fort to confound himfelf with his beard, which was fo dear to him that it difpleafed the inhabitants of Antioch. After all, the title of a book frequently refers to fome paſſage only in the work.
        LA BLETERIE.

Inſtead of abuſing, or exerting, the authority of the ſtate, to revenge his perſonal injuries, Julian contented himſelf with an inoffenſive mode of retaliation which it would be in the power of few princes to employ. He had been inſulted by ſatires and libels; in his turn, he compoſed, under the title of " The Enemy of the Beard," an ironical confeſſion of his own faults, and a ſevere ſatire on the licentious and effeminate manners of Antioch. This imperial reply was publickly expoſed before the gates of the palace, and the Miſopogon ſtill remains a ſingular monument of the reſentment, the wit, the humanity, and the indiſcretion of Julian.   GIBBON.

The ſatire of Julian, and the homilies of St. Chryſoſtom, exhibit the ſame picture of Antioch.   *Ibid.*

In like manner, Hadrian, it is obſervable, was alſo much offended with the levity and petulance of the Antiochians, and had thoughts of disjoining Phœnicia from Syria, that their city might not continue the metropolis of ſo many others.

A Lyric

THE MISOPOGON.

Archilochus * of Paros, were favoured by the Gods with a Muse who had a talent for mirth and pleasantry; for when they were oppressed with misfortunes, they had recourse to the Muses, and alleviated the weight of their cares by railing at their enemies. The law, however, forbids me, as well as every one else, to accuse any by name ‖,

even

---

† A Lyric poet of Teos, a city in Ionia, who wrote many more odes than are transmitted to us, as Horace says,—*persæpe cavâ testudine flevit amorem.* Epod. xiv. 4.

‡ We read in the editions, "Anacreon made many "serious and ludicrous poems," χωιλη σιμια και χαριεντα. Whether this poet wrote any thing but songs, is the question. By saying, that "Anacreon made some serious verses," Julian would say the direct contrary of what he meant. I think therefore that the text shoul be corrected, and the word τερπνα substituted, or that we should only read χαριεντα. In one of the MSS. of the King's library, which has been lent me, the words σιμια και are not to be found; and the other informs the reader, that there are some MSS. in which those words do not occur. La Bleterie.

§ A native of Mitylene. From him the Alcaïc verses derive their name. His pieces were severe satires against the tyrants of Lesbos, Pittacus in particular. His style, according to Quintilian, was lofty, and much resembled that of Homer.

* See p. 131.

‖ The Roman laws, beginning with those subsequent to the xii tables, condemn severely the authors of defamatory libels. Julian, though in joke, is glad to shew that he has a republican spirit. He considered the Emperors as justly subject to all the laws, except those with which they had specifically dispensed. La Bleterie.

Personal satire was condemned by the law of the twelve tables.

Si mala condiderit in quem quis carmina, jus est Judiciumque. Hor.

Julian owns himself subject to the law, and the Abbé de la Bleterie has eagerly embraced a declaration so agreeable

THE MISOPOGON.

even of those, who, as I have, in no respect injured them, are hostile aggressors. And, besides, the mode of education, which is at present pursued by persons of fashion *, deprives me of the harmony

able to his own system, and indeed to the true spirit of the Imperial constitution. GIBBON.

* I do not remember elsewhere to have read that poetry was then so much decried. However that might be, in Greece the age of verse was not then over: witness St. Gregory Nazienzen, whose sublime and truly Homeric poems prove that genius and enthusiasm require not the assistance of fable. Julian himself was a poet; and Libanius informs us, that there was a collection of verses made by that prince to celebrate the arrival of some men of learning at his court. Two small pieces of his writing are all that now remain. In one of them, he elegantly and forcibly describes an organ, consisting, like ours, of pipes, bellows, and stops. The other is an epigram " against beer." It must have been made in the Gauls.

LA BLETERIE.

Of the latter, M. de la Bleterie has given a paraphrase, or imitation, in French. The following are close translations of them both. The originals, as literary curiosities, are annexed.

The Emperor Julian on an Organ.

Reeds strike my wond'ring eyes, unknown before,
Sprung from some brazen soil, some foreign shore;
Fruitless our efforts, for in vain we blow,
Till, from a cave of leather, winds below
To hollow pipes harmonious powers impart:
Then, if some master, in th' Orphean art
Experienc'd, touch the well-according keys,
Instant they warble, and responsive please.

Ιελιανε Βασιλεως εις το οργανον.

Αλλοιην οροω δοναχων φυσιν· ητα απ' αλλης
Χαλκειης ταχα μαλλον ανεβλαςησαν αρυρης.
Αγριοι, ουδ' ανεμοισιν υφ' ημετεροις δονεονται,
Αλλ' υπο ταυρειης προθοςων σπηλυγγος αητης

THE MISOPOGON.

mony of numbers. For it seems now as dishonourable to cultivate poetry, as it was in former times to be unjustly rich.

I will

Νερθεν ευτρητων καλαμων υπο ριζαν οδευει.
Και τις ανηρ αγερωχος *, εχων δοα δακ]υλα χειρος,
Ιςαται αμφαφοων κανοιας συμφραδμονας αυλων †·
Οι δ' απαλον σκιζωνιες αποθλιβουσιν αοιδην.

Mersennus has inserted a Latin translation of this epigram, in his lib. III. *De Organis*, p. 113. and Zarlino, who wrote in 1571, is of opinion, that the organ here mentioned was essentially the same with the organ of his time. But the introduction of it into churches is generally ascribed to Pope Vitellianus, who was advanced to the Pontificate, A. D. 663. Dr. Priestley indeed (History of the Corruptions of Christianity, vol. II. p. 122.) by some mistake, supposes it to be introduced into churches by Marinus Sanutus so late as 1312. An organ is mentioned by Gervase the monk, who wrote in 1200, as having been sometime erected in Canterbury Cathedral, over St. Michael's chapel (*ubi organa solent esse*), and the foundation of its loft remains to this day. An hydraulic organ (of which Sir John Hawkins has given a sketch from Kircher) is described by Vitruvius, who lived in the reign of Augustus. The following note is from Dr. Burney.

The most ancient proof of an instrument resembling a modern organ blown by bellows, and played by keys, very different from the *Hydraulicon* (or water-organ) which is of much higher antiquity, is a Greek epigram in the *Anthologia*, attributed to the Emperor Julian the Apostate, who flourished about 364 ‡.

I shall here give a literal translation of this epigram, which, though it contain no very beautiful or poetical images, will answer the historical purpose of ascertaining

---

* A tall sturdy fellow, " alluding to the force necessary to beat down that kind of clumsy carillon keys of this rude instrument of new invention. BURNEY.

† The rulers of the pipes, literally *keys*. *Ibid.*

‡ This is a small chronological mistake, as Julian died in June, 363.

the

I will not, however, totally disclaim the assistance of the Muses. I have seen the barbarous nations beyond the Rhine delighted with the melody of savage music, whose notes resemble the dissonant screams of birds. Bad musicians disgust

the existence of an instrument in the fourth century, which in many particulars resembled a modern organ.
" I see reeds of a new species, the growth of another
" and a brazen soil; such as are not agitated by our winds,
" but by a blast that rushes from a leathern cavern be-
" neath their roots; while a robust mortal, running with
" swift fingers over the concordant keys, makes them, as
" they smoothly dance, utter concordant sounds."
Nothing material is omitted in the version of this epigram, or rather enigma, upon the organ, though not a very ingenious one; for the word αυλων, *the pipes*, discovers the whole mystery. BURNEY.

The Emperor Julian on Barley-wine.

Who, what art thou? thy name, thy birth declare:
Thou art no Bacchus, I by Bacchus swear.
Jove's son alone I know, I know not thee;
Thou smell'st like goats, but sweet as nectar he.
In Gallia, thirsty Gallia, thou wert born,
Scanty of grapes, but prodigal of corn.
Bromus, not Bromius, styl'd, thy brows with corn,
As sprung from Ceres, not from Jove, adorn.

The turn, or pun, at the conclusion, cannot be preserved in English. *Bromius* was one name of Bacchus, from Βρεμω, " to rave," like the Bacchanals. And Julian gives the name of *Bromus* to beer, from Βρομος, " oats." Such, however, is the improvement of climates, that modern Gaul produces as much and as good wines as Italy; and Britain more and better beer than ancient Gaul.

Ιυλιανω Βασιλιω; οινω απο κριθης.
Τις; ποθεν εις, Διονυσε; μα γαρ τον αληθεα Βακχον,
Ου σ'επιγιγνωσκω· τον Διος οιδα μονει.
Κεινος νεκταρ οδωδε· συ δε τραγον. η ρα σε Κελτοι
Τη πενιη βοτρυων τευξαν απ' αςαχυων.
Τω σε χρη καλεειν Δημητριον, ε Διονυσον,
Πυρογενη μαλλον, και Βρομον, ε Βρομιον.

their hearers, but they are naturally pleasing to themselves. Reflecting on this, I have been wont to whisper to myself, not indeed with equal address, but, I am certain, with equal magnanimity, what Ismenias * said of old, " I will sing for the Muses ". and myself." But my song is in prose, and will contain many bitter sarcasms, not on others, by Jupiter, (for how can that be, as they are illegal?) but on the author himself. For no law forbids my writing a panegyrick or satire on myself; though if I were desirous of praising myself, I could not, but blame I can in many instances.

And, first, I will begin with my face. To this, formed by nature not over beautiful, graceful, or becoming, my own perverseness and singularity have added this long beard †, to punish it, as it were,

---

* Ismenias was a very skilful player on the flute. Julian is the only one who ascribes to him this expression. Cicero, [in his Brutus, c. 50.] puts one very like it in the mouth of Antigenidas, another player on the flute, who, in order to encourage one of his scholars, whom the public did not relish, said to him, " Play for the Muses, and for me."

LA BLETERIE.

† Some friends, for whose understanding and taste I have the highest respect, supposing themselves to speak in the name of the nation, requested me to suppress entirely the idea which Julian here conveys. It is only by sufferance that they have allowed me to intimate it by one rapid word. For my own part, I was afraid of giving a handle to infidelity. Will the French delicacy go so far as to falsify authors? The more disgusting this passage of Julian is, the more it characterises him; and every thing that characterises, when it does not offend good manners or religion,
should

THE MISOPOGON.

were, for no other reason but because Nature has not made it handsome. Therefore I suffer lice to scamper about it, like beasts through a thicket: I cannot indulge myself in eating voraciously, and must be cautious of opening my mouth wide when I drink, lest I swallow as many hairs as crumbs. As for kissing, and being kissed, they give me not the least trouble.

Yet amongst other inconveniences of my beard, this is one, that it prevents my joining pure lips to smooth, and, I think, much sweeter lips, as was formerly observed * by one, who, inspired by Pan

---

should be sacred to a translator. As the notes admit any thing, here follows a faithful translation of the passage in question; excepting that the original calls the things by their name. [In the French translation therefore φθειρων, " lice," are rendered by *de petits animaux incommodes*, " some " little troublesome animals," which might as well be fleas. And why not *des insectes*, or *de la vermine* ?] That a Roman emperor should boast of such a circumstance, and that he should boast of it falsely, as I suppose, is, literally speaking, a singular stroke, which paints Julian better than a thousand volumes. LA BLETERIE.

The friends of the Abbé de la Bleterie adjured him, in the name of the French nation, not to translate this passage so offensive to their delicacy. Like him, I have contented myself with a transient allusion; but the little animal, which Julian names, " is a beast familiar to man, " and signifies love." [Shakspeare, 2 Hen. IV.] GIBBON.

Mr. Gibbon's " transient allusion" is " the shaggy and " populous beard," and " *la barbe longue et peuplée*" is the " rapid word" of M. de la Bleterie.

* Theocritus, Idyll. XII. 32.

Ὡς δε κε περσμαξη γλυκερωτερα χειλεσι χειλη, κ. τ. λ.

He who shall lips to lips most sweetly join, &c.

speaking of a garland that was presented at the tomb of Diocles to the youth who gave the sweetest kiss.

and Calliope, made some verses on Daphnis [*]. You say, that " it is only fit to twist into ropes." That I would readily allow, provided you could so artfully extract the bristles, as to prevent their hurting your soft and tender fingers. Think not that this offends me; for I will give you a reason why I wear a chin like a goat, instead of making it smooth and bare like those of beautiful boys, and of all women by nature lovely. You, such is the delicacy, and perhaps simplicity, of your manners, even when old, imitate your sons and daughters by studiously shaving your chins, thus displaying the man by the forehead only, and not, like me, by the cheeks. But not contented with this length of beard, my head is also nasty and seldom combed, my nails are unpared, and my fingers are usually black with ink. And, to tell you a secret, my bosom too is rough and hairy, like the mane of the lion, king of beasts, nor have I ever made it smooth, such is my meanness and illiberality. If I had any wart, I would readily disclose it, as Cimon did, but at present in truth I have none.

---

[*] The son of Mercury, whose story is sung in the first Idyllium Diodorus Siculus supposes him to have been the first author of bucolic poetry; and, agreeably to this, Theon, an old scholiast on Theocritus, in his note on the first Idyllium, ver. 141. mentioning Daphnis, says, " he " was the inventor of bucolics." Be that as it may, this Daphnis was probably the first subject of bucolic songs.

FAWKES.

Theocritus has also an epigram " to Daphnis sleeping." The above is a note of the translator.

THE MISOPOGON.

Another circumstance, well known to you, I will also mention. Not satisfied with such an uncomely person, I lead a very rigid life. I absent myself from the theatres, through mere stupidity; nor do I allow a play at court, such a dolt am I, except on the calends of the year *, when I resemble a poor farmer bringing his rent, or taxes, to a rapacious landlord; and when I am there, I seem as solemn as at a sacrifice †. As it is not long since you saw him, you may recollect the youth, the genius, and understanding of my predecessor ‡; my way of life, so different from his, is a sufficient proof of my frowardness.

But to add something farther; I have always hated horse-races as much as a debtor hates the forum. Therefore I seldom resort to them, except on the festivals of the Gods, nor do I ever pass

---

* The calends of January were celebrated by the ancient Heathens with all kinds of public mirth and lasciviousness, and for a long time were devoted by the Christians to no very different amusements. PETAU.

† There is in the original a sentence which I omit. The passage is certainly faulty, and so it is thought to be by F. Petau. Literally translated it would be thus: " I " have no possessions; and though I am styled the great king, " like a præfect or duke, I am in fact a king, or general, of " players and charioteers." But this sense does not connect with that which precedes and follows it. The MSS. have here given me no assistance. LA BLETERIE.
For the same reason it is also omitted here.

‡ Constantius. It is needless to say, this is ironical. The " genius and understanding" of Constantius Julian despised; and as to his " youth," he was 44 years old when he died.

THE MISOPOGON.

the whole day there; as was the practice of my cousin *, my uncle †, and my brother ‡; but after seeing six races §, and that not with the keenness of a sportsman, but, by Jupiter, with disgust and aversion, I depart with joy. But enough of my public conduct. And yet how few of my offences against you have I mentioned!

As to domestic affairs, sleepless nights on straw, and food less than enough, give a severity to my manners, totally repugnant to a luxurious city ‖. Be not offended with me for this **. A great and foolish

---

* Constantius.
† Count Julian. See Epistle xiii.
‡ Gallus. Julian styles him (as he was) "his half-brother."
§ Out of four and twenty, which was the usual number. A twenty-fifth race, or *missus*, was added, to complete the number of one hundred chariots, four of which, the four colours, started each heat.

Centum quadrijugos agitabo ad flumina cursus.

It appears that they ran five or seven times round the *meta*, and (from the measure of the *Circus Maximus* at Rome, the Hippodrome at Constantinople, &c.) it might be about a four-mile course. GIBBON.

‖ The private life of Julian in Gaul, and the severe discipline which he embraced, are displayed by Ammianus. (xvi. 5) who professes to praise, and by Julian himself, who affects to ridicule, a conduct which in a prince of the family of Constantine might justly excite the surprise of mankind. *Ibid.*

** It may not be improper to add here the picture which Libanius draws of Julian's manner of life. "Always abstemious, and never oppressed by food, he applied himself to business with the activity of a bird, and dispatched it with infinite ease. In one and the same day he gave several audiences; he wrote to cities, to magistrates, to generals of armies, to his absent friends, to those who
"were

foolish mistake has from my childhood induced me to wage war with my stomach. I therefore never allow it to be filled with food. Consequently, to nothing am I so little addicted as to vomiting: and this, I remember, befell me once only since I became Cæsar; and that by accident, not repletion. It may not be amiss to relate the story, not that I think it entertaining, but as it was to me of the utmost consequence.

I happened to be in winter quarters at my dear Lutetia *; for so the Gauls call the town of the Parisians.

"were on the spot; hearing letters read that were addressed
"to him, examining petitions, and dictating with such ra-
"pidity, that the short-hand writers could not keep pace
"with him. He alone had the secret of hearing, speaking,
"and writing at the same time; and in this multitude of
"complicated operations he never mistook. After having
"dispatched business, and dined merely through urgent ne-
"cessity, shutting himself up in his library, he read and com-
"posed till the instant when affairs of state summoned him
"to other labours. A supper still more sparing than the
"dinner was followed by a sleep as light as his meals.
"He awaked in order to labour with other secretaries
"whom he had allowed to sleep on the preceding day.
"His ministers were obliged to relieve each other; but, as
"for himself, he knew no repose but the change of em-
"ployment. He alone was always labouring, he multi-
"plied himself, and assumed as many forms as Proteus.
"Julian was pontiff, author, diviner, judge, general of
"the army, and, in all these characters, the father of his
"country." *Liban. Orat. Parent.* LA BLETERIE.

* Leucetia, or Lutetia, was the ancient name of the city, which, according to the fashion of the ivth century, assumed the territorial appellation of *Parisii.*

The licentiousness and corruption of Antioch recalled to the memory of Julian the severe and simple manners of his
"beloved

Parisians. It is situated in a small island; two wooden bridges lead to it, and the river seldom rises or falls, but is generally of the same depth both in summer and winter. The water is very clear to the eye, and pure to the taste *. This is of great importance

" beloved Lutetia;" where the amusements of the theatre were unknown or despised. He indignantly contrasted the effeminate Syrians with the brave and honest simplicity of the Gauls, and almost forgave the intemperance which was the only stain of the Celtic character. If Julian could now revisit the capital of France, he might converse with men of science and genius, capable of understanding and of instructing a disciple of the Greeks; he might excuse the lively and graceful follies of a nation, whose martial spirit has never been enervated by the indulgence of luxury, and he must applaud the perfection of that inestimable art which softens, and refines, and embellishes the intercourse of social life. GIBBON.

Worthy patriot! Enlightened philosopher! Whatever "softens, refines, and embellishes" human life, in a proper degree, is certainly desirable. But why must France be commended with such warmth of approbation, as if she possessed this "inestimable art" exclusively? I think in this polished and enlightened age, the art is known and practised in England, as much as is consistent with the national character, and the preservation of that manly spirit which is necessary to the existence of civil liberty; an "inestimable" blessing, which enlarges, and ennobles, and secures all the natural rights and enjoyments of human nature.

I cannot think it consistent with a good citizen, and a lover of one's country, to admire and extol the "martial spirit" of that nation, which is at this moment most hostile to all we hold dear, and which in the present war has behaved with such perfidy as would stigmatise an individual in private life with perpetual disgrace.

KNOX.

* Julian gives the water of this river a better character than is usually allowed it, in modern times at least, and

importance to the inhabitants, as they are iflanders. The winter there is extremely mild, which is attributed to the warmth of the fea, it not being above ninety ſtadia diſtant *; fo that wholefome exhalations from the ocean are perhaps wafted thither, falt-water being warmer than freſh. Whether this be the reafon, or fome other unknown to me, fuch is the fact, the inhabitants of that country have mild winters; good wines therefore are produced there, and fome have even raiſed figs by covering them with mats by way of cloathing, and other fuch prefervatives from the inclemency of the weather.

The winter was then uncommonly fevere, and the river fupported blocks, as it were, of marble, (you know, without doubt, the Phrygian quarries, which large flakes of ice †, floating on each other, greatly refemble) forming a kind of continual paſſage and a ſtream of bridges. Being, on this occafion, more boorifh than ufual, I would not fuffer my fervants to warm the chamber in which I

---

and efpecially by foreigners. A late writer, a Frenchman too, expreſſes himſelf thus: " The Seine-water relaxes " the ſtomach of thoſe who are not uſed to it. Foreigners " generally ſuffer the inconvenience of a ſlight diarrhœa; " but they might avoid it if they had the precaution of " putting a fpoonful of white vinegar into every pint of " water." *Tableau de Paris.*

* The calculation is juſt; but I will not be anſwerable for the natural philofophy of the Pariſians of thoſe times.
La Bleterie.

† The inhabitants of Antioch had never feen the river bear. *Ibid.*

flept,

THE MISOPOGON.

slept, though the cold increased and grew every day more intense, left it should draw the damp out of the walls. I only ordered some lighted brands, and a few live coals, to be carried in and placed there. These exhaled so much vapour from the walls, that, my head being oppressed, I fell asleep, and narrowly escaped suffocation. But being carried into the air, and, by the advice of my physicians, disgorging the food that I had just swallowed, though I did not discharge much, I was immediately relieved, so as to pass an easy night, and on the next day I was again fit for business.

Thus, while I resided among the Gauls, like the Humourist * of Menander, I led an austere life. This, however, gave no offence to that rustic nation †. But such a rich, flourishing, and populous city as yours is justly displeased; a city, in which are many dancers, many pipers, more players than

---

* Δυσκολος, the title of a comedy of Menander.

† Though the Gauls had long become Romans, foreign manners had not yet penetrated into the northern parts of Gaul. Politeness, with its advantages and inconveniences, makes the tour of the world. If Julian were now to revisit his " dear Lutetia," would he take it for Antioch? No. He would find there so much love and respect for the sovereign, that he would be soon undeceived.

La Bletlrie.

Spoken like a Frenchman! Julian would never have thought highly of the sense, or sincerity, of a people who could " love and respect" such a sovereign as Louis XV. in whose reign the above note was written.

citizens, and no respect for sovereigns. A blush befits only the pusillanimous; but such heroes as you should revel in the morning, pursue pleasure at night, and not only teach by words, but shew by deeds, your utter contempt of the laws. Those therefore, who, like you, insult the prince, offer a still greater insult to the laws. That such is your delight you frequently and clearly demonstrate, particularly in the forum and the theatre; the people by shouts and clamour; the magistrates by their extravagance, which gains them more distinction and applause, from all to whom they have given these expensive entertainments, than Solon, the Athenian, obtained from his conversation with Crœsus, king of Lydia *. All there are handsome, smooth and beardless; all, both young and old, imitate alike the happiness of the Phæäcians †, and

Variety of dresses, baths, amours, they prefer, without hesitation, to what is just and right.

ANTIOCHIAN. And do you think, Julian, that your rusticity, savageness, and morofeness are suit-

* Every one knows the journey which Solon took to the court of king Crœsus, and the truths which he dared utter to that prince, intoxicated, as he was, with opulence and grandeur.   LA BLETERIE.

† The island of Phæäcia is now the island of Corfu. Homer, (Odyss. VIII. 249.) represents the Phæäcians as a nation given up to good cheer, luxury, music, dancing, and all kinds of pleasure.   *Ibid.*

able

THE MISOPOGON.

able to us? O thou most ignorant and odious * of all men, is your temperate, little animal, as some mean mortals have styled your soul, so mad and foolish, that you think it requires the ornaments and trappings of wisdom? In this you are mistaken; for, first, tell us, as we know not, what wisdom is? With the name only we are acquainted, but of the meaning we are ignorant. If it be that which you now practise, it consists in enforcing subordination to the Gods and the laws, in teaching equals to bear with equals, in observing moderation, in preventing the poor from being oppressed by the rich, and, for these purposes, stifling resentment, encountering enmity, anger, reproaches; in short, supporting all these with firmness, without being provoked, or giving way to passion, but keeping it, as much as possible, in proper bounds, and under due subjection. And if it should also be deemed a branch of wisdom to renounce even those pleasures which are not unbecoming, nor seem dishonourable, from a persuasion that it is impossible for any one to be temperate at home, and in private, who is dissolute abroad, and in public, and enamoured of the theatre; if this too be wisdom, you ruin yourself, and you would also ruin us. The very name of

* Φιλαπεχθημονεςατι, "who art most fond of being hated." This is one of the many Greek words which can only be rendered by a periphrasis. M. de la Bleterie has translated it *le plus haïssable*. It occurs again in the close of this satire.

servitude

servitude either to the Gods or the laws difgufts us.
Liberty is fweet in all things.

Of what prevarication are you guilty? You fay, you are not Lord *, nor can you endure the name.

You

* The word *dominus*, which the Greeks tranflated by κυριος and δεσποτης [or "lord"] properly fignified the power of mafters over their flaves. Under Auguftus, children already gave that name to their father, fometimes brothers gave it to their brothers, and wives to their hufbands, who returned them that of *domina*. Auguftus fuffered none but his flaves to give him that title, nor even his children and grand-children to treat him as "lord" by way of joke. *Dominum appellari fe nec a liberis quidem aut nepotibus fuis vel ferio vel joco paffus eft, atque hujufmodi blanditias inter ipfos prohibuit.* Suet. Aug. Satisfied with having deftroyed liberty, he fcrupuloufly banifhed every thing that could induce a thought of flavery. Some one having called Tiberius "Lord," he faid, with an angry look, that he did not like to be affronted. "I am," added he, "the prince of the fenate, and the general of the army; but I am lord only of my flaves." Caligula took the name of Lord, and even that of God. But none of the emperors who fucceeded him, not even Nero, followed his example, till Domitian, who exprefsly commanded himfelf to be called Lord and God, both in letters and in fpeech. One day, dictating an edict, he began it with thefe words, "Our Lord and our God ordains what follows." It appears, by the letters of Pliny the younger, that Trajan, averfe as he was to that impious pride, fuffered himfelf, neverthelefs, to be called Lord; but at that we muft not be furprifed. The more flavery augmented, the more complimentary the nation became. In the time of Seneca they gave each other the title of "Lord," almoft as commonly as we give one another the appellation of "Sir," which is much lefs fignificant. *Obvios, fi nomen non fuccurrit, dominos appellamus.* Men gave women that of *domina* as foon as they were fourteen years old. How it was ufed by the fucceffors of Trajan is not known. Certain it is, that Alexander, the fon of Mammea, rejected the title of Lord as too oftentatious.

You resent it so much, that you have induced many, who were formerly accustomed to it, to banish it from the empire, as invidious; yet you oblige us to obey the magistrates and the laws. How much better would it be for us to call you Lord, but in fact to be allowed freedom! O mild in appearance *, but in deeds most cruel! How unmerciful

tations. At last this name made part of the ceremonial of the court, and was inserted even in the public monuments. It is affirmed, that it is not found on any medal till those of Aurelian, and even on them it is rare: it is more common on those of Carus, and frequent on those of Diocletian, his collegues, and his successors. Julian had not time to abolish it. It is read on many of his.
           LA BLETERIE.
 As Julian never abolished, by any public law, the proud appellations of *Despot*, or *Dominus*, they are still extant on his medals, (*Ducange, Fam. Byzantin.* pp. 38, 39.) and the private displeasure which he affected to express only gave a different tone to the servility of the court. The Abbé de la Bleterie has curiously traced the origin and progress of the word *dominus* under the Imperial government. GIBBON.
 In the Hippolytus of Euripides, an officer says to that prince,
  My royal Master, (for the Gods alone
  Challenge the name of Lord,) &c.
on which Mr. Wodhull observes, after mentioning the practice of Augustus and Tiberius, that " we find, by the " Misopogon of Julian, that he followed their example at " Constantinople" [rather Antioch] " in much later times, " surrounded, as he was, by Asiatic slaves, inured to the " yoke, men to whom the sight of a philosopher on the " throne was so strange, that they ridiculed that moderation " in the conduct of their sovereign, which they felt them- " selves incapable of imitating."
 * In the original, ομματα (" eyes") perhaps for ονοματα (" names") for Julian was called by his friends πραοτατος και φιλοσοφωτατος, " the mildest and most philosophical." Theod. l. III. c. 15.   PETAU.
                     He

merciful is it to require moderation from the rich in the courts of justice, and to restrain the poor from slander! By abolishing the stage, the players, and the dancers, you have ruined our city, so that we have no consolation left, except, after having groaned under your oppressions for seven months *, that of referring our prayers for a deliverance from so great an evil to the old women † who constantly frequent the tombs of the dead. But we have succeeded by our scurrility, transfixing you with sarcasms as with arrows. If you are thus intimidated by our taunts, how, noble Sir, will you be able to sustain the darts of the Persians?

But we will now exhibit another charge. You resort frequently to the temples, perverse, morose, and abandoned as you are. On your account, the populace, and even many of the magistrates, flock thither, and welcome you with shouts, acclamations, and all the splendid applauses of the theatre. Why then are you not pleased? But, in-

---

He had probably in his view that line of Homer's Achilles,

—— Κυνος ομματ' εχων, κραδιην δ'ελαφοιο.
Thou dog in forehead, but in heart a deer,
as Pope translates it.

* Julian arrived at Antioch in the month of July, 362. He therefore composed the Misopogon in the month of January, or of February, 363.   La Bleterie.

† The churches were generally built over the tomb of some martyr. Julian supposes that the women, more assiduous at the churches than the men, requested God by the intercession of the martyrs to deliver them from him. In that there might be some truth.   *Ibid.*

stead

stead of approving, you endeavour, in this respect, to be wiser even than the Pythian *, by haranguing the people, and severely reproving those who clamour †; thus addressing the most active: " You " seldom enter the temples, through reverence to " the Gods, but when you resort to them on my ac- " count, you fill their sanctuaries with disturbance. " Men of sound minds should pray and ask bles- " sings of the Gods in silence, observing this rule " of Homer,

" Silently pray ‡.
" Remember too that Ulysses checked Euryclea ||,

---

* The priestess of Apollo, who delivered his oracles standing on a tripod called Cortina, which was placed on the mouth of a hollow in Mount Parnassus, whence proceeded a vapour that affected the head; and round this hollow was built the temple of Delphi.

† In his LXIVth Epistle Julian reproves the people of Constantinople on the same account.

‡ In the VIIth book of the Iliad, ver. 193, &c. Ajax, ready to fight with Hector, says,

Now while my brightest arms my limbs invest,
To Saturn's son be all your vows addrest.
But *pray in secret*, lest the foes should hear,
And deem your prayers the mean effect of fear.
Said I in secret? No, your vows declare,
In such a voice as fills the earth and air. Pope, 229.

How could Julian find, in these words of Ajax, a law which enjoins to " pray in silence ?" All the Greeks had the practice of quoting Homer at random. It is vexatious to see authors, infinitely more respectable than Homer, sometimes quoted with as little propriety. LA BLETERIE.

|| Euryclea was the nurse of Ulysses. See Odyss. XXII. 411.

" when

" when she loudly expressed her astonishment at
" the greatness of the deed;
 " Woman, experienc'd as thou art, controul
 " Indecent joy, and feast thy secret soul *.
" None of the Trojans in the Iliad, neither
" men nor women, are made suppliant to Priam,
" or to any one of his daughters, or sons, not
" even to Hector, though it is said they extolled
" him as a God: but to Minerva all the women,
" he says,
 " With hands uplifted, and imploring eyes,
 " Fill all the dome with supplicating cries †.
 " This, indeed, was suitable to Barbarians and
" women, but was no impiety towards the Gods,
" such as you commit by praising mortals like
" Gods, or rather flattering us more than Gods;
" when, instead of flattering even them, you had
" much better worship them wisely."

JULIAN. I repeat, you see, one of those remonstrances which I have been accustomed to make, and, instead of speaking boldly and freely, with my usual absurdity, I bear false witness against myself. Are these, and the like, proper lessons for those who would treat with freedom not only princes, but also the Gods? Can they deem any one a mild and benevolent parent, who is naturally wicked like me?

* Pope, 448.
† Iliad. VI. 301. Pope, 374.

THE MOSOPOGON.

ANT. It is plain then, Julian, that they hate you, and that they jeer you both in public and private, since those who see and applaud you in the temples you deem flatterers. You have not studied how to accommodate yourself to their ideas, lives, and manners. Well, but who can excuse this? You sleep almost every night alone *, nor can

---

* Καθευδεις ως επιπαν νυκλωρ μονος. "You sleep *almost always* alone." How is this "*almost always*" to be reconciled with the perfect continence which the Pagan authors ascribe to Julian, and which none of the Christian writers, not even St. Gregory Nazianzen himself, deny? Mamertinus scruples not to say that "the bed of that prince was " purer than that of the Vestals." If we believe Libanius, Julian never had the least frailty, either before his marriage, or after the death of his wife Helena. What that orator says is susceptible of no ambiguity or exception. I will content myself with quoting the Latin translation of Fabricius: *Nisi conjugii vinculis à Junone fuisset innexus, de mutuis hominum amplexibus, non aliâ ratione quam ex libris sermonibusque edoctus, moriturus fuisset.... Legitimam quidem luxit uxorem; aliam vero nullam, sive antea, sive post fœminam attigit,* &c.

It may be replied, that Mamertinus and Libanius are panegyrists. But what shall we say of Ammianus, whose testimony is as positive as that of Libanius? Ammianus is a most judicious historian, and does not spare Julian for any of his faults. He knew him perfectly, and seems even to have interrogated, on the point in dispute, those domestics of Julian to whom his frailties, supposing he had any, could not but be known. *Ita inviolatâ castitate enituit, ut post amissam conjugem,* nihil unquam *venereum agitaret ... ut ne suspicione quidem tenùs libidinis ullius vel* citerioris vitæ ministris *incusaretur.* Ammianus was of Antioch. Though he wrote in Latin, he was better acquainted with Greek. He had read the Misopogon. Perhaps then Martimius, the Latin translator of this satire, M. de Fleury, M. de Tillemont,

can any thing foften your favage and brutal difpofition. You have clofed up all the avenues of pleafure,

mont, and myfelf tranflate this paffage of Julian improperly, and the Greek words ω; ππωκι do not fignify here " almoſt always," but " always," abfolutely. At leaſt, it is certain that πππωκι occurs in both fignifications. In this cafe, I ought to have tranflated it, " You never ſhare " your bed with any one." I think, however, that it ought to be tranflated, as I have done, " You fhare fcarce ever." This reftriction feems to me a refined but fevere raillery againſt the inhabitants of Antioch, from which nothing can be inferred againſt the chaftity of Julian. It is in their name that he abufes himfelf. He muft therefore fpeak their language. Throughout the whole fatire he reprefents them as perfons immerfed in debauchery, and abandoned to the moft infamous pleafures. People of this character do not believe in virtue. They fuppofe all men to be vicious, and that they only differ in vice as to the more and the lefs. On the part of Julian, whofe morals were fuperior to all fufpicion, it is a ſtroke of pleafantry to reprefent his enemies as perfuaded that his wifdom fuffered eclipfes, and making, neverthelefs, his excefs of wifdom a crime in him. M. de Tillemont, who underſtands the text in queſtion literally, and confiders it as a confeffion, which Julian himfelf makes, of his incontinence, obferves, in order to ſtrengthen this pretended avowal, that Julian, in an Epiſtle to the philofopher Jamblicus [the XLth] fpeaks of the man " who nurfed his children." This learned writer adds, that Codin, in his Antiquities of Conſtantinople, mentions fome ſtatues of Julian and his children. " Now," fays M. de Tillemont, " he never " had any legitimate, excepting a fon, who was deftroyed " by the midwife that was fuborned by the emprefs Eufebia : " the fact is certain ; he therefore had fome illegitimate."

Let us briefly examine thefe two difficulties, always remembering that the Pagans, on the one fide, pafs an elogium on the chaftity of Julian, the completeſt, the moft forcible, and the moft exclufive of the leaſt reftriction; and that, on the other fide, the Chriſtians, far from controvert-

pleasure, and, which is the greatest of evils, you delight in leading such a rigid life, and make pleasure the subject of your detestation. In short, you are angry at the mention of this, though you ought rather to thank those who have kindly and harmoniously admonished you in anapæsts, first, to shave those cheeks, and then, having begun with yourself, to exhibit all pleasurable entertainments to this laughter-loving people, such as players, dancers, and, in particular, lewd women, public assemblies, and festivals, not sacred indeed, in which wisdom and temperance must be observed *, for these are as abundant as acorns, so as to occasion a general disgust.

JULIAN. The Emperor, I allow, sacrificed once in the temple of Jupiter, and afterwards in that of

---

ing those elogiums, have not said a word that can render them suspected. This established, what stress ought to be laid on the mere indication of a modern Greek, such as George Codin, who is known to have survived the taking of Constantinople by Mahomet II.? If Julian had had bastards, would he have erected statues to them? Would he, who said, that " incontinence is sufficient to tarnish " the best life," have published his own shame, and that of his children, in tender age? &c.   LA BLETERIE.

For what is said on the passage above-mentioned in the XLth Epistle, see the notes on that Epistle.

This suspicious expression (ὡς ἐπιπᾶν) is explained by the Abbè de la Bleterie, with candour and ingenuity.

GIBBON.

* This is not absolutely contrary to what is related of the extravagant processions of Julian on the festivals of Venus and others. All the Pagan festivals were not so licentious as those of Venus.   LA BLETERIE.

Fortune.

Fortune *. He also went thrice to that of Ceres.
I forget how often I went to the temple of Daphne,
that auguſt fabrick which was betrayed by the
treachery of the keepers, and by the preſumption
of the impious †. On the Syrian calends ‡, Cæſar
goes

* Genius and Fortune were *Dii Contubernales*, and had temples dedicated to them jointly. See *Pauſan. Bæotic.* p. 313. Hence what Ammianus calls *Genii templum* (xxiii. 1.) Julian here ſtyles τυχης, the one a male, the other a female, deity; the images of both being ſet up together. Modern antiquaries, as well as artiſts, by a kind of mythological ſolecifm, have confounded that diſtinction, who call a female deity the Genius of a city.   BOWYER.

† After Babylas (a biſhop of Antioch, who died in priſon in the perſecution of Decius) had reſted near a century in his grave, his body, by the order of the Cæſar Gallus, was tranſported into the midſt of the grove of Daphne. A magnificent church was erected over his remains; a portion of the ſacred lands was uſurped for the maintenance of the clergy, and for the burial of the Chriſtians of Antioch, who were ambitious of lying at the feet of their biſhop; and the prieſts of Apollo retired, with their affrighted and indignant votaries. As ſoon as another revolution ſeemed to reſtore the fortune of Paganiſm, the church of St. Babylas was demoliſhed, and new buildings were added to the mouldering edifice which had been raiſed by the piety of Syrian kings. But the firſt and moſt ſerious care of Julian was to deliver his oppreſſed deity from the odious preſence of the dead and living Chriſtians, who had ſo effectually ſuppreſſed the voice of fraud or enthuſiaſm. The ſcene of infection was purified, according to the forms of ancient rituals; the bodies were decently removed; and the miniſters of the church were permitted to convey the remains of St. Babylas to their former habitation within the walls of Antioch. The modeſt behaviour, which might have aſſuaged the jealouſy of an hoſtile government, was, on this occaſion, neglected by the zeal of the Chriſtians. The lofty car, that tranſported the relics

of

of Babylas, was followed, and accompanied, and received by an innumerable multitude; who chanted with thundering acclamations, the Pſalms of David the moſt expreſſive of their contempt for idols and idolaters. The return of the ſaint was a triumph; and the triumph was an inſult on the religion of the Emperor, who exerted his pride to diſſemble his reſentment. During the night which terminated this indiſcreet proceſſion [22 Oct. 362.] the temple of Daphne was in flames, the ſtatue of Apollo was conſumed, and the walls of the edifice were left a naked and awful monument of ruin. The Chriſtians of Antioch aſſerted, with religious confidence, that the powerful interceſſion of St. Babylas had pointed the lightnings of heaven againſt the devoted roof; but as Julian was reduced to the alternative of believing either a crime or a miracle, he choſe, without heſitation, without evidence, but with ſome colour of probability, to impute the fire of Daphne to the revenge of the Galileans. GIBBON.

Julian (in Miſopogon) rather inſinuates, than affirms, their guilt. Ammianus (XXII. 13.) treats the imputation as *leviſſimus rumor*, and relates the ſtory with extraordinary candour. *Ibid.*

I do not find that Ammianus treats this report in the manner here affirmed. All that he ſays of it is this: *Suſpicabatur enim id Chriſtianos egiſſe, ſtimulatos invidiâ, quòd idem templum inviti vidébant ambitioſe circumdari periſtylio.* "For "he ſuſpected the Chriſtians to have been the perpetrators, "urged to it by envy on ſeeing reluctantly that temple "ſurrounded by a ſpacious periſtyle." Then follows, *Ferebatur autem, licèt rumore leviſſimo, hâc ex cauſâ conflagraſſe d. lubrum*, &c. "But it was reported, though *on the ſlighteſt* "*grounds*, that this was the cauſe of the fire: The phi- "loſopher Aſclepiades, being on a viſit to Julian, and "going to that ſuburb, as he was uſed to carry with him, "wherever he went, a ſmall ſilver image of Juno, placed "it at the feet of the great image, and lighting wax tapers, "as uſual, departed; from which, in the middle of the "night, when no one could attend or aſſiſt, ſparks flying "adhered to the very ancient materials," &c. To this ſtory therefore, and not that of the Chriſtians, the *leviſſimus rumor* is app'ied.

‡ As in the concluſion of the Miſopogon, Julian reckons the Macedonian month *Loüs* the tenth of the Syrian year, this

THE MISOPOGON,

goes again to the temple of Jupiter Philius *. Then comes the general festival †, and Cæsar goes to the temple of Fortune. Omitting an inauspicious

this year began with the month *Dius*, In the Syrian year, which is used by Eusebius, St. Epiphanius, Eusgrius, Malela, &c. the month Dius answers to the month of November. But perhaps the city of Antioch had a Syrian year that was peculiar to it. In different Macedonian cities, the month Dius answered to different Roman months. It is certain that the Syrian year of Antioch began in autumn. We cannot, however, positively assert in which of the Roman months, September, October, or November. This is the result of some learned and judicious observations communicated to me by a friend to whom I owe several of my remarks. LA BLETERIE.

* The patron of friendship, the same with *Hospitalis*, "a bearded face, with a placid look, to denote," says Tristan, "that true friendship is the result of age." He had a temple at Antioch, where Julian sacrificed to him more than once, during his residence there; pleased, no doubt, to have so good an authority for his beard, which, as the inhabitants little regarded in Jupiter, no wonder they ridiculed in the Emperor. BOWYER.

† The calends of January [mentioned above, p. 231.] when the consuls entered on their office, and the priests, in a solemn procession, offered vows for the public safety of the empire, or of the Roman senate and people.

This therefore Libanius, in like manner (in his description of the calends), styles "a general festival to all who live under the Roman government." SPANHEIM.

This day was deemed a festival throughout all the Roman world, though all did not begin the year with it. For instance, the Romans then commenced the year with Dius, which answers to the Julian November: Therefore, in the above passage of Julian η Συρων Νεομηνια, ("the Syrian calends,) are the first day of the month Dius. This passage has been misunderstood by Martinius, the [Latin] translator. VALOIS.

day,

THE MISOPOGON.

day [*], he again pays his vows in the temple of Jupiter Philius, after the manner of his ancestors [†]. Who can endure Cæsar's going so frequently to the temples, when the Gods should be troubled only once or twice to celebrate those festivals, which are common to all the people, and of which not only they who honour the Gods, but they also with whom the city is filled, participate [‡]? What an exquisite pleasure and delight does every one constantly enjoy in the sight of a number of dancing men, dancing women, and dancing boys!

Reflecting on these things, I cannot but think you happy in such diversions, and yet I am by no means dissatisfied with myself; for the life I lead, by the influence perhaps of some God, is to me agreeable. Believe me, therefore, far from being offended with those who reprobate my life and manners, I even add to their sarcasms as many as possible, and accumulate on myself more reproaches for being such a fool as not to perceive at first what were the manners of this city, especially as none of my contemporaries, I am certain, are more conversant with books than myself.

---

[*] Jan. 2. The days immediately following the calends, nones, and ides were reckoned inauspicious. *Ov. Trist.* I. 55. *et seq.*

[†] On Jan. 3, when solemn vows were offered for the safety of the prince,

[‡] He means the games and shews at which the Christians, as well as the Gentiles, were present, to the great offence of the most holy prelates; which St. Chrysostom, among others, frequently mentions.   PETAU.

It

It is related that the king who was namesake to this city, or rather, to whom it owes its name (for it was built by Seleucus [*], but takes its name from his son), Antiochus I mean, from an excessive indulgence in luxurious delights, always loving and being loved, was at length illegally enamoured of his mother-in-law [†]. He wished to conceal his passion, but could not; his body being emaciated, and secretly decaying, his strength failing, and his mind being languid. His case seemed mysterious, the disorder having no apparent cause, and the nature of it not being known. The young man's illness, however, being certain, the great difficulty proposed to a Samian physician [‡] was, to discover what the distemper was. He, suspecting from Homer what are "the limbs-consuming cares [§]," and that anxiety of mind, not weakness of body, is often the cause of bodily decay, and observing the youth, as well by years as constitution, to be not averse to love, took this method to discover the disease. He sat down by the bed-side, and looking the young man stedfastly in the face, he desired some beautiful women to be introduced, beginning

---

[*] Seleucus Nicator.
[†] Stratonice, the daughter of Demetrius Poliorcetes, and wife of Seleucus.
[‡] Erasistratus.
[§] Γυιοβοροι μελεδωνες, "the anxieties that devour the body." I do not find the word γυιοβοροι in the Index of Homer, made by Wolfgangus Seberus. If the Index be not faulty, Julian is mistaken, or quotes some work of Homer which we do not possess.   LA BLETERIE.

with

with the queen. As soon as she appeared, or as soon as he saw her, the youth betrayed some symptoms of his disorder; he breathed short, as if he had been asthmatic; with his utmost endeavours he could not avoid trembling, great was the evident agitation of his mind, and his face was covered with blushes. The physician, observing this, applied his hand to his patient's breast, and found his heart beat violently, as if it would burst forth. Such were his sensations, while the queen was present. But when she had withdrawn, while the others were passing by, he remained tranquil, and seemed in perfect health. Having thus discovered his malady, Erasistratus communicated it to the king, and he, being an affectionate father, said, he would resign his wife to his son. He then refused it; but his father dying not long after, the present, which, when offered him before, he nobly declined, he then very eagerly seized. Such was the conduct of Antiochus.

That his descendants therefore should imitate their founder, or, at least, their namesake, is not blameable. For, as in plants, it is probable that the qualities are widely diffused, and perhaps those which are produced altogether resemble those

---

* Plutarch relates the story differently in his life of Demetrius. For he says, that Antiochus, the son of Demetrius Poliorcetes, married his mother-in-law in the life-time of his father.   PETAU.

which

which produce them; so, among men *, the manners of the descendants are likely to be similar to those of their ancestors. Of the Greeks I think the Athenians the most liberal and humane; though all the Greeks, I have observed, are the same, and I can truly affirm of them, that of all men they are the greatest lovers of the Gods, and most hospitable to strangers; but of the Greeks, I give this testimony chiefly to the Athenians. And if they retain in their manners the resemblance of ancient virtue, why may not the same similitude be traced in the Syrians, the Arabians, the Gauls, the Thracians, the Pannonians, and that nation which is situated between the two latter on the banks of the Danube? I mean the Mysians, the stock from which I am descended †, who are absolutely inelegant, boorish, austere, uncivilised, and obstinately tenacious of their opinions, all which are proofs of lamentable rusticity.

First, therefore, I ask pardon for myself, for imitating the manners of my ancestors, and then I grant it to you for the same offence; nor do I mention, as a reproach, your being

In lying and in wanton dances skill'd ‡.

---

* The inhabitants of Antioch were nothing to Antiochus. The kind of argument which Julian here employs must not be understood seriously. It is a mere joke. LA BLETERIE.

† Eutropius, the great grandfather of Julian, and the father of Constantius-Chlorus, was of the province of Mysia. *Ibid.*

‡ Iliad. xxiv. 261. Priam's reproach of his nine surviving sons.

On the contrary, your following the examples and studies of your fathers I think much to your honour. Thus Homer also, praising Autolycus, says that he excelled all men

In thieving and in swearing *.

* Homer, in the xixth book of the Odyssey, v. 396, says, that Autolycus, the maternal grandfather of Ulysses, excelled other men, κλεπ7οσυνη θ'ορκωΊι, " in theft and oaths." Mad. Dacier, on this passage, says, in effect, that the word κλεπ7οσυνη may signify not only " theft," but also " cunning, " address, stratagem, skill to conceal the knowledge of " his schemes, to penetrate the secrets of others, &c. " and that Homer meant to say that Autolycus was a very " acute politician, an artful prince, an able negociator, who " knew how to make treaties to his advantage, but, on the " whole, was faithful to his word, and one who respected " his oaths." Admitting the charitable explanation of Mad. Dacier, it is unfortunate for him to have been praised by Homer in equivocal terms; for the knavery of Autolycus has grown proverbial. Martial, speaking of a thief, says, *Non fuit Autolyci tam piceata manus.* LA BLETERIE.

Dr. Clarke (on the above line in the Odyssey) understands it, however, as a commendation; and Fenton, agreeably to the same interpretation, has, in his translation, ascribed to Autolycus

——————— a mighty name
For spotless faith, and deeds of martial fame. 456.

Shakspeare, on the contrary, has given his name to a roguish pedlar: " My father," says he, " named me " Autolycus, who being, as I am, littered under Mercury, " was likewise a snapper-up of unconsidered trifles."

Winter's Tale, Act IV. Sc. II.

Euripides had two dramas (now lost) named Autolycus, the first satyric (as we learn from Julius Pollux) of which a fragment is preserved by Galen and Athenæus. Barnes and Dr. Musgrave suppose that it derives its name from this Autolycus; but from what is transmitted to us, Mr. Wodhull, who has translated it, thinks, with more probability, that another Autolycus, a champion in the public games, was its hero.

And

And so, you say, do I in rusticity, obstinacy, morosenefs, in not being easily softened by supplications, or induced by intreaties or clamours, to mind my businefs. With these reproaches I am not in the least offended. Which of us is the most excusable is known to the Gods, but no man can determine between us, such is our self-love; every one admiring his own endowments, and despising those of others. But he, who bears with indulgence a course of life the reverse of his own, seems to me the most benevolent.

[On reflection, I find that, in some other particulars, I have been much my own enemy. For when I came to a free city, which could not endure the nastinefs of my hair, I came to it uncombed and bearded, as if barbers had been wanting *. You would have taken me for Smicrines or Thrasyleon †, a morose old man, or a frantic

---

* Soon after his entrance into the palace of Constantinople, Julian had occasion for the service of a barber. An officer, magnificently dressed, immediately presented himself. " It is a barber," exclaimed the prince, " that " I want, and not a receiver-general of the finances." He questioned the man concerning the profits of his employment; and was informed, that, besides a large salary, and some valuable perquisites, he enjoyed a daily allowance of twenty servants, and as many horses.   GIBBON.

Libanius says, that a thousand cooks, as many barbers (κυρίας ὐκ ιλαςίως), more cup-bearers, &c. were distributed in the several offices of luxury which Julian abolished or retrenched.

† These were probably two comic characters of Menander, as Casaubon (*Animadv. in Athenæum, l.* vi. *c.* 12.) mentions

frantic soldier, when I might have appeared, by the ornamental advantages of dress, a handsome boy, or, at least, a youth, if not in years *, in effeminacy and features †.]

ANT. You know not how to associate with men; you adopt not the maxims of Theognis ‡, nor imitate (as he recommends) the changeful polypus §,

mentions a comedy by that poet named Thrasyleon. He adds, that there was one of the same name in Latin by Turpilius, a translation, he supposes, from Menander, which is often quoted by Nonius.

* When Julian first came to Antioch, he was thirty-one years old.

† The paragraphs between [ ] are omitted here, and removed lower, by the French translator. They seem indeed a repetition of what was said at the beginning, yet I do not think myself warranted to transpose them, though I thoroughly assent to the propriety of the following remark of M. de la Bleterie, as an excuse for the incorrectness of the author, but not for the corrections of his translator: " In general, the Misopogon is a little unsewed,
" and the repetitions in it are too frequent. It was com-
" posed perhaps in the space of one or two nights. Julian
" was too much employed to be an author by premedi-
" tation. When an author scarce reads what he writes,
" we cannot wonder at tautology."

‡ Theognis, a poet of Megara, lived about 550 years before the Christian æra. We have some sentences, or maxims, by him, in elegiac verse.   LA BLETERIE.

§ Ulysses, clinging to a cliff, is compared to this fish by Homer, Odyss. V. 432. Aristotle, and others, suppose, that it changes its colour, in order more easily to catch its prey, or from fear. St. Paul, who, for good reasons *became all things to all men*, is on that account, compared to a polypus by Julian in his work against the Christian religion, preserved and confuted by Cyril. But its more extraordinary power of re-production was reserved for the speculation of modern naturalists.

which

THE MISOPOGON.

which assumes the colour of rocks, but, on the contrary, you behave to all with the proverbial rusticity, folly, and morosenefs of a Myconian *. Know you not, that we are widely different from the Gauls, the Thracians, and the Illyrians? This city, you see, abounds with shops. But you provoke the retailers by not suffering them to extort, both from natives and foreigners, what price they please for provisions. They complain of the landholders †; but these also you make your enemies,

---

* Archilochus of Paros writes, that Pericles used to come uninvited to the entertainments of others, after the manner of the Myconians, who inhabiting a barren island [in the Archipelago] were notorious for their avarice and rusticity. ATHENÆUS.
  On this proverb see Eustathius (*in Odyss.* XVII.) Suidas, and Zenobius. PETAU.

† This passage is obscure. What follows may explain it. Ammianus says (*l.* XXII.) that Julian, " with no " apparent reason, for the sake of popularity, endea- " voured to make all commodities cheap, which some- " times, by improper management, occasions dearth and " famine." Nor could the magistrates of Antioch dissuade him. By fixing therefore a lower price on things that were to be sold, he made the retailers his enemies. And when those retailers, being charged with the unreasonableness of their demands, complained that they bought corn and provisions dearer of the landholder, he compelled them also, by the same edict, to make abatements. This severity and rigour, exercised against these two ranks, extended to the chief men of the city and the magistrates, who supplied the markets, and owned the lands. And thus they were doubly mulcted. *Ibid.*
  The magistrates of Antioch perhaps condescended to sell wine themselves by retail, like some of the present nobility of Florence, as mentioned by Lord Corke, Dr. Smollett, and other travellers.

VOL. I.   S   by

by obliging them to be just. The magistrates, who, availing themselves of both these distresses, rejoiced before at receiving double profits, both as landholders and as retailers, now, on being deprived of both these advantages, are equally exasperated. The Syrians too, at being precluded both from drinking immoderately and dancing lasciviously, are no less enraged; but by giving them bread in plenty, you think they are sufficiently regaled. And so gracious are you, that you are not contented with procuring them oysters only.

When a complaint was lately made, that no fish, and scarce any poultry, could be procured in the markets, you said, with a sneering laugh, that "a frugal city ought to be satisfied with bread, "wine, and oil; that meat was a dainty; but "fish and poultry were more than dainties, and "would not have been indulged even to the suitors "in Ithaca." Thus you would have us deem pork and mutton luxuries, and subsist, like you, on vegetables *, thinking that in this you govern well,

and

---

* In the time of Julian, the philosophers of the reigning sect, who had blended the Ægyptian and Chaldean tenets with Platonism and the ruins of the doctrine of Pythagoras, transmitted by a very uncertain tradition, those philosophers, I say, or rather the most perfect among them, adopted a very austere mode of life, which made part of the doctrine which was revealed, in the mysteries, to the initiated. As Orpheus passed for the first institutor of the mysteries, it was pretended that this kind of life was that which

and are giving laws to your Thracian countrymen, or to those stupid Gauls, who, by their education, have made you a mere block of holm or maple, not a Marathonian but half an Acharnian * warrior,

one

which Plato and some other ancients have mentioned under the name of " Orphic life," Ορφικος βιος. This life, which Porphyry preaches in his book, *De abstinentiâ animalium*, consisted in the practice of moral virtues, added to the privation of things allowed in common life. The Orphics must have resembled the Ægyptian priests and the Bramins. Julian had not embraced the Orphic life, but he endeavoured to approach near it. To what I have elsewhere said of his extreme frugality, I will add here what I find in his funeral oration: See the *Bibliotheca Græca* of Fabricius, vol. VII. p. 309, 310. " What private philosopher
" in his cottage," says Libanius, " ever practised an ab-
" stinence so rigorous as that of this Emperor? Who de-
" prived himself more often than he, sometimes of one
" food, sometimes of another, in honour of Pan, of Mer-
" cury, of Hecate, of Isis, of all the deities? Who, like
" him, ever took delight in abstaining frequently from all
" nourishment? Thus he lived in an intimate connection
" with the Gods . . . his body not allowing him to raise
" himself to heaven, they descended on earth to converse
" with him. They came to instruct him in what he should
" do or forbear. . . . He had no occasion for human
" wisdom or understanding. The immortal beings, who
" know every thing, were both his council and his guard.
" By them he was almost always surrounded." After this quotation, to which I could add many similar, no one, I fancy, will have the least doubt of the fanaticism of Julian any more than of that of his panegyrist. LA BLETERIE.

* The Acharnians (so one of the tribes of Athens was called) were valiant, but rough and hardy. In the comedy of Aristophanes, entitled the Acharnian, some old men of that tribe are styled " men of oak and maple, soldiers " of Marathon ;" meaning invincible warriors. The inhabitants of Antioch, in allusion to this passage of the comic poet, reproach Julian for having the hardiness, the

unpolite-

one generally odious and difguftful. Was it not better for you to walk the forum, fcented with perfumes, and preceded by beautiful boys, and thus to attract the eyes of the citizens, and bands of women, fuch as you fee affembled every day *?

Jul. But to look wantonly, cafting my eyes on all fides, and to appear beautiful to you in perfon, not in mind, my principles will not allow me. "The true beauty of the mind confifts," you fay, "in the enjoyment of life." But my governor taught me, when I attended mafters, to behold the ground, not the ftage, and to cherifh the hairs of my chin more than thofe of my head. And even unpolitenefs, the roughnefs, of the Acharnians, without the courage of thofe brave Attic peafants. To thefe ideas, which are purely Greek, I have fubftituted fome that are equivalent. La Bleterie.

In this tranflation the Greek ideas are retained. As Julian is the fpeaker, let him fpeak as a Greek or Roman, and not like a Londoner or Parifian. Though it is not uncommon with us to fay, in like manner, of thofe who are hardy, that they are "made of iron and fteel;" and thus Charles XII. was ftyled by the Turks, "iron-head," and by Dr. Johnfon, "a frame of adamant, a foul of fire."

* Nothing could equal the feftivals of Venus, and other fuch folemnities, when, refufing to give audience to the officers and magiftrates, Julian conducted through the city the female proftitutes, and the other victims of the public incontinence. The women walked firft; after them came the effeminate youths. Between thefe two infamous troops, who burft into loud fhouts of laughter, and uttered all that debauchery could dictate, marched the reformer of Paganifm, with a burlefque gravity, heightening as much as poffible his puny ftature, extending a pointed beard, and affecting the ftep of a giant. His horfe followed at a diftance, and his guards clofed this extravagant pomp.

La Bleterie.

at

at that age I never went to the theatre privately and voluntarily, but twice or thrice only, to please Patroclus, by the prince commanded *, my intimate friend and kinsman. I was then a subject.

Pardon me therefore, and rather turn your resentment against that wicked governor, who was then so troublesome to me by inculcating those moral lessons. He has occasioned all your dislike to me by fixing, and, as it were, carving on my mind what I ought to shun. And, as if he meant to please me, he exerted himself with the utmost earnestness, calling rusticity gravity, and stupidity temperance, saying, that to resist the passions was fortitude, and that the gratification of them does not constitute happiness. My governor often said to me, when I was quite a boy, as Jove and the Muses can witness, " Do not suffer yourself to be " seduced to the theatre by the crowd of your " companions, nor be enamoured of such enter-" tainments. Do you wish to see a chariot-race? " It is elegantly described in Homer †: open the " book, and read. Do you hear of pantomime

---

* Πατροκλω επιηρα φερων, αρχων επιταιλει.

This, though not printed as such in the editions, or observed by the commentators, is an heroic verse; but it does not occur in Homer, nor is it clear whom Julian here means by " Patroclus." The prince (αρχων) must probably be his brother, Cæsar Gallus.

† In the xxiiid book of the Iliad, Achilles causes some games to be celebrated in honour of the funeral of Patroclus. Among them is a description of a chariot-race.

LA BLETERIE.

" dancers?

"dancers? Away with them! The Phæacian
" youths are less effeminate *. You have there
" the harper Phemius †, and the singer Demo-
" docus ‡. His trees too are more delightful to
" the ear than ours are to the eye.

" Thus seems the palm §, with stately honours
" crown'd,
" By Phœbus' altar ‖; thus o'erlooks the ground,
" The pride of Delos.

* See the dances of the Phæacians in the viiith book of
the Odyssey.   LA BLETERIE.
† Phemius was a musician of the island of Ithaca, whom
the suitors of Penelope forced to play on the harp during
their banquets.   *Ibid.*
‡ The Greeks must certainly have been very fond of
their Homer, as a governor so grave as that of Julian ad-
vises a child to read the scandalous romance of Mars taken
in the nets of Vulcan, which Demodocus sings at the feast
of Alcinous. See Odyss. viii.   *Ibid.*
Another grave and intelligent tutor, himself a proficient
in music, (who has lately given excellent " Advice to his
" pupils,") was also inattentive to these *furta Deorum*, as
Virgil modestly styles them, when he said, " The wise men
" of Heathen antiquity reserved the powers of music for
" the instilling moral instruction into youth." *Jones's Phy-
siological Disquisitions*, p. 354.
§ Odyss. vi. 162. Broome, 193. Nausicaa is compared
to this palm-tree by Ulysses.
Because the Ulysses of Homer said, that he " saw a tall
and tender palm-tree at Delos," the same is still shewn at
this day. *Cicero de Legibus*, I, 1.
The palm also of Delos is visible from the time of that
God [Apollo.] *Plin. Nat. Hist. l.* xvi. 44.
‖ In the original it is παρα βωμω. Casaubon, in his notes
on Athenæus, xvi. 9. quotes it περι βωμω. But Julian, in
the passage above, reads it, or quotes it by memory, παρα
βωμον.   CLARKE.

" And

" And the woody ifland of Calypfo, and the
" groves of Circe, and the garden of Alcinöus,
" be affured you will fee nothing more enchant-
" ing."

Would you know the name of this governor,
and his family? By all the Gods and Goddeffes,
he was a Barbarian, a Scythian, and name-fake to
him *, who perfuaded Xerxes to wage war againft
Greece and the renowned Argives. He was an
eunuch, a title, which twenty months ago † was
revered, but is now the fubject of fhame and reproach. He was educated by my grandfather ‡,
that

---

* It is well known that it was Mardonius, the fon of
Gobryas, who, in the council of Xerxes, gave his opinion
for making war with the Greeks, and whofe advice prevailed. Herod, VII. The governor of Julian had the fame
name. LA BLETERIE.

† He principally means Eufebius, the chamberlain of
Conftantius, [fee the Epiftle to the Athenians, p. 68] who,
in his reign, had the management of public affairs. Ammianus, (xxi. 15.) relates, that " Conftantius died Oct. 5.
" in the confulfhip of Taurus and Florentius," which was
A. D. 361. He alfo fays, in the next book, that " Julian
" compofed his Mifopogon towards the end of the year 362,
" and that he marched from Antioch againft the Perfians,
" March 1, 363." So that from the death of Conftantius to the time of his writing the Mifopogon there was
an interval of not quite fifteen months. But Julian reckons
twenty. Whether it is a miftake, or not, I cannot tell.
PETAU.
Julian probably fixes the epocha of the difgrace of the
eunuchs to the time of his declaring war againft Conftantius.
LA BLETERIE.

‡ The præfect Julian (probably Anicius Julianus, who was
conful in 322) the moft illuftrious private perfon of his age
by

that he might inftruct my mother * in the poems of Homer and Hefiod. I was her firft and only fon †, and a few months after my birth fhe died, leaving me an orphan, and oppreffed with many misfortunes. Young and tender, at feven years of age I was entrufted to his care. From that time, conducting me to proper mafters, he perfuaded me that this was the only right way; and as he himfelf would not know, nor would fuffer me to purfue, any other, he has expofed me to your refentment.

But, if you pleafe, we will now make peace, and terminate our animofity. For he had no idea of my coming hither, far from expecting that I

by his birth, his riches, and his reputation; and perhaps the firft Roman fenator who made a public profeffion of Chriftianity. He had been engaged in the party of Maxentius; but Conftantine, after the victory, revered the fuperior talents of this great man, and a virtue ftill fuperior to them. He made him conful, præfect, and at length his brother-in-law. LA BLETERIE.

* Bafilina. It is faid, that, when fhe was ready to lie in, fhe dreamed that fhe brought Achilles into the world; and that, upon her waking, while fhe related this dream, fhe was delivered of Julian, almoft without pain. This princefs died in the flower of her age. She appears to have been an Arian and a perfecutrefs, which is not furprifing, if fhe was related to Eufebius of Nicomedia. " It is certain that Julian was a diftant relation of this bifhop," fays Ammianus: probably by the fide of Bafilina, whofe mother, the maternal grandmother of Julian, might be of Ionia or Bithynia. *Ibid.*

† Gallus (as above-mentioned) was by another mother.

fhould.

should govern such an empire * as the Gods have bestowed, much against the will, believe me, both of the giver and receiver. For he who conferred † this honour, or favour, or whatever else you may please to call it, conferred it with reluctance, and by him who accepted it, the Gods well know, it was sincerely rejected. But their will is and must be obeyed. If my governor could have foreseen this, he would, without doubt, have endeavoured to make me acceptable to you. But now, whatever manners I may have previously contracted, whether gentle or boorish, it is impossible for me to alter or unlearn. Habit is said to be a second nature; to oppose it is irksome; but to counteract the study of more than thirty years is extremely difficult, especially when it has been imbibed with so much attention.

ANT. Allowing this, what induced you to investigate and determine matters of traffick? This, I imagine, was not taught you by your governor, as he did not foresee your reigning.

JUL. This also was owing to that wicked old man, whom, as the principal director of my studies, you so justly reproach as well as me; but know, that he was deceived by others. You have often

---

* Constantius, by the course of nature, might have had children, and Gallus was the elder brother of Julian, who was intended for the ecclesiastical state. LA BLETERIE.

† It is pretended that Constantius, on his death-bed, named Julian his successor. Julian believes, or affects to believe, it. *Ibid.*

heard,

heard, I suppose, the names of Plato, Socrates, Aristotle, and Theophrastus *, mentioned with derision. On these that old man had the folly to rely, and afterwards finding me young and capable of improvement, he told me, that, if in every thing I would make them my models, I should excell, he would not say all other men (for with them there was no competition), but myself. Thus guided by him, how could I act otherwise? Were it ever so desirable, I can now make no alteration, and when I reproach myself for not indulging every vice, I recollect what the Athenian stranger says in Plato †: " He is to be honoured who commits " no crime; he who prevents others from being " criminal is worthy of more than double honour: " the former is equal in dignity to a man; the " latter, who discovers to the magistrates the crimes " of others, is equal to many. But he, who, in " punishing, associates himself in authority with " the magistrates, is a great and perfect citizen, " and shall be deemed victor in the lists of virtue: " the same praise is due to temperance and pru- " dence, and to all those other good qualities " which are not only useful to the possessors, but " are also imparted to others."

* A Peripatetic philosopher, who succeeded Aristotle in his school. *Cic. in Orat.* xix. His books of plants and moral characters are all that remain of his composition; the rest of his works are enumerated by Diogenes Laërtius in his life. His name was changed by Aristotle, for his eloquence, from Tyrtamus.
† *De Legibus*, l. v.

"Such were the instructions that I received from one who thought that he was forming a private individual, not foreseeing the rank in which Jupiter has placed me. I should be ashamed of appearing worse as a prince than as a subject. I have indeed so far forgotten myself as to acquaint you with my rusticity. Another law of Plato, which has made me recollect myself, and be your enemy, says, that " the magistrates and elders should prac- " tise modesty and temperance, that their lives " may be lessons to the people." Singly, therefore, or rather with a few, I observe these rules; but the event has been different from what I expected, and has justly involved me in disgrace. Seven of us foreigners *, who have lately arrived among you, (but one, who has since joined us, is your own fellow-citizen †, dear to Mercury and to me, an excellent master of oratory,) have no connection with the rest of the world; we go out but seldom, and that only to the temples of the Gods. To the theatres we never resort, thinking them of all places the most ignoble, of all pursuits the most inglorious. If the Grecian

---

* In the number of the six friends, whom the Emperor had with him, must certainly be placed the philosophers Maximus of Ephesus, Priscus of Epirus, the sophist Himerius of Bithynia, and the physician Oribasius of Pergamus. It may be surmised that the two others were Sallust the second and Anatolius. But I do not think that Julian here speaks of any officer of the empire. LA BLETERIE.

† It is needless to observe that Libanius is here meant.
Ibid.

THE MISOPOGON.

sages will allow me to distinguish our society by the most remarkable circumstance that attends it, nothing seems so peculiarly our characteristic as an aversion to public entertainments *. Thus we solicit your hatred and resentment, instead of cajoling and endeavouring to please you.

ANT. Suppose a man is guilty of injustice. What folly is it in you to interfere! You might not only have ingratiated yourself with him, but have shared the emoluments of his injustice. Yet you prefer his enmity. You should have considered that one who is injured never complains of the magistrates, but only of the person who has injured him. But, when he has been punished, instead of blaming his accuser, he turns his resentment against the magistrates. With your usual wisdom therefore you should have refrained from compelling others to be just by force, and have allowed them all full liberty to act as they pleased, the manners of this city being remarkably free. Not attending to this, how can you think they will obey the dictates of prudence, or renounce that freedom which even the asses and the camels here enjoy? The drivers lead their camels through the porticoes, like so many brides, magnificently dressed †. As if the wide streets and narrow lanes

---

* There being no sense to be collected from the original, as it appears in the editions, both printed and MS. I have adopted that which M. de la Bleterie has substituted.

† A satirical stroke on the bad police of Antioch.

were

THE MISOPOGON.

was not intended for their ufe, they freely range the porticoes, and no one interferes, left he fhould be thought to abridge their liberty. Such is the freedom of this city; and yet you would have the young men here live peaceably, and think, or, at leaft fpeak, what it may give you pleafure to hear. But they are accuftomed to banquet freely every day, efpecially on feftivals.

Jul. The Romans formerly took vengeance on the Tarentines for affronting their ambaffadors at a Bacchanalian debauch *. But you, much happier than the Tarentines, inftead of a few days, revel the whole year †, and inftead of foreign ambaffadors, you

* In the year of Rome 473, the Romans fent an embaffy to the city of Tarentum to demand fatisfaction for an act of hoftility committed againft their fhips. Their ambaffadors had an audience in the theatre, which was the ufual place of affembly in all the Greek cities. The Roman ambaffadors defiring to fpeak in Greek were treated as Barbarians, infulted for their foreign accent and drefs, and at length driven out of the affembly. A buffoon, with beaftly impudence, foiled their robes, to the diverfion of every one, and was unanimoufly applauded. " Laugh now," faid Pofthumus, the chief of the embaffy; " you fhall weep " hereafter. This habit fhall be wafhed with ftreams of " blood." The Romans declared war againft the inhabitants of Tarentum. They called Pyrrhus to their affiftance; but Pyrrhus being forced to abandon Italy, the Tarentines furrendered at difcretion. The Romans defpoiled them of a confiderable part of their territory, obliged them to deliver up their arms and their fhips, deftroyed the walls of the city, and made it tributary.   La Bleterie.

† Let Julian fay what he will, I do not imagine that the inhabitants of Tarentum were at all inferior to thofe

of

you insult your own princes, and, in particular, deride their beards, and the devices of their coin[*]. I congratulate you, most modest citizens, some for indulging these sportive conceits, and others for applauding and admiring them. Those, it is certain, are not more delighted with uttering, than these are with hearing, such ribaldry. Such a harmonious concurrence is wonderfully pleasing to me, and happy is this one city in being actuated only by one mind.

To check and restrain the petulance and licentiousness of youth is by no means right or laudable. For to deprive men of the power of saying and doing whatever they please is an offence against liberty of the deepest die. Thoroughly convinced that you ought in all respects to be free, first, you allow your wives to be their own rulers, that they may be as licentious as possible; and, next, you devolve upon them the education of your children, lest by our laying restraints upon you, they also should at length be enslaved; or, when they advance to maturity, they should be taught to respect their elders, and then by degrees should reverence their princes; and, lastly, should thus be classed, not among men, but slaves, and by becoming temperate, just, and honest, should be corrupted and

---

of Antioch. It is said of the former, that they had more feasts and public festivals than there were days in a year.
LA BLETERIE.

[*] The inhabitants of Antioch ridiculed the marks of idolatry that appeared on the coins of Julian. *Ibid.*

ruined.

ruined. As to the women, they seduce their children to their religion by the charms of pleasure *, which is deemed the greatest good not only by men, but brutes. In consequence of this, you are most happy when you renounce all subjection; first, to the Gods, secondly to the laws, and, lastly, to us, the guardians of the laws. And if the Gods thus connive at this licentious city, and take no vengeance on its crimes, for us to be indignant and enraged would be folly in the extreme.

Neither the *Chi* nor the *Kappa*, you say, have hurt your city. This ænigma of your wisdom it is difficult to understand. But from some interpreters, of your city, I have learned, that these letters are the initials of certain names, the one of Constantius, the other of Christ †. Allow me, on this subject, to deliver my sentiments with freedom. The only instance, in which you were injured by Constantius, was his not putting me to death when he made me Cæsar. Would to heaven, that you alone, of all the Romans, had many Constantii, or rather might experience the rapine of his favourites! As for him, he was my relation

---

* It is an accuser who speaks. However, it is easy to suppose, that, in the reign of a prince so eager, as Julian was, to make proselytes, fathers and mothers were extremely indulgent to their children, lest they should embrace the religion of their sovereign. It is said, that, among the modern Greeks, the children of the lowest of the people, when they are ill-treated by their parents, threaten to turn Turks, and sometimes keep their word. LA BLETERIE.

† Χριτος and Κωνςαντιος.

and

and friend; but after he converted his friendship to enmity, and the Gods had terminated our dispute by gentle means *, I became a more sincere friend to him than, before our rupture, he could have expected. Why then should you think me displeased with those who praise him? On the contrary, I am offended with those who disparage him.

But you love Christ, and adore him as a tutelar deity, in the room of Jupiter, Daphnæan Apollo, and Calliope, who has detected your imposture †. . . . Did the Emesenians ‡ shew their love of Christ by burning the sepulchres of the Galileans? But have I ever offended the Emesenians? On the contrary, whom have I not offended of you? Most, if not all, of you, the senate, the rich, the populace? Or, rather, all the people, being attached to impiety, are displeased with me

---

* There was no blood shed in the war. Constantius died of a fever, (see p. 104, note.) while he was marching against Julian. LA BLETERIE.

† Though neither the printed editions, nor the MSS. take notice here of any chasm, the passage seems to me defective. I suspect that there were some blasphemies here, which the transcribers have retrenched. *Ibid.*

‡ The inhabitants of Antioch placed to the account of the other people of Syria, and in particular of the city of Emesa, the songs and satires which they composed against the Emperor. But Julian was not duped by them: the other cities of Syria testified a zeal for Paganism, which would not admit a suspicion that they wished to dishonour the restorer of their religion. The inhabitants of Emesa had set fire to the churches built over the tombs of the martyrs, and had spared only the principal, which they converted into a temple of Bacchus. *Ibid.*

for

THE MISOPOGON.

for adhering to the laws and ceremonies of my ancestors; the rich, because I prevent their exacting unreasonable prices; and all on account of the dancers and players, not because I abolish them, but because I regard them no more than the frogs of the lakes *. After having excited so much hatred, may I not be allowed to accuse myself?

The Roman Cato (what kind of beard he wore I know not †, but of this I am certain) excelled all who were most renowned for temperance, magnanimity, and, which is the greatest of all, bravery. When, therefore, he visited this populous, luxurious, and wealthy city, seeing in the suburbs the young men under arms, and the magistrates in their robes, he thought all this parade was exhibited by your ancestors in compliment to him; and alighting immediately from his horse ‡, he hastened forward, and blamed his friends, who had entered the city before him, for apprising the

---

* A proverbial hyperbole, meaning that the business is nothing to us §. And it is justly also applied to detractors, when we mean to say we hold their calumnies in contempt. As though frogs croak continually, and bark at the passers-by, repeating incessantly that odious ditty, Βρεκεκεκεξ κοαξ κοαξ, yet no one is offended. ERASMUS.

† Julian must surely have known that, in the time of Cato of Utica, the Romans wore no beards. It may be said that he is sorry that Cato had not one as long as his own. LA BLETERIE.

‡ Plutarch says, that "Cato was on foot, as was his "usual custom, and his friends, who accompanied him, on "horseback. On this occasion, he made them dismount."

§ Rather that we totally disregard it; as many do not regard what greatly concerns them; and, on the contrary, pay great attention to matters with which they have no concern. STEPHENS.

VOL. I.   T   citizens

citizens of his approach, and persuading them to go and meet him. While Cato thus hesitated, and seemed abashed, the master of the ceremonies coming up to him, said, " Stranger, how far off " is Demetrius ?" He was a freed-man of Pompey, and was possessed of much wealth. You will ask me how much *, as I know nothing more likely to excite your curiosity. For this I must refer you to my author, Damophilus † of Bithynia, who collected many such stories from various writers, which are very entertaining both to young and old who have a taste for such subjects. For old age seems to renew the curiosity of youth in the most incurious; to which, I imagine, it is owing, that both old and young are equally fond of stories. But to return. Would you know what answer Cato gave? Suspect not that I traduce the city. The story is not mine. If the name of a certain native of Chæronea ‡ has reached your ears, of that vile sect, as it is called, of insolent philosophers, into which I have not indeed yet been admitted, though such is my folly, I have

---

* Bishop Warburton, in a note on ver. 390, of Pope's Epistle to Arbuthnot, " What fortune, pray," [had your parents] where " his friend's personating the town, and " assuming its impertinent curiosity, gives great spirit to " the ridicule of the question," quotes this passage of Julian as " a parallel stroke."

† Damophilus lived, it is said, in the reign of Marcus Aurelius. Julian gives us no high idea of this compiler, and ridicules him by the way.   LA BLETERIE.

‡ Every one knows that Plutarch was of Chæronea in Bœotia. He relates this story in the Life of Pompey. *Ibid.* He relates it also in the Life of Cato.

wished

wished it; he, I say, relates that Cato made no answer, but only exclaimed, like a madman, "O miserable city!" and departed.

Wonder not therefore at my behaving to you in the same manner, especially as I am more savage, and as much bolder and prouder, than Cato as the Gauls are than the Romans. He lived almost all his life in his native country. But I was scarce arrived at manhood when I was sent among the Gauls and Germans, and into the Hercynian forest *; and having spent much time there, fighting with savages, like a hunter chasing wild beasts, I contracted such a disposition as cannot fawn nor flatter, but can live on terms of simplicity and equality with all men. As in the days of my early youth I travelled through the works of Plato and Aristotle †, I had no talents for this civil life, and no taste for pleasure. When I became a man, and my own master, I lived among the most fierce and warlike nations, who had no connection with Venus, the Goddess of love, but in the way of marriage, and for the sake of an off-spring; nor with Bacchus, the God of wine, but for the sake of drinking as much as they could. In their theatres, they have no obscenity, no insolence, no lascivious dances. It is said, that not long ago a certain Cappadocian fled thither from hence. You know whom I mean; the same who

---

* See a Fragment on this forest at the end of the epistles.
† Η τι ιν μειρακιοις οδος δια των Πλατωνος και Αριστοτελους λογων. Literally, "my way lay through the discourses," &c.

was educated in your city by a goldsmith. He had imbibed, I know not where, some dissolute principles, which, I know not how, he had reduced to practice *. Being introduced to one of their kings †, remembering what he had seen here, he first entertained them with a number of dancers, and afterwards with many other curiosities of this city. At length, being in want of a cotylist ‡,
(with

* In the original, μαˊων οπε και εμαθεν, ως ε διον ομιλειν γυναιξι, μειρακιοις δ᾽ επιχειρειν, εκ᾽ οιδα οποσα ενθαδε δρασας και παθων. I have substituted, with the French translator, more decent general expressions.

† Παρα τον εκεισι βασιλια, *ad regem qui illic*. Must we understand, by this, a Barbarian king, for instance, the chief of some tribe of Franks, who, in the time of Magnentius, settled themselves in a district of Gaul? Magnentius, who derived his origin from the Franks, might have called some of them to his assistance. Besides, Constantius had sent word to the people beyond the Rhine, that they might enter into the Gauls, and that he would cede to them all the conquests that they might make there. The Barbarians seconded his views too well. Julian had much difficulty to make them repass the Rhine. Perhaps too it may be supposed (but this sense seems to me less natural) that it relates to one of the Emperors, or Cæsars, who resided in the Gauls before Julian. The name of βασιλευς was given to the Emperors and Cæsars. It is sometimes given to them even by Julian, notwithstanding his republican ideas.
LA BLETERIE.

‡ The word *cotylistes* occurs in no other passage of Julian. We are totally ignorant of what he means. However, as κοτυλος and κοτυλη signify a kind of cup, κοτυλιστης, their derivative, may signify perhaps "a player with cups, or "a jugler." Seneca calls these goblets *præstigiatorum acetabula*. It is remarkable that κοτυλη and *acetabulum* have another meaning, which is common to them. They both signify the cavity of the *os ischion*, in which the head of the thigh is inserted. As *acetabulum* means " a cup to " p'ay tricks," there is great probability that κοτυλη is used

in

(with this you are well acquainted both in word and deed) he sent for one also from hence, such was his attachment to your respectable way of life. Though the Gauls were strangers to a cotylist, for this was the first time that any one had been seen at court, yet, when the dancers exerted their skill in the theatre, they deserted it, thinking those performers fools or mad.

To me a theatre seems no less ridiculous. But there, the few were derided by the many; here, I with the few am derided by you all. This, however, does not offend me; for it would be unjust in me, after concurring with them, not to bear with patience this treatment from you. I was so beloved by the Gauls, for the similitude of my manners, that they not only took up arms for me, but also made me many presents; on my refusing them, they frequently obliged me to accept them, and in every thing readily obeyed me. From thence, which was of the utmost importance, my name was often transmitted to you with glory; and all exclaimed, that I was brave, prudent, just, equally expert in peace as in war, mild, and courteous.

Of this the manner in which you have treated me has been quite ther everse. First you say, " I " have subverted the world *." In answer; I know

of

in the same sense. I am indebted for this erudition to the learned M. Falconet.   LA BLETERIE.

   * According to Socrates, (*l.* III. *c.* 17.) the saying, that " Julian had subverted the world," was owing to a bull and an altar appearing on his coins. F. Petau, M. Fleury,

of nothing that I have subverted, either by design
or inadvertence. Next, that " my beard should
" be twisted into ropes." And, lastly, that " I

and M. de Tillemont suppose, that Socrates says, the bull
lay on his back. But the historian says no such thing. We
know of no medal of this prince on which is seen a bull
thrown down, or even a bull with an altar. We are acquainted with some on which appears a bull standing, above
which are two stars. At the feet of that animal is an eagle,
who holds a crown in his beak, and seems to present it to
the bull; but there is no altar. Supposing that Socrates is
not mistaken, he alludes to some medal that is unknown to
us. A victim, ready for sacrifice, stamped on the coins of
the Emperor, shewed that the empire had changed its religion; and that is what the inhabitants of Antioch might
very well call the " subversion of the world." After all,
Julian, by his restless and reforming genius, by the various
changes which he introduced, both in the state and religion,
sufficiently deserved the above reproach, without its being
necessary to think that this reproach was relative to any
one of his coins.   La Bleterie.

One medal of Julian with a bull and an eagle and another
with a bull and two stars, are described by Occo. Among
the Imperial brass coins belonging to the library of Christ-
Church, Canterbury, are three, which are supposed to
be Julian's. One of them, which seems to have his head, has
t is inscription, DN Constanti . . . . " from which"
(says the expositor) " one would think this coin a Con-
" stantine; but the head does not resemble either of the
" Constantines, and I do not find that Julian took the
" name of Constantinus, or any name like it. His titles
" were Flavius Claudius Julianus. The reverse is a war-
" rior on foot, directing his javelin against a horseman,
" with his horse falling to the ground. Fel. Temp. . . .
" Dufresne describes this reverse on a coin of Julian, as
" doe also Occo, and I find no such of either of the Con-
" stantines. I should think Constanti . . . might possibly be
" filled up Constantinopolis, but DN, *Dominus noster*, shews
" it to be the emperor's name, and not the city's."

Constanti . . . on this coin may perhaps mean Constantius, as a coin of his, described by Occo, has the reverse here mentioned.

                                                   " wage

THE MISOPOGON.

" wage war against the *Chi* *, and that you regret
" the *Kappa* †." I wish that the guardian-gods of
this city would give you two such *Kappas*, and thus
revenge your slanderously imputing the libels
against me to many of the neighbouring holy cities,
which agree with me in worshipping the Gods;
cities, which, I am certain, have more affection for
me than for their own children, as they immediately restored the temples of the Gods, and, at
a signal lately given by me, destroyed all the
tombs of the atheists ‡, being so ardent and zealous

to

---

* Christ.   † Constantius.

‡ The cruelties, which were exercised against the Christians by those " holy cities," may be seen in the ecclesiastical history. At Heliopolis, a city situated at the foot of Libanus, men were seen to gnaw the entrails of the sacred virgins, to tear out the liver of a deacon named Cyril, and to eat it publickly. The inhabitants of Gaza in Palestine tore some of the Christians to pieces, and committed the same barbarities on the remains of their bodies which in other places were practised on the relics of the martyrs. The like enormities happened at Arethusa, &c. I know that Julian did not command those barbarities; but he could not be ignorant of what the populace are capable. When we loosen the reins, we are responsible for their fury. Julian should at least have punished these excesses, instead of apologising for them.   LA BLETERIE.

 This imperfect and reluctant confession may appear to confirm the ecclesiastical narratives, that in the cities of Gaza, Ascalon, Cæsarea, Heliopolis, &c. the Pagans abused, without prudence or remorse, the moment of their prosperity; that the unhappy objects of their cruelty were released from torture only by death; that, as their mangled bodies were dragged through the streets, they were pierced (such was the universal rage) by the spits of cooks, and the distaffs of enraged women; and that the entrails of Christian priests and virgins, after they had been tasted

by

to punish those who had transgressed against the Gods, as even to exceed my wishes.

As to you, many of you, whom my lenity has scarce been able to pacify, have overthrown the altars lately erected. But after we had sent the dead body * back from Daphne †, some of you, who worshipped

by those bloody fanatics, were mixed with barley, and contemptuously thrown to the unclean animals of the city. Such scenes of religious madness exhibit the most contemptible and odious picture of human nature.

GIBBON.

* Of Babylas, a Christian bishop of Antioch, mentioned in a former note, p. 247.

† At the distance of five miles from Antioch the Macedonian kings of Syria had consecrated to Apollo one of the most elegant places of devotion in the Pagan world. A magnificent temple rose in honour of the God of light, and his colossal figure almost filled the capacious sanctuary, which was enriched with gold and gems, and adorned by the skill of the Grecian artists. The deity was represented in a bending attitude, with a golden cup in his hand, pouring out a libation on the earth; as if he supplicated the venerable mother to give to his arms the cold and beauteous DAPHNE; for the spot was ennobled by fiction; and the fancy of the Syrian poets had transported the amorous tale from the banks of the Peneus to those of the Orontes... . The temple and the village, insensibly formed by the perpetual resort of pilgrims and spectators, were deeply bosomed in a thick grove of laurels and cypresses, which reached as far as a circumference of ten miles, and formed in the most sultry summers a cool and impenetrable shade, ... The groves of Daphne continued for many ages to enjoy the veneration of natives and strangers; the privileges of the holy ground were enlarged by the munificence of succeeding Emperors; and every generation added new ornaments to the splendor of the temple. GIBBON.

The whole of the garden at Rousham [in Oxfordshire] laid out by Kent, for General Dormer, is as elegant and antique,

THE MISOPOGON.

worshipped the Gods, by way of expiation, gave up the temple of the Daphnæan God to others who were enraged on account of the relics of the dead. And these, by their negligence or connivance, kindled those flames, and exhibited to foreign nations a sight most horrid, but to your citizens most pleasing, and by the senate hitherto disregarded. The God indeed seems, in my opinion, to have deserted the temple long before the fire *. This, at my first entrance, the statue declared to me; and I appeal to the great Sun, as a witness of it against unbelievers.

I must now remind you of another of my offences, and then, as I have done before, I will censure and condemn myself. In the tenth month †,

antique, as if the Emperor Julian had selected the most pleasing solitude about Daphne to enjoy a philosophic retirement.   WALPOLE.

* Ecclesiastical critics, particularly those who love relics, exult in this confession of Julian, and that of Libanius, (*Nænia*, p. 185.) that Apollo was disturbed by the vicinity of one dead man. Yet Ammianus (XXII. 12.) clears and purifies the whole ground, according to the rites which the Athenians formerly practised in the isle of Delos.
  GIBBON.

† F. Petau thinks, that we should read " the eleventh " month," and not " the tenth ;" supposing that the month Hyperbereteus was the first of the Macedonian year. But Suidas and Zenobius, from a Macedonian proverb, inform us, that this month was the last; and consequently the month Dius was the first. The following is the order in which the physician Ætius, and all the ephemerists, place the Macedonian months. I will annex the Roman months to which they answer in the Syrian year, which the ecclesiastical writers

according to your reckoning, (you call it, I think, Lous), is the ancient feſtival of this God, when great crowds uſed to aſſemble at Daphne. I therefore haſtened thither from the temple of Jupiter Caſſius *, expecting to ſee a profuſion of wealth and

have adopted; but, as I have ſaid before, it was not perhaps that of Antioch:

1	*Dius*,	November.	7 *Artemiſius*,	May.
2	*Appellæus*,	December.	8 *Dæſius*,	June.
3	*Audinæus*,	January.	9 *Panemus*,	July.
4	*Perittius*,	February.	10 *Löus*,	Auguſt.
5	*Dyſtrus*,	March.	11 *Gorpiæus*,	September.
6	*Xanthicus*,	April.	12 *Hyperberetæus*,	October.

LA BLETERIE.

* Jupiter was called Caſius, or Caſſius, from a very high hill of that name in Syria, which bounds Antioch to the ſouth, about fifteen miles diſtant. This was a day's journey; but Julian performed it ſeveral times during his reſidence in that city. Nothing was difficult to him when it was to viſit a place revered by the Pagans. One day, while he was ſacrificing there, he ſaw at his feet a man proſtrate on the ground, who humbly intreated him to geant him his life. He aſked who he was. " Theodotus," he was anſwered, " formerly chief of the council of " Hierapolis, who, when he conducted Conſtantius back, " then preparing to attack you, complimented him be- " fore-hand on his victory, and with ſighs and tears " conjured him to ſend immediately to Hierapolis the " head of that rebellious, that ungrateful wretch; thus " he ſtyled you." ' I have heard this long ago,' ſaid the Emperor, ' and I have heard it from more than one.' Then addreſſing himſelf to Theodotus, who was half-dead with fear, he added, ' Return home in ſafety, and diſmiſs all ' apprehenſions. You live under a prince, who, accord- ' ing to the maxim of a great philoſopher, ſtudiouſly en- ' deavours to diminiſh the number of his enemies, and to ' increaſe that of his friends.' *Ibid.*

Trajan,

and splendor. Already I feigned to myself, and saw there, as in a dream, the solemn pomp, the victims, the libations, the dances, the incense, and the boys, with minds properly disposed to the God, arrayed in white and elegant garments. But when I entered the temple, I found there neither incense, nor cake, nor victim. This much surprised me, and I concluded that you were waiting without the gate, by way of respect, for a signal from me as sovereign Pontiff *. I therefore asked the priest what offering the city intended to make on that solemn anniversary? He replied, " I have brought " the God a sacred goose from my own house, " but the city has provided nothing." Odious as I am apt to render myself, I expostulated, on this occasion, with the senate in severe terms, which it may not be unseasonable here to repeat: " Shameful," said I, " it is, that so great a city " should contemn the Gods more than any village in " the remotest parts of Pontus, and though posses- " sed of a territory so extensive, on the late annual " festival of your tutelar Deity, the first since the

---

Trajan, in his progress against the Parthians, made an offering to Jupiter Casius; on which account his temple is represented on several of his coins, and those of other emperors afterwards. He is supposed to be the same with the God Terminus among the Romans. BOWYER.

Others derive this name of Jupiter from a hill in Palestine near Ægypt, where that God had a temple, and Pompey a tomb. See Luc. vii. 451. and Plin. v. 12.

* Julian discovers his own character with that *naiveté*, that unconscious simplicity, which always constitutes true humour. GIBBON.

"Gods dispelled the cloud of impiety, should not
"have brought him even a single bird, when
"every tribe ought to have sacrificed an ox! Or,
"if that had been too expensive, the whole city
"might have joined to have offered him a bull.
"None of you scruple being profuse of expence
"on your private entertainments, and many of
"you, I know, lavish large sums on the festival of
"the Maïuma *; but none, either as individuals or a
"community,

* I know not whether we must believe, on the authority of Suidas and of some comments, that the Maïuma was originally a Roman festival. Suidas says, that in the month of May, the magistrates of Rome, followed, no doubt, by all the people, went to celebrate it at Ostia, and that, amidst diversions and licentiousness, they pushed one another into the sea. But we find in no other author that this festivity was ever celebrated in Italy, or in any other part of the West. It even seems to have been peculiar to the Orientals, and particularly to the Syrians. As places where there was much water were chosen for its celebration, such as the suburb of Daphne near Antioch, and we know not that it was celebrated in the month of May, it is more probable to suppose that it was called *Maïuma*, because that word in Syriac signifies "waters." All that is known of this festival is, that it lasted seven days, and that it "was the essence of it not to abstain "from any kind of infamy." This is the expression of Libanius, who, a thorough Pagan as he is, often mentions it with horror. Godefroy thinks that the infamous spectacle against which St. John Chrysostom inveighs with so much zeal must refer to the Maïuma. In the middle of an amphitheatre, in a reservoir filled with water, the common women swam and gambolled in the sight of the whole city. If Godefroy be not mistaken, as we also know that the city of Maïuma in Palestine, situated on the sea-shore, was particularly devoted to the worship of Venus, I should suspect that the festival of the Maïuma had originally for its
object

" community, sacrifice for their private or the
" public safety. The priest alone has sacrificed,
" who, in my opinion, ought rather to have car-
" ried home some part of your offerings. For
" the Gods require the priests to honour them
" only by their probity, and attention to virtue,
" and their decent ministration of the sacred duties;
" but the city, I think, should sacrifice both in
" public and private. Instead of this, all of you
" suffer your wives to squander your substance on
" the Galileans, who, by feeding the indigent at

object the celebration of the birth of that Goddess, who, according to the fable, sprung from the waves. But it appears that, in the time of Julian, the Maïuma was no longer considered as part of the religious worship of the Pagans. However, it is no less strange to see the Christians of Antioch partake of this scandalous festivity. But, as M. de Tillemont says, " a great nation is often more zealous " to defend the name of Christianity than to practise its " morality." " A wise prince," says Libanius, (he is supposed to mean Constantius) " had suppressed the festival " of the Maïuma." But it was tolerated in the reigns of Julian and Valens, and till the last years of Theodosius I. who forbade it some time before his death. Arcadius, in 396, allowed it to be celebrated on condition that nothing should be done there contrary to decency. *Clementiæ nostræ placuit, ut* Maïumæ, *provincialibus lætitia redderetur; ita tamen ut servetur honestas, et verecundia castis moribus perseveret.* But as it was impossible to exact this, the same emperor forbade it three years after. *Ludicras artes concedimus agitari, ne ex nimiâ harum restrictione tristitia generetur. Illud vero quod sibi nomen procax licentia vindicavit,* Maïumam fœdum atque indecorum spectaculum, *denegamus.* xv. *Cod. Theod. tit.* vi. *de Maiumâ.* Some remains of this festival were found nevertheless at Constantinople in the 1xth century, in the reign of Leon the son of Constantine Copronymus. l A BLETERIE.

" your

"your expence, exhibit a wonderful proof of
"impiety to their poor, who seem to abound
"every where. But you, though you contemn
"the worship of the Gods, think yourselves blame-
"less. No one supplies the altar with necessaries,
"not being able, I suppose, to defray the expence.
"Yet when any one of you celebrates his birth-
"day, he provides a suitable entertainment, and
"magnificently treats his friends. While on a
"solemn festival no one brings the God a libation,
"nor a victim, nor even oil for his lamp, nor
"incense. In what manner this may appear to
"any good man among you, I know not; but
"that it cannot please the God, I am certain."

Such, I remember, were my expostulations, and these the God, by his testimony, approved; which I wish he had not, but, instead of deserting the suburb in which he had so long resided, had in the late tempest turned the hearts, and opened the hands, of the magistrates *. But I was so absurd

as

* In the original, των κρατουντων. Who these κρατουντες are is not sufficiently clear to me; unless he means the guardian genii of the place [Daphne] whose attention and power were baffled by a divine interposition, which, in order to avenge the people of Antioch, occasioned that conflagration.   PETAU.

The following is the manner in which the whole passage ought, I think, to be translated, by repeating a negation that occurs a little before. " In that horrible event, " Apollo would not have diverted the attention of the tutelar " genii of the place; he would have stopped the hands of
" the

as to be angry with you, when I ought rather to have been silent, like many who entered the temple with me, and to have made no inquisitive enquiries nor reproaches. But such was my precipitation, and so ridiculous my flattery, (for it cannot be supposed that the speech which I addressed to you was dictated by friendship, but by a vain-glorious affectation of reverence to the Gods, and of a sincere regard for you, which of

" the incendiaries." For my part, I am convinced that κραταιης signifies here " the people in power, the magistrates," and if I thought, that, by " the storm," we should understand " the burning of the temple of Apollo," I would translate it " he would not have diverted the attention of " the magistrates." But I think it more natural to understand by this " storm," or " agitation," εν εκατη τη ζαλη, the commotions and disorders that happened at Antioch on account of the scarcity which Julian mentions in the sequel. The avarice of the magistrates, and the most powerful persons of the city, was the cause of that scarcity. Thus Julian would say, that Apollo, if he had still been in his temple, would have prevented or stopped the disorders, by touching the hearts of those rich misers, by forcing them to open their hands to distribute the corn which they locked up in their granaries. This is the explanation which I have adopted. I will not venture, however, to affirm that it is the true one. La Bleterie.

I adopt the same explanation, though I choose to translate the words literally. M. de la Bleterie renders them, " In the commotions by which it has lately been agitated, " he would have forced the magistrates to open their " granaries, he would have inspired them with sentiments " more humane." Τρεψας αλλαχου την διανοιαν seems very analogous to our scripture expression, ος αποκαταστησει καρδιας, κ. τ. λ. he shall turn the heart, &c. Mal. v. 6.

all

all flatteries is the most ridiculous,) that I rashly inveighed against you.

Justly therefore you now repay me for those invectives, though not in the same place. For I reproached you before the God, at the altar, at the feet of the statue, and in the presence of few; but you are thus sarcastic on me in the public markets, before all the people, and by the mouths of some of your worthy fellow-citizens. For, be assured, all who speak have a communication with their hearers; but he who eagerly listens to calumnies enjoys equal pleasure, with more safety, and is no less culpable than he who utters them.

Thus the whole city hears your lampoons on this unfortunate beard, and on its wearer, who has never shewn, nor will ever shew you, what you call a good example. For he will not lead such a life as you lead yourselves, and as you expect your princes should lead. As to the aspersions which you have both privately and publickly thrown upon me in scurrilous anapæstic verses, I also condemn myself, and very readily allow you still farther liberty. I will never expose you, on that account, to the danger of death, stripes, bonds, imprisonment, or to any other punishment. What purpose would that answer? But as the temperate life which I here lead with my friends seems to you despicable and loathsome, and exhibits a sight by no means agreeable, I have determined to remove

move and quit your city *, not from a perfuafion that my perfon and manners will be more acceptable where I am going, but becaufe I think it expedient, fhould I fail of being thought good and virtuous, to give others fome fhare of my difagreeablenefs, and no longer to difguft this happy city with the ftench, as it were, of my moderation, and of the temperance of my friends. For none of us have purchafed fo much as a field or a garden here, or have married, or given in marriage, or have been enchanted with any of your amufements; nor have we coveted the Affyrian wealth, nor been lavifh of our patronages †; nor have we fuffered any of the magiftrates to fhare with us the dominion over you; nor have we allured the people by the ruinous feftivity of banquets or plays. On the contrary, we have made them fo voluptuous, that, free from any apprehenfions of indigence, they have compofed anapæfts on thofe to whom they are indebted for fo much affluence. No gold have we exacted, no filver have we demanded, nor have we

---

* Julian had refolved to return after the Perfian campaign, and to pafs the winter at Tarfus in Cilicia.
LA BLETERIE.
This not being permitted, he ordered his corpfe to be interred there, in the fuburbs.

† Ουδ' ενεμαμιθα τας προφασιας. In the Latin, *Neque præfecturas depafti fumus.* Rather, *Neque patrocinia diftribuimus.* For he means the guardianfhip and protection of certain orders, and bodies, or the negociation of bufinefs with the Emperor, the foliciting which was very lucrative to the great. PETAU.

VOL. I. U increafed

increased the taxes; but, besides the arrears now
due, we have remitted to all a fifth of what they
used to pay.

Not contented with being regular myself, I have
also, (by Jupiter and all the Gods, I am firmly
persuaded) a most temperate usher *; who has
been much censured, however, by you, because
though old, and rather bald on the fore part of
his head, yet such is his perverseness, that he
is not ashamed to wear his hair on the back part,
like the Abantes † of Homer. Two or three more,
in no respect his inferiors, I may say four, I have also
at my house; and if you desire even a fifth, such
was my maternal uncle and namesake ‡, who governed

---

* I know not whom Julian here means. La Bleterie.
Εισαγγελευς. One who introduces persons to a king or
prince. Robertson.
This answers to the English word and place of gentle-
man-usher, or master of the ceremonies.

† Among the Greeks who went to the siege of Troy,
Homer reckons the Abantes, to whom he gives the epithet
of οπιθεν κομοωντες, *retrò comati*, because they threw their hair
back. La Bleterie.
Down their broad shoulders flows a length of hair. Pope.

‡ Julian, Count of the East, brother to Basilina. After
the profanation and destruction of Daphne, (see p. 248.)
being ordered by the Emperor to shut up the cathedral of
Antioch, then possessed by the Arians, his zeal induced
him to exceed his commission by shutting up all the other
churches, and even by beheading a presbyter, named Theo-
doret. For this rash act being reprimanded by his nephew,
he was seized, a few days after, with an inveterate ulcer,
of which he languished two months, and then died. " His
" seasonable death," says Mr. Gibbon, " is related with
" much

verned you with the strictest justice, as long as the Gods allowed him to continue and co-operate with us, though he did not manage the affairs of the city with the utmost prudence. For those governors who rule with mildness and moderation seem to me highly laudable, and this, I hoped, would have atoned for my want of beauty. But since the length of my beard, the negligence of my hair, my dislike to the theatres, my gravity in the temples, and, above all, my adherence to equity in the courts of justice, and my earnest endeavours to banish extortion have given you such offence, I shall with pleasure leave your city. If I were to attempt to alter my conduct, I should probably exemplify the old fable of the kite. For the kite, it is said, having originally a voice like other birds, was desirous to neigh like a high-bred horse; but not being able to attain the one, and losing the other, he was afterwards deprived of both, and in voice became inferior to them all. In like manner, I am very apprehensive of being neither rustic nor polite. For, as you yourselves perceive, I am now, by the will of the Gods, on the verge of that age, when, according to the Teian poet,

Grey hairs will mingle with the black *.

But

" much superstitious complacency by the Abbè de la Ble-
" terie." To the above-mentioned indiscretion of his uncle the Emperor probably here alludes. See Epistle XIII. which is addressed to this Count Julian.

* Ευΐι μοι λευκαι μελαιναις αναμεμιξονται τριχες.

The poems of Anacreon, now preserved, are said to have been first discovered by Henry Stephens; but where or how

But tell me now, I conjure you, by the immortal Gods, and by Jupiter, the guardian of your city, what has occasioned this ingratitude? Has any private or public offence of mine so provoked you, that, not being able openly to revenge it, you lampoon me in the forum, in anapæstic verses, as the comic poets treat and represent Hercules and Bacchus *? Is it because, though I have abstained from injuring you by my deeds, I have offended you by words, that you take your revenge in the same manner? Can this have occasioned your enmity and resentment? But certain I am, that nothing injurious, nothing offensive, has been done, nor any thing reproachful said, by me, either

---

is scarce known. His first edition of them, which was published at Paris in 1544, was deemed a happy discovery by some of the learned, and suspected by others. Stephens, falling into a kind of distraction in the latter part of his life, suffered his two MSS. which he had carefully collated, to perish, without communicating them even to Casaubon, his son-in-law. This we learn from M. de la Monnoie in Bayle's article Anacreon. And M. de Pauw, who published an edition of that poet at Utrecht in 1732, in 4to, is fully persuaded that the odes were composed by different authors; and, besides, doubts whether Anacreon was really the author of any single ode in the whole collection. Julian has quoted from him one passage (as above), and refers to another in his xviiith Epistle. But neither of them are to be found in Stephens's edition.

* We need only open Aristophanes, and cast an eye, in particular, on his comedies of The Frogs and The Birds, to be convinced of the licentiousness with which the Greek poets treated the Gods. The most abused, and those whom they represented in the most ridiculous characters, were Bacchus and Hercules. LA BLETERIE.

privately

privately against individuals, or publicly against the community. I have even bestowed commendations, whenever I thought them due; and I have, in some respects, been serviceable to you, as became one who was desirous of being, to the utmost of his power, a general benefactor. It was impossible, you may be assured, that all the taxes should be remitted to those who pay them, and that by those who used to receive them all should be returned. As therefore it appears that I have not diminished the public largesses, which used to be defrayed at the Imperial expence, though I have remitted you several taxes, does not this seem mysterious? But it is more proper for me to be silent as to what I have done for all the citizens in general, that I may not seem studiously to publish my own panegyric, after declaring that I would compose a bitter satire on myself. The instances of my rashness and imprudence towards you, though they ought not to have incurred your displeasure, it is, I think, incumbent on me to mention, as they are really disgraceful to me, and being more true, and relating wholly to my mind, are much more important than my personal defects, I mean the roughness of my visage, and my unpoliteness *.

---

* Και της αναφροδισιας. *Veneris odium* in the Latin translation, not properly. To αναφροδιτον is opposed to επαφροδιτον. But this means " agreeable and elegant." That therefore is " disagreeable and inelegant ;" and αναφροδισια " rusticity, " unpoliteness." PETAU.

And, first, I highly extolled you, before I was acquainted with you, or was apprised on what terms we should be, on this consideration only, that you were descended from the Greeks, as I, though by birth a Thracian, am in manners and disposition a Greek. I presumed, therefore, that we should have a mutual regard for each other. In this one instance I judged rashly. Afterwards, though you were the last who sent ambassadors to me, not excepting the Alexandrians, who are so remote as Ægypt, yet I remitted you much gold and silver, and many taxes, in particular, more than to any other city. I also augmented the number of your senators * to two hundred, and I exempted none †,

my

---

* Zosimus, *l.* III. " The Emperor, indulging the city, as " was just, and granting it a large number of senators who " were descended from parents of that rank, who were born " of the daughters of senators, (which, we know, was al- " lowed to few cities.)" But this was not so agreeable and honourable to those who were enrolled as to the city itself. For it was rather burthensome to be returned to the senate, and generally declined on account of the weight of assessments. Therefore, soon after, he says, he enrolled those two hundred in the senate, " sparing no one," φεισαμενος ουδενος. For the more powerful and opulent thought it, as has been observed, a burthen; and therefore they were to be compelled. *Ibid.*

† Every city had a senate, which was called in Latin *Curia*, the name of *Senatus* being usually appropriated to the senates of Rome and Constantinople. Two annual magistrates, named *Duumviri*, were at the head of that assembly, whose members bore the name of *Curiales* or *Decuriones*. The decurions, among other burthensome functions, were charged with collecting the taxes in the district

of

THE MISOPOGON.

my view being to increase and aggrandise your city. I allowed you therefore to choose them from among the richest of my treasurers *, and the officers of the mint. You did not, however, make choice of those who were best qualified, but, when an opportunity offered, your conduct was that of an ill-governed city, and not unlike yourselves. Shall I remind you of one instance? Having nominated a certain senator, before he was enrolled on the list, and while the process of his election was yet depending, you dragged him from the streets into the senate, indigent as he was, and thus admitted into your society one of the lowest of the people, of those who are every where else disregarded, but whom you chose to purchase at any price †. Such

is

---

of their city, and with making good the payments. Individuals therefore avoided those places as much as they could. But it was equally the interest of the empire, and of the cities, to have the curiæ numerous and filled with responsible persons. *Curiales servos esse reipublicæ, ac viscera civitatum, nullus ignorat, quorum cœtum recte appellavit antiquitas minorem Senatum,* says the Emperor Majorian. *Novell. Theod. l.* IV. *tit.* 1. Julian therefore gave a proof of his zeal for the public good, and of his affection for the city of Antioch, by allowing it to augment the number of its senators, and to choose them from among the officers of the Emperor, who pretended that they were exempted.   LA BLETERIE.

* Απο των επιτροπευσαντων τας θησαυρυς. He means the Præfects and Counts of the treasuries, of whom the Notitia treats; who were under the direction of the Counts of the sacred largesses. Thus οι εργασαμενοι το νομισμα are the officers of the mint.   PETAU.

† Martinius and Spanheim consider this as two instances of popular licentiousness; the one, that of a man, who

was

THE MISOPOGON.

is your difcernment. Many of your elections have been equally irregular, but, as I cannot connive at them all, the remembrance of my paſt favours is loſt; and for the refuſal of what juſtice would not allow me to grant, you are incenſed againſt me. But theſe were of little importance, and by no means ſufficient to irritate the whole city. What follows was my chief offence, and gave the greateſt provocation *.

When I firſt came hither, the people, oppreſſed by the rich, began with exclaiming in the theatre, "There is plenty of all things, yet all things are "extravagantly dear." Next day I difcourſed with your magiſtrates, and endeavoured to convince them of the propriety of ſpurning unjuſt

---

was enrolled into the ſenate, while he had a ſuit depending, whoſe iſſue ought to have been expected; the other, that of a poor man, taken from the dregs of the people. Their miſtake ſeems to ariſe from the words μιτιωρυ της δικης υσης, which they apply to a law-ſuit, and Αλλον, which, as uſually printed, begins the next ſentence. But the former words may as well refer to the proceſs of the ſenatorial election yet undetermined, and accordingly M. de la Bleterie tranſlates them, *lorſque le procès, dont ſa nomination fut ſuivie, étoit encore pendant.* And for Αλλον (" Another " man") I would ſubſtitute αλλα or αλλ' (" but"), and cloſe the former paragraph with a comma only, or ſemicolon. That Julian meant to produce no more than a ſingle inſtance appears from his introductory words, Βυλεσθι ινος υμας υπομνησω; " Will you allow me to remind you of *one* of them?"

* Julian proceeds to make his apology on account of the kind of famine which Antioch ſuffered, while he reſided there. Let him ſay what he will, the conduct, which he then purſued, does leſs honour to his prudence than to his diſintereſtedneſs and good intentions.   LA BLETERIE.

gain,

gain, and of obliging their fellow-citizens and foreigners. They promised to attend to what I said; but after waiting with confidence for three months, such was their negligence that I despaired of any good effect. Finding therefore that the popular clamour was just and reasonable, and that the markets were straitened not by dearth, but by the avarice of the rich, I fixed a moderate price on every commodity, of which I ordered public notice to be given. And as there was great plenty of wine, oil, and all other provisions, except wheat, whose scarcity was owing to the drought of the preceding year, I determined to supply that deficiency from Chalcis, Hierapolis, and other neighbouring cities. From them I imported for your use four hundred thousand measures; and when they were consumed, I brought from my own house, and gave to the city, first, five thousand, then seven thousand, and now, lastly, ten thousand *modii*, as you style them, all which wheat was sent me from Ægypt, for my own consumption, and fifteen measures I ordered to be sold at the same price that used formerly to be given for ten *. If ten measures

---

* With a salutary view, the Emperor ventured on a very dangerous and doubtful step, of fixing, by legal authority, the value of corn. . . . The consequences might have been foreseen, and were soon felt. The Imperial wheat was purcased by the rich merchants; the proprietors of land, or of corn, with-held from the city the accustomed supply; and the small quantities that appeared in the market were secretly sold at an advanced and illegal price.

measures cost you an *aureus* * in summer, what could be expected, when, as the Bœotian poet says, —— cruel famine rages in the house †? Would you not have accepted five measures ‡, or less, in such a severe winter as followed? Why then did your rich merchants clandestinely sell their standing corn for more, and thus take advantage of the public distress? Notwithstanding this, besides the citizens §, numbers also from the country

price. Julian still continued to applaud his own policy, treated the complaints of the people as a vain and ungrateful murmur, and convinced Antioch, that he had inherited the obstinacy, though not the cruelty, of his brother Gallus. The ignorance of the most enlightened princes may claim some excuse; but we cannot be satisfied with Julian's own defence [as above], or the elaborate apology of Libanius, *Orat. Parent. c.* XCVII. *p.* 321.   GIBBON.

* From Mr. Greaves's elements, in his excellent discourse on the *denarius*, we may fix the currency of the *aureus* at somewhat more than eleven shillings.   *Ibid.*

† Καλιπος γιγνεσθαι τον λιμον επι δωμαϊι.

"If I have searched well," (as M. de la Bleterie says of another passage), these words are not to be found in any of the works of Pindar that have been transmitted to us.

‡ Julian states three different proportions of five, ten, or fifteen *modii* of wheat, for one piece of gold, according to the degrees of plenty and scarcity. From this fact, and from some collateral examples, I conclude, that, under the successors of Constantine, the moderate price of wheat was about thirty-two shillings the English quarter, which is equal to the average price of the sixty-four first years of the present century.   GIBBON.

§ Και υχ η πολις μονον. Something, I think, is wanting here. For the sentence seems abrupt, and rather incomplete. Understand it thus. Julian made the price of corn only, and the making of bread, cheap; that is, he sold fifteen *modii* of corn for one *solidus*. But the Antiochians, besides

country came hither in crowds to purchafe bread, the only commodity that is plentiful and cheap. But which of you remembers, even in the moſt favourable feafons, fifteen meaſures of corn ſold ſo cheap as for one *aureus*? I was therefore hated by you becauſe I would not ſuffer wine, vegetables, and fruit to be ſold at an exorbitant price, nor corn, which the rich had hoarded in their granaries, to be immediately converted by them into gold and ſilver. They infamouſly ſold it to foreigners, and, in conſequence, expoſed you to famine,

—— that cruel ſcourge of mortals, *

as it is ſtyled by a God, who ſeverely reprobates ſuch tranſgreſſors. Thus, by my attention, the

---

beſides corn, wiſhed to have plenty alſo of wine, vegetables, and fruit. Compare this with another paſſage (p. 258.) where he mentions their complaints againſt him for occaſioning a plenty of bread only, and not alſo of wine, fiſh, and poultry. But here, he ſays, he was reproached for not ſuffering garden-ſtuff and fruit ἀποδόσθαι χρυσῶ, " to " be ſold for gold." Where χρυσός, that is " gold," not χρυσός, " a piece of gold ſo called," I ſuppoſe to be meant. For when the common people had hitherto purchaſed from the rich, at an extravagant price, not only corn but wine, and other articles leſs neceſſary to ſubſiſtence than corn, Julian, by ſupplying the people with plenty of corn alone, in this particular alleviated their wants. But when by his edict he had lowered the prices of meat, wine, and other things, they were no longer publickly ſold by the rich; which not being regarded by the Emperor occaſioned the popular complaints. PETAU.

* Λιμὸς ἀλοιήτερα βρότειων. This is the concluſion of an heroic verſe, though not ſo diſtinguiſhed in the editions. I ſuppoſe it to be taken from one of the Didymæan oracles (ſo called) from which Julian has given another quotation in his Duties of a Prieſt, p. 130, and in his LXIIId Epiſtle.

city

city abounded in bread, but in nothing else. Such conduct, I was well aware, would not be generally pleasing; but this gave me no concern, as I thought it my duty to relieve an oppressed people, and also the foreigners who accompanied me hither, and the officers who attended me. But since they are now departed, and the whole city has combined against me, being hated by some, and from others whom I have supported, having no return but ingratitude, relying on divine Nemesis, I will remove to another nation, another city, without reminding you of your acts of justice on yourselves nine years ago *, when the populace, with furious clamours, set fire to the houses of the magistrates, and massacred the governor; and, in return, were punished by a resentment just in the motive, but rigorous in the execution †.

* In 354, when Gallus set out for Hierapolis, the people of Antioch begged him to order an importation of corn. Gallus contented himself with replying, that " he left them " Theophilus, governor of Syria, who very well knew " how to procure it for them." The people, remembering these words, made Theophilus responsible for the dearth. On account of a quarrel that happened at the games of the Circus, they attacked and murdered the governor, and diverted themselves with dragging his body through the streets. Eubulus, one of the principal persons of the city, and his son, narrowly escaped the same treatment. But the people set fire to their house. Constantius sent Strategius to punish the rioters. Julian hints that it was at the desire of the magistrates. LA BLETERIE.

† Libanius, however, in his oration on this sedition, much applauds the clemency of Constantius.

In

THE MISOPOGON.

In short, what part of my conduct has given you so much offence? Is it my supporting you, from my own house, at an expence which no other city has seen equalled? Is it my augmenting the number of your senators? Is it my pardoning the frauds which I have detected? Lest this should be deemed a rhetorical fiction, let me specify one or two. Three thousand lots of land, you said, were vacant *, and desired the grant of them; but when they were granted, the rich alone divided them. This, on enquiry, being clearly proved, I took them from those unjust possessors, and making no scrutiny into the former exemption of those who had no right to it, applied them to the principal expences of the city. Thus those of you who annually breed horses have about three thousand exempt portions, owing partly to the prudence and good management of my uncle and namesake †, and partly to my generosity, who, for thus punishing thieves and cheats, am justly thought by you to have subverted the world ‡.

---

* He here charges the Antiochians with another instance of ingratitude. For when three thousand κληροι, or lots, of land, were vacant, having fallen in by the deaths of the heirs, Julian, at their request, gave them to the citizens. But as the few rich divided them among themselves, he soon after resumed them, and restored them to the public towards the expence of their games and entertainments, especially those of the Circus; which, he says, was the act of his uncle Julian. PETAU.

† Count Julian, of whom above, p. 290.

‡ See p. 277.

For, believe me, lenity to such offenders encourages and hardens the wicked *.

This is the whole of my meaning, and with this I shall close my discourse. My misfortunes originate from myself alone. They are owing to the ingratitude of those whom I have obliged, and are therefore the effect, not of your liberty, but of my folly. This will teach me to act with more discretion for the future, and for the kindness which you have publicly shewn me, may you be properly requited by the Gods †!

* Julian, it is observable, is silent as to his sending the whole body of the senators of Antioch, consisting of two hundred of the most noble and wealthy citizens, under a guard, from the palace to the prison, for their disrespectful and interested boldness. But he suffered them to return to their respective houses before the close of the evening. "Their short and easy confinement," says Mr. Gibbon, "is gently touched by Libanius, (*Orat. Parent.* c. xcviii. pp. 332, 333.")

† Though Julian affected to laugh, he could not forgive. His contempt was expressed, and his revenge might be gratified, by the nomination of a governor [Alexander, of Heliopolis] worthy only of such subjects; and the Emperor, for ever renouncing the ungrateful city, proclaimed his resolution to pass the ensuing winter at Tarsus in Cilicia. Libanius, in a professed oration, invites him to return to his loyal and penitent city at Antioch. GIBBON.

Soon after writing this satire, viz. March 5, 363, Julian began his march towards Persia, of which he has given the particulars, as far as Hierapolis, in his xxviith Epistle (the latest extant), to Libanius, " one citizen of Antioch," as the above cited historian expresses it, " whose genius and virtues might atone, in the opinion of Julian, for the vice and folly of his country."

XVI Epistles of LIBANIUS* to JULIAN.

EPISTLE I. †

MAY the present health and strength, that, you say, you possess, be your constant portion! For your grief may God supply a remedy! Or rather your grief requires in part only the assistance

A. D.
358.

* The sophist Libanius was born in the capital of the East [Antioch]. He publickly professed the arts of rhetoric and declamation at Nice, Nicomedia, Constantinople, Athens, and, during the remainder of his life, at Antioch. The preceptors of Julian had extorted a rash but solemn assurance, that he would never attend the lectures of their adversary: the curiosity of the royal youth was checked and inflamed; he secretly procured the writings of this dangerous sophist, and gradually surpassed, in the perfect imitation of his style, the most laborious of his domestic pupils. When Julian ascended the throne, he declared his impatience to embrace and reward the Syrian sophist, who had preserved, in a degenerate age, the Grecian purity of taste, of manners, and of religion. The Emperor's prepossession was increased and justified by the discreet pride of his favourite. Instead of pressing, with the foremost of the crowd, into the palace of Constantinople, Libanius calmly expected his arrival at Antioch: withdrew from court, on the first symptoms of coldness and indifference; required a formal invitation for each visit; and taught his sovereign an important lesson, that he might command the obedience of a subject, but that he must deserve the attachment of a friend... The voluminous

affiſtance of God, for ſome part of it yourſelf can alleviate. You are able, if you pleaſe,
to re-build the city ‡; but for your concern on
account

---

minous writings of Libanius ſtill exiſt; among them, near
two thouſand of his letters *... His birth is aſſigned to
the year 314. [In a letter to Priſcus] he mentions the 76th
year of his age (A. D. 390.) and ſeems to allude to ſome
events of ſtill later date. GIBBON.

Libanius was a great admirer of Julian, fond of Gentiliſm,
and averſe to Chriſtianity, but not an enemy to all Chriſtians. He did not embrace Chriſtianity, having been educated in great prejudices againſt it, and having never examined its evidence. Nevertheleſs, I cannot but eſteem
him an uſeful man. For, as Socrates acknowledges, he
was an excellent ſophiſt; he was continually employed in
teaching polite literature; and had many ſcholars; ſome
of whom were afterwards men of great eminence. Among
them, Socrates and Sozomen reckon John Chryſoſtom,
Theodore of Mopſoueſtia, and Maximus biſhop of Seleucia
in Iſauria. LARDNER.

By comparing their works, we find in reality that Julian
reſembles Libanius, but it is with a handſome likeneſs, and
in the ſame manner as a perſon of quality, who ſpeaks
well without affecting to do ſo, may be ſaid to reſemble a
rhetorician who makes it his ſtudy. "Hence, I imagine,"
ſays Libanius, "his ſubſequent writings have ſome affinity
"to our ſtyle, as if he had been one of our ſcholars."
Julian ſubmitted to his criticiſm both his actions and writings. He was thought to have aſſiſted him in the compo-
ſition of the Miſopogon. "Libanius," ſaid he, "loves
"me more than ever my mother did; he is not attached
"to my fortune, but to my perſon." LA BLETERIE.

† This Epiſtle is one of the three firſt publiſhed by
Fabricius, with a Latin tranſlation, in his Bibliotheca
Græca, vol. VII. p. 397. In the edition of Wolfius, it is
the xxxIIId.

‡ Nicomedia, the capital of Bythinia, which, from the
beauty of its ſituation, the magnificence of its buildings,

* In his Life, his letters, he ſays, were innumerable.

its

account of the dead, may Heaven afford you consolation! Nicomedia, ruined as she is, I deem most happy. Her safety indeed would have been most desirable; but even thus she is honoured * by your tears. Nor are these inferior to the lamentations which the Muses are said to have uttered for Achilles †, or to the drops of blood which Jupiter, in honour of his dearest son, poured down at the approaching death of Sarpedon ‡. That she therefore, who was lately a city, may again be a city, will be your concern. Elpidius §, always

its grandeur, and its riches, had been looked upon as the fifth city in the world, was destroyed by an earthquake, Aug. 24, 358, followed by a fire which lasted five days. A monody, by Libanius, on this subject, I have inserted in vol. II. Julian was then only Cæsar; but he visited the city, and gave orders for re-building it, in his way from Constantinople to Antioch, May 15, 362, after his accession to the empire. Another earthquake, which was also felt at Constantinople and Nice, swallowed up the remains of Nicomedia, on January 1, 363.

* Τιλμηλαι δι ομως I have added, to complete the sense, from the [French] king's largest MS. where these words are written in the margin, but in a more modern hand. That of the Vatican also has on the side τιλμηλαι δι ομως πισυσα. For the city might be honoured indeed, but could not be restored from its ruins, by the tears of Julian. Valois quotes this passage of Libanius, in his notes on Ammianus, XXII. 9. p 319.   WOLFIUS.

† Alluding to Homer, Odyss. XXIV. 60.
Round thee the Muses, with alternate strain,
In ever consecrating verse, complain.   POPE, 77.
‡ Iliad. XVI. 459.
Then, touch'd with grief, the weeping heavens distill'd
A shower of blood o'er all the fatal field.   POPE, 559.
§ A philosopher, to whom Julian has addressed his LVIIth Epistle. Libanius also has addressed several Epistles to him, and has mentioned him in several others.

EPISTLES OF LIBANIUS.

a man of distinguished probity, has now made wonderful improvements. Thus it is not only true, as Sophocles says, that

Wise kings are form'd by converse with the wise *, but the wisdom of a king improves also his friends in virtue. So serviceable have you been to Elpidius, making him not only richer but better. Though younger than he, you have been his instructor in these laudable pursuits, in equity, in an eager desire to assist his friends, to treat courteously those whom he knows not, and by so treating them, always to retain their friendship. For all, who have approached and conversed with him, have first admired and then instantly loved him, or rather have discovered your ideas in all that you have entrusted to him. I often discourse with him; and all our discourses turn on you, on the understanding that you possess, and the important affairs in which you are engaged. The manner in which you will complete them, and how you will ward some impending dangers, we have sagely discussed. I seemed, as it were, conversing with yourself. With particular pleasure I received the intelligence of your having defeated the Barbarians †, and that you had related your victories in a commentary.‡, thus acting

---

* Σοφοι τυραννοι των σοφων συνεσια.

I have searched Sophocles in vain for this verse. WOLFIUS.

† Probably his victories over the Salian Franks and Chamarians. See the Epistle to the Athenians, p. 87.

‡ We should add him to the number of celebrated historians, if his Memoirs of the Gallic war had been transmitted to us.   LA BLETERIE.

EPISTLES OF LIBANIUS.

at once as an orator and a general *. Achilles required a Homer, and Alexander many fuch †, but your trophies, your own voice, which has erected them, will tranfmit to pofterity. Thus you furpafs the fophifts, by propofing to them not only actions for them to celebrate, but the orations, which you have compofed on your actions, for their emulation.

To thefe your trophies I wifh you to add that of reftoring Pompeianus ‡ to his rights; and think not this an unworthy contention. For this is the man, whom formerly, in Bithynia, when he was ambaffador from hence, you faw with pleafure, and, on being informed of what he had been defrauded, gave him hopes of recovering his property. Of this promife, O prince §, I intreat you to be mindful.

* See the Epiftle to the Athenians, p. 88, note *.

† Τίλανὸν [the common reading] has no meaning. Spanheim has συγγραφόντων, perhaps for συγγραφέων, " writers." M. V. la Croze preferred Σειρήνων, (" Sirens.") To me it is not yet clear. Suppofe we fhould read τοιούτων, (" fuch,") which I have expreffed in my tranflation? Salvinius has " Titenibus." WOLFIUS.

‡ Pompeianus, who had been præfect of Bithynia, is mentioned with elogiums by Libanius in many other Epiftles, and fome are alfo addreffed to him.

§ Ὦ Βασιλεῦ. Though Julian was then only Cæfar, as appears from fome paffages above, both Fabricius and Wolfius have tranflated this *Imperator*. But Βασιλεύς was often applied to the Cæfars.

EPISTLE II.*

A. D. 362.

ARE you then forgetful of us? But Phœnicia does not suffer us to be forgetful of you, as she celebrates your reign in immortal hymns †. From your ‡ Asia also flows the fame of your actions, increasing our expectations. For nothing that we have heard, great as all these actions are, is so great as to exceed the hopes that we have formed. We, on account of our relation to the Ionians §, rejoice, trusting that you will proceed in the right road, and that your authority both over them and us will be more firmly established. But this must be left to the providence of God.

Andragathius, in requesting to be the bearer of this, has rather conferred than asked a favour of me.

---

* This is another of the Epistles preserved by Fabricius. In the edition of Wolfius it is the ccxxivth.

† Godefroi, in one of the indexes to his edition of the Theodosian Code, quotes this passage; but supposes this letter (then unpublished) to be addressed to Count Julian, Consular of Phœnicia.

‡ Υμιλιξας. In the Barocc. MS. Ημιλιξας. Our reading is supported by four others; and justly, as Libanius appeals to the accounts sent him, of the actions performed by Julian, from foreign and distant parts. Addressing Julian, he styles Ionia (which is soon after eloquently named) "*Your* Asia," meaning a district of Asia Minor, in which, having left Phœnicia, he then was.   WOLFIUS.

§ For this relationship, of which Libanius, an orator of Antioch, here boasts, the scholiast thus accounts: "The "Ionians near Smyrna formerly sent a colony to Antioch, "and therefore he styles them relations."   *Ibid.*

For

For he will not be more gratified by the pleasure of seeing you than I am by thus being enabled to accost you. This youth will have these three recommendations to you; an energy of speech, which he has displayed before the præfects; a courtesy of behaviour, which endears him to all with whom he converses; and such an intimacy with me, as, in that respect, to exceed all the friends that I have had since my childhood.

EPISTLE III. *

YOU have gained a double victory †, one by your arms, the other by your eloquence. One trophy is erected to you by the Barbarians, and the other by me your friend; a trophy this most pleasing even to a conqueror. For all parents wish to be excelled by their children ‡, and you,

A. D. 358.

---

* The Barocc. MS. to the name Ιουλιανω adds, Καισαρι, ("Cæsar,") but the Medic. B. τω Καταρατω ("the execrable.") Ezech. Spanheim quotes the beginning of this epistle in his preface to the works of Julian, p. 4. WOLFIUS.
In the edition of Wolfius, this is the CCCLXXIId.

† Thus our author, in his cccxcivth epistle, a: "The excellent Anatolius has gained two victories over us."
              Ibid.

‡ A comparison by no means foreign to this passage, as the sophists used to style their scholars their sons. See Eunapius, in Julian, and Damascius in the Life of Isidorus in Photius on Zenodotus; " alone thought worthy of being called the darling child of Proclus." Our author also in his epistles has frequently the same expression. That Julian had been instructed in the art of speaking by the precepts of Libanius, is evident from this as well as from other passages. *Ibid.*

who by me have been instructed in writing, have in that excelled your instructor. But now for the brevity * of my epistle, I, the orator, must account to you, the general, or rather to one no less consummate in the art of oratory than in that of war †. After the Emperor ‡ had given you a share in the government, I thought myself bound to lay some restraint on my freedom, and not to indulge it, as I had been accustomed, to a man so exalted. For knowing, as we do, in our declamatory skirmishes, how to accost Pericles, Cimon, and Miltiades, it would have been shameful in real life to neglect those laws. And as you yourself say, that the letters of generals, on account of their avocations, should be short, this induced me to contract my

* Julian loved long epistles, as appears from his second to Prohæresins: "Sages, like you, may make long and verbose orations, but from me to you a little is sufficient."

† This union of war with eloquence and the other arts is applauded by Libanius in other places, but especially in his IIId oration to Julian, p. 183. "You alone comprehend the accomplishments that are divided among others; and no orator, nor warrior, nor judge, nor sophist, nor mystic, nor philosopher, nor prophet can admire himself when compared with you. For in your actions you excell those who act, in your speeches those who speak." WOLFIUS.

‡ That Constantius, who, when he was oppressed with the difficulties of the Gallic war, though by no means a friend to Julian, rather thinking that he had cause to fear him, yet yielded to the exigence of the times, and associated Julian in the empire. For this reason, in the Barocc. MS. this epistle has the addition of "Cæsar." *Ibid.*

epistles,

EPISTLES OF LIBANIUS.

epistles, sensible, that he whose business prevents him from writing long letters, by one who sends him long letters must be much interrupted. But now, as you order me to be diffuse, I will obey.

And, first, I congratulate you, that, with arms in your hands, you have not suspended your application to oratory, but wage war, as if war were your only study, and attend to books, as if you were a stranger to arms. And next, that he *, who has given you a share in the empire, has had no cause to repent of his having given it, but considering him as your cousin, and collegue, and lord, and master, in all your actions you promote his glory, and exclaim to your falling enemies, " what " would be your fate, if the Emperor were pre- " sent?" All this I applaud, and also your not having changed your manners with your dress, nor lost, by gaining power, the remembrance of your friends. Many blessings attend you for shewing that, when I celebrated your talents, I was not a liar, or rather for having shewn that I was a liar in promising nothing equal to what you have performed! This is all your own, and copied from no model. For though some, together with the empire, have assumed the love of money, contracting desires to which before they were strangers, and others have given more indulgence to their former inclinations, you alone, when raised to the throne,

* Constantius. See the last note, p. 310.

have shared your fortune * among your friends,
giving one a house, another slaves, land to this,
money to that, and, when a subject, were more
wealthy than now when you are prince. Nor do
you exclude me from the number of your friends,
though I am not one of those who have shared
your favours. For I can assign a reason of my
alone having received nothing. As you would
have cities abound with every thing that can promote their happiness, you deem nothing more
essential to this than oratory, knowing that, if that
were extinct, we should resemble the Barbarians.
Apprehending therefore, that, if I abounded with
riches, I should neglect my art, you thought it
right for me to remain poor, that I might not be
tempted to desert my station: Such, at least, is my
solution. Not that you have said, " Amphiaraus
" and Capaneus are something †; but this man
" has neither name nor place ‡." But your not
having

* This may illustrate what our author, in his Life, p. 42,
relates of Julian, viz. that " Libanius loved himself, but
others loved his riches." WOLSIUS.

† This is a proverbial expression, which I do not remember to have read elsewhere. In other passages of the
ancients, Capaneus is applied to a faithful friend, because
Capaneus, amidst great wealth, living with frugality and
œconomy, was most attentive to his friends. *Ibid.*
It is needless to add, that Amphiaraus and Capaneus
were two of the seven chiefs against Thebes.

‡ Ουτ' εν λογω ετ εν αριθμω. This oracle of Apollo, to the
inhabitants of Ægina, is quoted by the scholiast on Theocritus : Υμεις δ', ω Μεγαρεις, ετ' εν λογω, κ. τ. λ. Compare the
Chiliades of Erasmus, p. 437. *Ibid.*

The

having given me any thing is owing to your regard for the public. Therefore though we are indigent of money, we abound with words. This is your concern; may we not disgrace the part that is allotted to us, nor you your illustrious rank!

EPISTLE IV. *

I SENT you a short oration on an important subject. You can add to its length, by supplying what is essential to that purpose. If you give that, you will shew that you think I have a talent for encomiums. If you do not give it, I shall be induced to entertain some other suspicions.

EPISTLE V. †

UNLESS you were well apprised how long ago my friendship with the excellent Macedonius ‡ was contracted, and for what reasons it has been since improved, of these I would

---

The inhabitants of Ægina, say some, of Megara, say others, after gaining a naval victory, enquired of Apollo who was the bravest of the Greeks; to which he gave a depreciating answer, concluding as above.

* This, in the edition of Wolfius, is the DXXVth. It is also one of those preserved in Latin by Zambicari. See a note on Epistle XV. To what oration Libanius here alludes does not appear.

† This is the DLXXXVIth in the edition abovementioned.

‡ The son of Pelagius, of Cyrus, a city in Syria, an orator, and a philosopher. Libanius mentions him with great encomiums in several other epistles, and has addressed three to him, one of which is a congratulation on his marriage.

first

first apprife you; but knowing, as you do, its foundation, you will not wonder that I, who would decline no danger for my friends, fhould devote to his fervice this letter. He has indeed prevailed with me to ask a favour of you, not that you grant favours cafily, or grant all that are afked; but fuch as are juft and right you willingly confer. And, in truth, whoever does not oblige his friends, in matters thus irreproachable, blames the daughter* of Jove for retaining the Graces in her veftibule. But that you favour thofe who ask nothing unreafonable is evident to all. Now obferve whether my requeft is fuch as can be cenfured.

Macedonius married a wife who had a fon by a former husband. That fon is now dead. I wifh therefore that the mother †, in preference to the grandfather, may fucceed to his eftate, if a regard to honour can induce the grandfather to wave his right, and to prefer praife to a compliance with the law. Be it therefore your endeavour to con-

---

* The Greek mythologifts ftyle her Δικη, ("Juftice,") whom he virtually condemns, that does not return to a friend the favour which he could and ought. WOLFIUS.

† The mothers, among the Romans, had not, in the beginning, any fhare in the fucceffion of their children, whether they were emancipated or not. In procefs of time, the mothers did fucceed, but differently according to the different times, and the whimfical changes that many laws made in their right of fucceffion. In England, if, after the death of a father, any of his children die inteftate, without wife or children, in the life-time of the mother, the mother, in that cafe, fucceeds jointly and equally with the brothers and fifters of the deceafed and their reprefentatives. STRAHAN.

vince

vince him, that it is more creditable for him to decline than to take these effects. You will be doubly persuasive, as, besides the powers of oratory, you possess supreme dominion. And I hear that this old man is vain of a good reputation, and had rather accumulate fame than wealth. Delay not therefore to send for and confer with him, and thus perform an action more humane than any law. Nor think that we will admit, as an excuse, your alleging that the discussion of such matters does not belong to you, or, by way of subterfuge, that you are unable to persuade him. To be the instrument of conferring wealth on the mother, and fame on her father, will do you no dishonour. Every word from you makes a strong impression on the hearers.

EPISTLE VI. *

THE laws and myself will take care that that most abandoned servant shall be punished for what he has said and done. But you, together with the empire, shew that you possess also such benevolence as the excellent Priscian † displayed to Seleucus ‡. Acting thus, you will induce the

* This, in the edition of Wolfius, is the DXCIft.
† Priscian was an excellent orator, and on that account was invited by Julian to Constantinople. Libanius has addressed several Epistles to him.
‡ Seleucus is also mentioned as a friend of Libanius in many of his Epistles, and many are addressed to him.

preceptors

preceptors of Arrhabius, I mean Calliopius *, and his father, to treat him with more indulgence. For Seleucus married the daughter of one, and the sister of the other. Him therefore, whom in your letters you so highly honour as to style him your son, assist, I intreat you, in his literary improvements.

EPISTLE VII. †

WOULD you have me believe that you do not take the least concern in the affairs of Ulpian and Palladius ‡, that you neither regard them as friends, nor esteem them as orators, nor recollect that they may assist you with their friendly offices? Such reports, which it does not become me to repeat, are circulated by many. On the contrary, I contend that none of them, as far as you are concerned, are true. Write therefore, and confute them. You will thus confer a favour on yourself, as well as on me.

* Calliopius, by some of the Epistles to him, appears to have been an orator.
† This in the edition of Wolfius is the DCIId, a.
‡ Two orators, frequently mentioned by Libanius.

EPISTLE VIII. *

I HAVE discharged my obligations to Aristophanes †; but you, in return, have given me such splendid tokens of a vehement affection as are conspicuous both to Gods and men. So that now I seem almost to soar into the sky, elevated by your epistle, which has inspired me with such hopes, and has so decorated my oration ‡, that all things else, the wealth of Midas, the beauty of Nireus §, the swiftness of Crison ‖, the strength of Polydamas **, the sword of Peleus ††, seem little in my sight.

A. D. 362.

---

* This Epistle is one of the three first published by Fabricius. In the edition of Wolfius it is the DCLXXth.

† This oration for Aristophanes, a Corinthian, the son of Menander, who had been severely fined by the præfect of Ægypt, on account of his consulting astrologers, is preserved in the works of Libanius, vol. II. p. 210, &c.
WOLFIUS.
It is said in this oration, that he had been fined, scourged, and imprisoned.

‡ The Epistle of Julian to Libanius, to which this is an answer, is the LXVIIIth, or last, in vol. II.

§ See Homer. Iliad. ii. 671.

‖ Crison was that native of Himera, who gained three victories in the Olympic games. See the Prolegomena of Erasmus Schmidius on Pindar, p. 31. Add. Pausan. Eliac. p. 172. WOLFIUS.

** A famous Thessalian wrestler, who strangled a lion on mount Olympus, tamed a wild bull, and stopped a chariot drawn by the strongest horses. He was crushed to death by a rock under which he took shelter from a storm; and this was owing to his indiscretion in flattering himself

that

fight. Even the nectar of the Gods, were I allowed to enjoy it, could not give me greater delight than I now feel, when my prince, such a one as Plato formerly fought and could scarcely find *, has commended my sentiments, admired my oration, and has not only promised that he will give something, but, which is much greater honour, that he will consult with me what to give. They who observe the rising of the celestial goat †, do not always obtain their wishes; but I, though I have not attended to this, have been most successful. And if I want any other favour, the Emperor, imitating the Deity, is ever gracious. Your epistle therefore shall be prefixed to my oration, to inform all the Greeks, that my dart has not been launched in vain, for by what I have written, Aristophanes will be honoured, as I am by what you have returned; or rather both of us shall

<hr>

that he could support the rock, which was beginning to fall, when his companions fled.   MORERI.

Libanius mentions him also in his xvith Declamation.

†† Peleus received a sword from Vulcan, with which he could defend himself against all attacks, as we learn from the scholiast on the ivth Nemean of Pindar, ver. 88, &c.   WOLFIUS.

* Alluding to the famous saying of Plato, that " go-
" vernments would be happy, if kings philosophised or
" philosophers reigned."   Ibid.

† A proverbial expression, often used of those with whom every thing succeeds happily, and as they wish; because it was of old a vulgar opinion that they who saw that goat, who was the nurse of Jupiter, and on that account was made a constellation, obtained whatever they desired.

   ERASMUS.

shall

EPISTLES OF LIBANIUS.

shall glory in what has been written and will be given by you, for each of us is honoured by each of these.

But now it may divert you to hear how Aristophanes has been terrified. One of your usual evening-attendants informed us that, on coming to your door, he was refused admittance, because he was told, you were busy in composing an oration. This immediately occasioned an apprehension that you had determined to controvert my oration *, and confute your preceptor, and would thus overwhelm Aristophanes like the Nile †. We hastened therefore to the excellent Elpidius, who, on hearing the cause of our alarm, burst into a loud laughter. Thus we recovered our spirits, and soon after I received your elegant epistle ‡.

---

* Libanius means the oration, which he, who had formerly been the preceptor of Julian, had spoken for Aristophanes.   WOLFIUS.

† Alluding, I imagine, to the inundation of the Nile, and, at the same time, to the torrent of Julian's eloquence, which might over-power Aristophanes. Thus Suidas ascribes to Chrysostom " cataracts like those of the Nile," and Tzetzes mentions " Nile-like floods," both applied to eloquence. See p. 305.   *Ibid.*

‡ This Epistle of Julian to Libanius is here subjoined in a note, by Wolfius, from Fabricius. But I have added my translation of it to his other Epistles in Vol. II.

EPISTLE

EPISTLE IX. *

A. D. 361.

HOW much soever I condemned that journey (fatiguing as it was) †, I no less, or rather more, condemned myself for returning so soon, instead of going to the place appointed, and there indulging my eyes, the next morning, at sun-rising, with the sight of his divine visage. And so unfortunate is the city, that she could not afford me the least consolation. I style her unfortunate, not on account of the dearth of provisions, but because she has been and is adjudged wicked, invidious, and ungrateful ‡ by him whose prudence

---

* To the name Ιουλιανω, Αυτοκρατορι ("Emperor,") is prefixed in two MSS. And in another, τω τρισκαταρατω ("most "execrable,") is annexed to it. WOLFIUS.
In the edition of Wolfius it is the DCCXIIth. It is also one of those preserved in Latin by Zambicari.

† What fatiguing and fruitless journey Libanius had taken, does not appear. Perhaps it was to Mount Cassius, (see the Misopogon, p. 282.) where Jupiter had a temple, fifteen miles, or a day's journey, from Antioch, which, however, Julian performed several times during his residence in that city. For "from thence," says Ammianus, (XXII. 14.) "at the second cock-crowing, is first "seen the rising of the sun."

‡ Meaning Antioch, at that time not only afflicted with famine, but exposed to the resentment of the Emperor for disregarding his edict for lowering the price of provisions, and not abstaining from sarcasms on himself. This appears from the embassy (πρεσβευτικος) our author sent to Julian for

the

EPISTLES OF LIBANIUS.

prudence surpasses his dominions, extensive as they are. While Alcimus * was with me, I had one who would hear with indulgence my s.l.-reproaches and my boasts of the distinction shewn me by you. But after his departure, considering the cieling as my only friend, I looked up to it, as I lay in my bed, and said, "Now the Emperor sent for me: "now I entered and sat down (for that he allowed "me); now I pleaded for the city, as I was per- "mitted to intercede with him for those who "had offended him. But he prevailed, so just "was his charge, and so powerful his elocution. "And though I opposed him, I was neither dis- "liked, nor ejected." With this banquet I regale myself, and I intreat the Gods, first, that they will give you the superiority over your enemies, and, secondly, that they will render you as propitious to us, as you were formerly. I have also a third petition, which they have heard, but I will not here mention. I ought not, however, even to have said that I will not mention it. For you are ingenious enough to conjecture this third article from my wishing to conceal what I wish. And, in-

---

the Antiochians, which is in the second volume of his works, p. 151, and also from his oration to the Antiochians *de Imperatoris irâ*, which, before unpublished, our learned Fabricius has inserted in his Bibliotheca Græca, vol. VII. p. 207.
WOLFIUS.
See also the Misopogon, p. 296, &c.

* A native of Nicomedia, and a man of learning, as appears from several letters addressed to him by Libanius.

Vol. I.   Y   deed,

deed, I apprehend that the contrary will be your choice *.

Now then pafs the rivers; rufh on the archers † more impetuoufly than a torrent; and afterwards think on what you faid you would think. But fail not to folace me, in your abfence, as much as you can. I, for my part, will fend epiftles to extort your anfwers from the midft of the battle, as I am convinced that you have a genius that can at once command an army, fight an enemy, and correfpond with a friend. I am fo infirm, that I am obliged to hear what I ought to fee. Happy is Seleucus ‡ in this glorious fight, and in preferring the honour of ferving fuch a prince to that which he derives from a good wife, and a moft beloved daughter!

* I fhould underftand this of marriage, to which Julian was averfe. WOLFIUS.

† Meaning the Perfians, Julian being then engaged in that expedition. *Ibid.*

‡ Seleucus has been mentioned in Epiftle VI. p. 315.

EPISTLE

EPISTLE X.*

THAT Alexander † was appointed to the government, it first, I confess, gave me some concern, as the principal persons among us were dissatisfied. I thought it dishonourable, injurious, and unbecoming a prince; and that repeated mulcts would rather weaken than improve the city. But now the good effects of this severity are so manifest, that I recant ‡. For they, who formerly bathed and slept at noon, now, imitating the

A. D. 363.

---

* This, in the edition of Wolfius, is the DCXXIId.

† This is the Alexander of whom Ammianus says, (XXIII. 2.) " When Julian was going to leave Antioch, he made " one Alexander of Heliopolis governor of Syria, a tur-" bulent and severe man, saying, that ' undeserving as he ' was, such a ruler suited the avaricious and contu-' melious Antiochians." Consult Valois on that passage, who refers to this Epistle, then unpublished. WOLFIUS. See the Misopogon, p. 302. note †.

‡ Ἄδω παλινῳδίαν. This proverb is taken from a transaction of Stesichorus, the Lyric poet, mentioned by Plato in his Phædrus. For having slandered Helen, in a poem, he was deprived of his eye-sight; but Achilles, by her desire, as Pausanias relates, in his Laconica, having acquainted him with the cause of his blindness, he immediately sung a recantation, by praising Helen, whom before he had censured; and thus he recovered his sight. Socrates says, in joke, that " he wishes to imitate him, and would rather sing a recan-" tation in favour of love, which he had blamed, than " lose his eyes." ERASMUS.

manners of the Lacedæmonians *, labour indefatigably not only in the day-time, but no small part of the night, nailed, as it were, to the gate of Alexander. And when he clamours from within, every thing is instantly in motion. Thus the sword will never be wanted, since his threats alone are sufficient to render the impudent modest, and the slothful industrious. Calliope is also honoured, agreeably to your wishes †, not only by horse-races, but theatrical exhibitions; and sacrifices are offered to that Goddess in the theatre, without our making the least alteration. Loud applause is given, and amidst this applause the Gods are invoked. With this applause the governor seems so delighted, that he urges many more to add to it. Of such importance, O prince, to mankind is divination ‡, as it teaches every one the best manner of governing a family, a city, a nation, and a kingdom.

* For the Lacedæmonians were far from being delicate. Hence arose the proverb, Λακωνικως διπνειν, ("to sup Lacedæmonially,") on which see Erasmus, p. 268. WOLFIUS.

† This must probably be ironical, as Julian was far from being a favourer, or frequenter, of the circus, or the theatre. See the Misopogon, pp. 232, 261, and 268.

‡ Libanius here flatters Julian, as if he had learned by divination that Alexander was such a one as ought to govern Syria and the Antiochians. WOLFIUS.

EPISTLE

EPISTLE XI.*

ON all accounts I was pleased to see Ablavius †, but principally because he brought me a letter from you. For sooner than blame you I should detest myself; such has been your attention to the promotion of my interest, amidst this tedious war, which you could not have been, if any one had spoken to my disadvantage. In seeming to laugh, and in pardoning those who, in order to flatter one, calumniate another, you acted like yourself. Flattery is their trade, and as necessary to their subsistence as rowing is to that of sailors. That sage, with whose morals Ablavius acquainted me, though he would not disclose his name, gave me no concern on any account, this only excepted, that in mentioning me he was guilty of a solecism; and I, though guilty of no offence, was sent by him among the Barbarians ‡. Inform him of this, and caution him to avoid such mistakes for the future; he may then, if he pleases, speak evil of me, for then, at least, he will not speak ill §. But this

---

* This, in the edition of Wolfius, is the MXXXVth.

† Libanius has two Epistles to Ablavius, by which it appears that he was an orator.

‡ Libanius ridicules the man, by whose speaking barbarously of him, he himself was, as it were, made a Barbarian. WOLFIUS.

§ This play on the words λεγειν κακως, and ερει κακως, I have endeavoured to retain in English, by the equivocal meaning of "evil" and "ill," as applied to slander and to language.

man is unalterable *. If, however, by his calumnies he should still offend you, and you wish to punish him, you easily may, by confining him to his house, in an afternoon, and obliging him to sup at home; and when he again grows insolent, through repletion, and drinks your own wine against you †, you need only repeat that punishment; you cannot inflict a greater. This will effectually curb his licentious tongue; but, whatever be his name, let me know it, that, when I write his elogium, it may not be anonymous.

EPISTLE XII. ‡

A. D. 358.

ALAS! alas! how insatiable is your desire of farther attainments! You possess the palm of eloquence, snatched from others, at once

A matchless prince and a most potent sage §.

Other

---

* Σταδιος, in Greek, usually signifies "firm, immoveable." I understand, therefore, this passage of a man who cannot be changed, but always remains the same. WOLFIUS.

† Πινε τον σοι οινον κατα συ. It should seem by this passage, that it was customary to drink health, or confusion, in those times as it is in ours.

‡ In the edition of Wolfius this is the MCXXVth.

§ Αρχων τ' αγαθος, κρατερος τε σοφιστης.
In allusion to Homer. Iliad III. 178.

Αμφοτερον βασιλευς τ' αγαθος, κρατερος τ' αιχμητης.

Great in the war, and great in arts of sway. POPE, 236.
That Libanius here did not flatter Julian, in praising him for his eloquence, his orations and epistles still extant attest. To which may be added what Spanheim says in his preface to the works of Julian, c. 2. "Among the "Emperors his predecessors, or those who followed him "in

Other princes have acted, and we applauded; but you excell in both those capacities. For how can we speak so highly in commendation of your actions as you do of that short letter *? Hence I conjecture what you will do, when you have subdued Phœnicia †, as already you administer justice to your subjects, wage war with the Barbarians, and in the composition of orations far exceed the common rank. Though I am not solicitous as to the future, I shall be as much pleased with this slaughter as with a victory. For when the vanquished and the victor are friends, the vanquished has a share in the triumph; as friends, it is said, have all things common ‡.

" in the same exalted station, I cannot see any, who as to the
" extent, or copiousness, of their learning, or the bright-
" ness of their genius, or the power of their eloquence,
" can in those arts, and in the talent of writing, contest
" with him the superiority." Libanius bestows a similar elogium on Julian in his own Life, p. 41. styling him " the
" most temperate, the most oratorical, and the most war-
" like." WOLFIUS.

* Julian also highly commended other orations of Libanius. See on this subject the remarkable Epistle of Julian, before unpublished, mentioned in p. 317. now the [LXVIIIth.] *Ibid.*

† I should understand this of the orators of Phœnicia. *Ibid.*

‡ Κοινὰ γὰρ, φασὶ, τὰ τῶν φίλων. This proverb is quoted by Euripides in his Orestes, in the same words. See the Chiliades of Erasmus [p. 13.] and Gregory Nazianz. Ep. LXIV. *Ibid.*

" No proverb," says Erasmus, " is more salutary, or
" more celebrated, than this."

EPISTLE

EPISTLE XIII. *

GEMELLUS † is my relation and my friend, and by his manners is no disgrace to his family. If he had been possessed of money and a large estate, he would long ago have been employed on some public function. But as his fortune is small, he has, by my advice, taken a method which may exempt him from tears and chains, the usual attendants of those whom public employments have reduced to poverty.

Happy he is in discharging this office under your inspection; as you never fail to reprobate injustice, and to honour what is just and equitable. Many there are who look upon justice and equity as meanness, and accordingly despise them. But far different is your conduct; for you were well born, and well instructed, and therefore glory more in being virtuous than in the numerous nations which you govern. Of this Gemellus has proofs; and, that he may have more, let him be obliged for those to you, but for these to me. For if he should receive any greater favours in consequence of my letter, he will certainly be indebted for them to my advice.

* In the edition of Wolfius this is the MCCCXCIVth.
† To this Gemellus Libanius has several epistles.

EPISTLE XIV.*

WE have made a mutual agreement, that I should write to you in behalf of my friends, and that if their requests are reasonable, you will assist them. Of your assistance let this Hyperechius † first reap the advantage. He has long been harrassed and oppressed by those whose chief study is unjust gain. He was one of my scholars in my former prosperity. Such I deem the time of my residence at Nicomedia ‡; not on account of the wealth, but of the excellent friends, that it procured me, many of whom are no more. This man, whose hopes now rest on you, then came from Ancyra §. In eloquence, none excelled him; in manners, none equalled him. I love him therefore with a parental affection. I cannot see him injured without assisting him myself, and urging others to assist him also. And if in this you think that I act no bad part, shew by your deeds that you approve my conduct.

* In the edition of Wolfius this is the mccccxcth.
† An orator, the son of Maximus, a native of Galatia. Libanius has addressed several epistles to him.
‡ Our author affirms, in his Life, p. 21, that he spent five years with pleasure at Nicomedia, and calls that time "the spring of his life."   WOLFIUS.
§ The same city which Libanius, in his xxvith oration, p. 599, styles "the principal and largest city in Galatia."
Ibid.

EPISTLES OF LIBANIUS.

EPISTLE XV.*

A. D. 363.

THE oration †, which contains some account of your glorious actions, you honour not only with praise, but admiration. And as you are ranked among the learned, you maintain, I am told, that Demosthenes could not have written more forcibly, Socrates more agreeably, or Plato more copiously, on the occasion. You affirm also, that greater glory will redound to you from my writings, than from the fortunate event of your actions. My opinion is far different. For though, with my most studious and elaborate endeavours, I strove to exalt your name; yet, as my strength was unequal to such a weight, what I performed I performed with great pleasure. But so brilliant are your praises, that the rudest genius may seem

---

* This is the 111d of the IId book of the Epistles of Libanius, collected in Greece by Francisco Zambicari of Bologna, and published, in his Latin translation only by John Somerfeld, at Cracow, 1504. It is also inserted by Fabricius, in his Bibliotheca Græca, vol. VII. p. 390.

† His Προσφωνητικος, or panegyrical address to Julian, when he was at Antioch, just before he set out on his Persian expedition. It is the Vth in the IId Vol. of the works of this Sophist, published by Morell. How agreeable it was to the Emperor Libanius mentions in an Epistle to Celsus [the DCXLVIIIth], as well as in the above.

FABRICIUS.

sufficiently decorated by the dignity of the subject. Your actions therefore were the noblest ornaments of my oration. And though I attempted to illustrate those actions which in their own nature were most splendid, I rather illustrated myself. So that you have no cause to return me thanks, or to think that they are due to me. But that I may acquire such a splendor by recording your exploits, whatever success may attend you in future fail not to communicate to me by a letter.

EPISTLE XVI.*

I CAN scarce believe that, than which nothing can be more certain. Departing from you, in obedience to your order, and on an urgent occasion, I am both willingly and unwillingly absent from you. For I think I could be sooner negligent of my life than of your commands. Any labours, however great, seem trifles; however small, when desired to undertake them for you, I have been used to think them sweeter than ambrosia. To this it is owing, that, were you to command me, I would depart not only from you, but from myself. But as I consider you as my deity, without you nothing seems pleasing. You constantly occur to my mind: whatever I hear repeats the voice of

* This also is published only in Latin by Zambicari. It is the XLVth of his IId book.

Julian; whatever I see reflects the image of my venerable deity. And when a sweet slumber refreshes my languid limbs, you seem so present to me, that, by the kindness of the immortal Gods, separated and loosed from the body, my mind seems to fly to you, to embrace, accost, in short, to worship you; so that if I were to be deprived of life, I would wish that to be my last day. Farther, that I may no longer be thus tormented, I intreat you to give me your permission to return to you, and in your presence to adore your deity, which absent I at once admire and venerate. If not, as by your indulgence it may be effected, I could easily consent to be banished, not only from the city I so much love, but also from the world *.

* In the Latin, *non modo interdici mihi optatissimâ urbe, sed ipsâ etiam urbe facilè patiar*—which I do not understand. Perhaps *ipsâ urbe* should be *ipso orbe*. I have ventured so to translate it.

*** These are all the Epistles of Libanius to the Emperor that are extant. Of the others addressed to Julian (of which there are ten more), one is to his uncle the Count of the East, and the rest to some other person, or persons, of the same name.

INDEX.

INDEX

TO
VOLUME I.

| A. | Page |

ABANTES, a people of Greece   290
    Acharnians, a tribe of Athens   259 (note)
———————- a comedy of Aristophanes   *ibid.*
Adonis, gardens of   202
Æmilian, Emperor, omitted by Julian in the Cæsars
     165 (note)
Æschylus, quotation from   139 (note) imitated 198
Ætius, an Arian bishop, duped by Julian   3 (note)
Africanus, fate of   70 (note)
Agrippina (Cologne) retaken by Julian   84
Alcæus, the poet   223, 4 (note)
Alexander the Great   11, 50, 51, 183, 187, 203, &c.
——————— Severus, Emperor   163
——————— governor of Syria   302 (note) 323
Allegorical Fable   xxxi. 195
Amphiaraus, his modesty   138
Anacreon, the poet   223, 4. quotation from 291. account of his supposed poems   *ibid.* (note)
Anaxagoras, the philosopher   21. 41. 42. 44.
Andragathius, recommended to Julian by Libanius   309
Antinous, his deification   159 (note)
Antioch, inhabitants of, their character and manners.
    See the whole Misopogon
Antiochus gives his name to Antioch. History of his
    marriage   251, 252
Antisthenes, the philosopher   20. 34

Vol. I.   A a   *Antoninus,*

INDEX.

	Page
Antoninus, Pius, Emperor	160
———— Philosophus (see Marcus Aurelius)	
Antony, Mark	191. 194
Apollo, his festival ill celebrated at Daphne 283. Complaints and reproaches of Julian on that subject	ibid.
Araxius and Areta, friends of Julian	14
Archilochus, the poet, reprobated by Julian	131. 224
Areus, a friend of Augustus	25, 26. 193
Aristides, the Just	61, 62
Aristophanes, the poet, imitation of '	167
———— of Corinth, defended by Libanius	317
Aristotle, his thoughts on sovereignty 16. his definition of law 17. his work on the nature of God	24
Athenians, Epistle to the XVII. 59. What Julian thought of them	253
Athenodorus. A bold action of that philosopher 193 (note)	
Augustus (see Octavianus)	
Aurelian, Emperor (misprinted *Aurelius*)	168
Autolycus, equivocal elogium on, by Homer	254 (note)
———— a roguish pedlar in Shakspeare	ibid.

B.

Babylas, bishop of Antioch, his corpse removed	247 (note)
Balbinus, Emperor, omitted in the Cæsars	165 (note)
Basilina, the mother of Julian	264
Beer, verses against, by Julian	227 (note)
Berenice, queen. Her wisdom at least equivocal	150 (note)
injured the reputation of Titus	ibid.
Bleterie, Abbé de la, account of his Life of Julian, and History of Jovian v. translation of the former VI. his account of the works of Julian IX.	
Byzantium. The crescent was from all antiquity its arms	200 (note)

C.

Cæsar Julius, disputes before the Gods against Alexander	183
Cæsars. Elogium on that work	XXIII 146 (note)
Caligula, Emperor	153
Callisthenes, the philosopher	34
Caracalla, Emperor	163

Carus,

INDEX.

Carus, Emperor, and his sons   170
Cato of Utica 9, elogium on   273
   what happened to him at Antioch   ibid.
Chamavians reduced by Julian   87
Charity enforced   122. 142
Charmides, a beautiful Athenian   38
Christianity is revenged by the ridiculous opinions of those who attack it xviii. The obligations which unbelievers have to it 22 (note) does not favour the corruptions of mankind, whatever the Pagans may say   218 (note)
Chrysippus, a Stoic philosopher   8. 133
Claudius I. Emperor   153
———— II.   167, 220
Cnodomar, king, taken prisoner by Julian   85
Coins of Julian   277, 8 (note)
Commodus, Emperor   161. 210
Constans, Emperor   105 (note)
Constantine the Great, harangues before the Gods 105. 199. 201. 213. 215
———————— the Younger   105 (note)
Constantius-Chlorus, the grandfather of Julian   172
Constantius, Emperor. Julian writes to him 54. his cruelties 63, 64. his death   104 (note)
Cotylist, a kind of juggler   276 (note)
Crispus, Cæsar, son of Constantine the Great   216
   put to death by his father   ibid. (note
Curia. What it was   294 (note)
Curiales. Their functions.   ibid.
Cyril, of Alexandria, St. His books against Julian account of, xxi.

D.

Dalmatius, brother of Constantine   63 (note) 106 (note)
———————— nephew of Constantine   ibid.
Damophilus, a compiler, ridiculed by Julian   274
Daphne, the burning of its temple 248 (note) the suburb of described   282
Demetrius, a freed-man of Pompey   274
Democritus, the philosopher   21
Didymæan oracle quoted   127. 130
Diocletian, Emperor   171
Dion Siculus   9

Dominus,

INDEX.

Dominus. What emperors refused to take that title
              239 (note)
Domitian, Emperor   156
Duties of a priest   118, &c.
Dynamius, an informer   71

E.

Elagabalus, Emperor   163
Elpidius, his praises.   306
Emesa, the inhabitants of, burn the Christian churches 272
 the Antiochians ascribe to them the libels which
 they made against Julian   *ibid.* (note)
Epictetus, a Gallic bishop, sent to Julian by Constantius 101
Epicurus, his advice controverted   8
 his tenets exploded   134
Epistles of Julian, account of   xxxi
――――XVI of Libanius to Julian   303, &c.
Erasistratus. How he knew the malady of Antiochus 251
Euemerus, the librarian of Julian   78
Euripides, quotations from 139 (note) 166. 205. 240 (note)
Eusebia, Empress. Her kindness to Julian   69. 71. 75
Eusebius, chamberlain to Constantius . 68. 71. 263 (note)
Eutropius, the great grandfather of Julian   253 (note)

F.

Fausta, the wife of Constantine, destroys Crispus by her
 calumnies, and perishes herself   216 (note)
Florentius, præfect of Gaul   87
 His inveteracy against Julian   92
Florian, Emperor, justly omitted in the Cæsars 169 (note)
Fragment, a long account of   17. 118 (note)
Friends, six, of Julian, their conduct and characteristic 267
 their names   *Ibid.* (note)

G.

Galba, Emperor   155
Galileans, a term of reproach   133 (note)
Gallicisms military   89 (note)
Gallienus, Emperor   166
                Gallus,

INDEX.

	Page
Gallus, Cæsar, writes to his brother Julian 1. Account of him *ibid.* (note). What his Christianity was 4. (note). His catastrophe 65. 68. Occasions a sedition at Antioch	300 (note)
—— Emperor, omitted in the Cæsars (omitted also by mistake in this page)	165 (note)
Gaudentius, an informer	70. 92
Gauls, elogium on by Julian	275
Adventure of a Cappadocian at the court of one of their kings	276
Gemellus, a relation and friend of Libanius	328
Geta, Emperor	163
Gods. The licentiousness with which the comic poets treated them	292
Gordians (the three) Emperors, omitted in the Cæsars	165 (note)
Gregory Nazianzen, his poems commended	225 (note)

H.

Hadrian, Emperor 158. Compared with Julian *ibid.* (note)
Hannibalianus, nephew of Constantine 63 (note) 106 (note)
Helena, wife of Julian 97. 106 (note) 108 (note)
Heraclius, a Cynic. Julian addresses a discourse to him xiii
Hesiod, quotation from 40
Hipponax, the poet, reprobated by Julian 132
Homer, often quoted by Julian at random 3 (note) 35 (note) 242 (note). passages from him 3. 10. 15. 20. 32. 35. (note) 39. 44. 46. 48. 49. 50. 53. 78. (note) 110. 111. 121. (note) 139. (note) 148, 149. 210. 237. 241. (note) 242, 243., 251. 253, 254. 262. 305. (note) 325.

Humourist of Menander	236
Hunting-matches in the theatres	141
Hymettus, mountain	33
Hyperechius, a Galatian, recommended to Julian by Libanius	329

I. and J.

Ismenias, a player on the flute. A saying which Julian ascribes to him	228

A a 4 JULIAN,

INDEX.

JULIAN, Emperor. La Bleterie's opinion and character of all his works, IX. Annals of his life, XXXV. his pedigree, XL. confined in Cappadocia, 65. declared Cæsar, 77. sent into Gaul, 79. his first campaign, 80. recovers Agrippina, 84. takes king Cnodomar prisoner, 85. his second and third campaigns, 86. declared Augustus, 55. 98. his proposals to Constantius, 56. acknowledges God's providence, 111. is initiated at Ephesus, 113. (note) his temperance, 140. (note) writes verses, 225. (note) his strange picture of himself, 228. his rigid life, 231. hates the circus and the theatre, 232. his danger at Paris, 236. cannot endure to be called Lord, 239. quotes Homer improperly, 242. (note) was he so chaste as is said? 244. (note) accused of having subverted the world, 277. expostulates with the senate of Antioch, 283. makes his apology on account of the famine in that city, 296. his commentaries, 88. (note) 306. his excellence both in arms and oratory   307. 309, 310. 327

Julian, Count, uncle to the Emperor   232. 290
Julius Constantius, the father of Julian   63 (note)
Jupiter Philius   249
———Cassius   282

K.

Knights of Aristophanes   153

L.

Laws, Roman, against defamatory libels   224
Libanius, the sophist; his picture of Julian's manner of life, 232 (note). his Epistles to Julian 303. his character *ibid.* (note). his panegyric on Julian praised by that prince   330
Lice, a remarkable passage concerning   229
Licinius, Emperor   174
  vanquished by Constantine   199
Logos of Plato. What it was   xi
Lucian, quotation from   182
Lucius Verus, Emperor   160

Lupicinus,

INDEX. 339

	Page
Lupicinus, a general in Gaul 89. 93. sent to Britain	89 (note) 94
Lutetia, or Paris. Its situation and climate	234
Mr. Gibbon's encomium on it 234. (note) censured by Mr. Knox *ib.* Julian is in danger of losing his life there,	236
Luxury, deified by Julian	216
Lycurgus, the lawgiver of Sparta	6

M.

Macedonius, recommended to Julian by Libanius	313
Macrinus, Emperor	163
Magnentius the tyrant 175. Resemblance of that prince and Julian	*ibid.*-(note)
Maiuma, the festival, history of	284 (note)
Marcellus, a general in Gaul, 81. 91. his perfidy	61
Marcus Aurelius, Emperor 160. 198. blamed for his conduct towards his wife and son	161. 210 (note)
Mardonius, an eunuch, the governor of Julian	73. 261
Marriages between cousin-germans exploded	108
Maxentius, the tyrant	174. (note) 199
Maximian-Herculius, Emperor	172 (note)
———— Galerius, Emperor	*ibid.*
Maximin I. Emperor	165
———— II. surnamed Daïa	174 (note)
Misopogon, account of xxix. 223 (note). The meaning of that word *ibid.* when Julian composed that satire	241 (note) 263 (note)
Months, Macedonian and Roman	248 (note) 281 (note)
Musonius, a Roman knight and Stoic philosopher, ill-treated by Nero	25 (note)
Mycon, island of,	257 (note)

N.

Nebridius, præfect of Gaul, his resolution	94 (note)
Nepenthes, drug	32
Nero, Emperor	154
Nerva, Emperor	157
Nicolaus, of Damascus, a philosopher	25
Nicomedia, city of, destroyed by an earthquake	304
grief of Julian	305

Octavi-

INDEX.

O.
	Page
Octavianus (or Augustus) Emperor 150. harangues before the Gods	192
Oration, A confolatory	xx. 30
Orations of Julian, account of	10
Organ, verfes on, by Julian	225 (note)
Oribafius, the phyfician of Julian	78
Orphic life	258 (note)
Otho, Emperor	155

P.
Palace of the baths at Paris — 97 (note)
Paul, a flanderer — 92
Pentadius, his innovations — ibid.
Pericles, his friendſhip for Anaxagoras 41. a fuppofed fpeech of — 42, &c.
Pertinax, Emperor — 162
Petau, Dionyſius, his Latin tranflation of Julian viii. an account of him — ibid. (note)
Phæacians, the idea which Homer gives of them 237 inhabitants of the ifland now called Corfu ibid. (note)
Philanthropy recommended — 120
Philips (the two) Emperors, omitted in the Cæfars 165 (note).
Philofophy incapable of reftoring mankind — 22 (note)
Phœnicia, her praifes of Julian — 308
Pindar, quotation from — 298
Pittacus, one of the wife men of Greece — 6
Plato, quotations from 11, 12. 37. 266. 318 (note)
Plutarch, an extract from — 274
Polemo, the philofopher — 34
Pompeianus, fon-in-law of Marcus Aurelius — 161
Priefts fhould be honoured 125. how they fhould act 126
Probus, Emperor — 169
Pruſſia, king of, compared with Julian — 158 (note)
Pupienus, Emperor, omitted in the Cæfars — 165 (note)
Pyrrho, his tenets exploded by Julian — 134
Pythagoras, the philofopher 21. 40, 41. 51. 133. a faying of — 40

Quintillus,

INDEX.

Q.

	Page
Quintillus, Emperor, omitted in the Cæsars	168 (note)
Quirinus (see Romulus)	

R.

Repentance deified by Julian	192
Rhine, passed by Julian thrice	88
a fourth and fifth time	162 (note)
Rodney Lord, his pious magnanimity	29 (note)
Romulus (or Quirinus) his banquet	148

S

Salians, surprised by Julian	87
Sallust, oration on his departure 15. 30 (note) his virtues recalled	37. 91, 92
—— the second, præfect of the East	31 (note)
Saturnalia, account of	146 (note)
Scipio Africanus, his friendship with Lælius	39. 41
Seleucus Nicator, the founder of Antioch	251
Severus, Emperor	162
Simonides, the poet, an expression of	208
Socrates withdrew from the bar many indifferent orators 8 preferred to Alexander 21. incapable of reforming mankind 22 (note) Dæmon of 47. Mr. Nares's idea of it	*ibid.* (note)
Solon, one of the wise men of Greece	6. 18. 237
Sophocles quoted	306
Soul, immortality of, inculcated by Julian	117,
believed by all nations	196 (note)
Spanheim Ezekiel, account of VIII (note) Character of his translation of the Cæsars VII. XXVIII.	
Strasburgh, battle of	85
Stratonice, the wife of Seleucus, marries her son-in-law	252
Sylvanus, revolt of	71, 72. (note)

T.

Table of the Emperors from Julius Cæsar to Julian	222
Tacitus, Emperor, omitted in the Cæsars	169 (note)
Tarentines, punished by the Romans for insulting their ambassadors	269
Taurus, præfect of Italy, banished	101 (note)

Themistius,

Themistius, Epistle to, account of xxxii. 4 (note) a
    senator of Constantinople ·   26 (note)
Theocritus, quotation from   229
Theognis, the poet, his maxims   256
Theophrastus, the philosopher   266
Thrasyleon of Menander   256 (note)
Thrasyllus, the philosopher   259
Tiberius, Emperor   152
Tillemont M. de, understands too rigorously an expression
    of Julian ·   \   245 (note)
Titus, Emperor, too harshly treated by Julian   156 (note)
    Justified,   *ibid.*
Trajan, Emperor 157. harangues before the Gods   195
——— Decius, Emperor, omitted in the Cæsars 165 (note)
Translations of Julian by La Bleterie v. Petau viii
    Spanheim viii. xxviii.

V.

Vespasian, Emperor   155
Vindex C. Julius. Julian seems to reckon him among
    the Emperors 155. Rebells against Nero *ibid.* (note)
Vitellius, Emperor   155

W.

Walpole Mr. his elogium on Rousham   280 (note)
Warburton Bishop, compares a passage of Pope to
    one of Julian   274 (note)

Z.

Zamolxis, his incantations 38. 152. his doctrine   196
Zeno, the philosopher   39. 133. 151

END OF THE FIRST VOLUME.

The Translator's distance from the press, he is sorry to find, has occasioned the following ERRATA.

Page	Page
v. l. 3. r. 'Julien'	143. note † l. 14. r. 'τρωτον'
xxvii. l. 11. r. 'responsible'	165. note l. 16. after 'TRA-
xxxi. note † l. 1. for	JAN-DECIUS' add 'GALLUS'
'LXXI' r. 'LXXX.'	168. l. 5. r. 'AURELIAN'
xxxvii. l. 3. fr. the bottom,	195. note l. 5. r. 'Dion-
r. 360.'	Chrysostom'
2. l. 2. r. 'ancestors'	197. l. 7. For 'with' r. 'by'
7. note † l. pen. after 'ap-	224. note ‡ l. 2. r. 'μιλη.'
prehension', put a comma	227. note l. 6. fr. the bot-
10. note † l. 1. r. 'asterisks'	tom. r. 'μα γαρ'
13. note § l. 1. r. ανηυθω	— l. 9. fr. the bot-
§ 2. r. δη	tom r. 'wine'
17. note ‖ l. 1. r. ανθρωπος	243. is mispaged
κελινων	247. note * l. 4. r. 'Τυχης
20. note * r. επιςορα	248. note ‡ l. ult. r. 'Löus'
38. note ‡ l. 4. r. 'Critias	304. note ‡ l. 1. r. 'Bithynia'
here says'	312. note * l. 3. r. 'WOLFIUS'
49. note §. After 'Θεοφιλη'	317. note ‡ l. 2. dele 'or last'
put a full stop	323. l. 3. For 'it' r. 'at'
93. note † l. penult. r.	— note * r. MDCCXXIId.
'opening of'	328. l. 6. For 'on' r. in.

www.ingramcontent.com/pod-product-compliance
Lightning Source LLC
Chambersburg PA
CBHW030341230426
43664CB00007BA/487